BEYOND TRAVEL

A Road Warrior's Survival Guide

Marcey Rader

Talk Doesn't Cook Rice. - *Ancient Chinese Proverb*

This book is dedicated to my late grandpa and biggest fan, Wally Bertram.

He didn't understand my business, but he sure thought I was the best at it.

Also by Marcey Rader

Hack the Mobile Lifestyle: 6 Steps to Work Well and Play More! [TM]

Acknowledgments

Thank you to Diana M. Needham, my book marketing coach, for helping me get through my launch. Thank you to Leslie Flowers, my editor, for keeping my voice. Thank you to the creators of Grammarly, because I have an issue with commas. A special shout out to Extended Stay America Hotels for being a partner in my quest to prevent Pound Packing. Thank you to the generous people who read my manuscript to give endorsements and testimonials. Thank you to everyone who bought my first book and ignored all the errors of a self-published book.

Super High-Five Fist Bump to my current and former clients who have trusted me with their mental, physical, emotional and digital mess. You are my inspiration.

Foreword

With Americans making more than 405 million long-distance business trips annually, staying fit and healthy on the road can prove to be a daunting task. With junk food lurking in every airport and hotel gym equipment dating back to the era of bell-bottoms, the light at the end of the healthy and productive tunnel seems rather dim. We're told to eat healthy, work out, be productive and do our job well. Yet, no one tells us exactly how to do these things. That's where Marcey Rader has stepped up to the plate, bridging the gap between knowing what you should do, and knowing how to execute it effectively.

With more than fifteen years of business travel under her belt, Marcey knows what she's talking about. Business travel isn't just a part of her job — It's a lifestyle.™ Being in the hospitality industry at Extended Stay America, we're always on the move. We are constantly improving our travel routines and the routines of our guests. Once an airport sprinter, grab-anything-and-go diner, email inmate and task juggler herself, Marcey knows well what many of us consider an average day. Shared with empathy, she is familiar with the numerous 'triggers' of business travelers. While her personal convictions on health, diet, fitness and productivity may not mirror the masses, Marcey's adversities, from her varied health diagnoses to confronting and altering her personal life habits, give her the experience to break it down to the basics and appeal to those travelers most resistant to change.

With Marcey's guidance, it's time to stop waiting for the "right time" (that conveniently never comes) to start making these changes. Staying productive and maintaining a healthy lifestyle even away from home is an absolute essential to climbing the ladder - whether corporate or personal. Accomplishing this on a daily basis is and will always prove to be a challenge.

This is where *Beyond Travel: A Road Warrior's Survival Guide* steps in. With this book in hand, excuses to keep a healthy life at bay …

vanish. Marcey brings the process of making positive lifestyle changes brilliantly to life, in a manner we can all understand and incorporate into our lives. Just like a car that's never had an oil change, you know it will never run to its full potential. And eventually over time, the engine burns out. And like the human body, with proper care and maintenance, it has the potential to run beautifully.

Marcey's latest book hones in on the practical and personal reasons to focus on making the switch to a healthier and more productive lifestyle. She points out key factors that influence our decision - the triggers and habits that warrant our less than beneficial behavior to perform at our best. Her goal in *Beyond Travel: A Road Warrior's Survival Guide* is for us to recognize what prompts these adverse actions and the steps to take to correct them. Then we will have the tools to minimize high stress levels while staying focused on the valuable aspects of our work and our lives.

For those that are working to restore their productivity to a healthy balance in the midst of a hectic traveling schedule, this book proves to be a tool with exponential insight from someone who has faced these challenges head on and succeeded beyond all expectations.

Rock on, Marcey Rader.

The Team at Extended Stay America Hotels®

Introduction

Business travel isn't part of your job. *It's a lifestyle.*™

During my second year in the field of business travel, we moved from Capitol Hill to Raleigh, North Carolina. I glanced at my itinerary and realized that I didn't need to arrive at the airport at 8:00am — my plane departed at 8:00am! It was 7:05am and we lived 12 minutes from the airport. In a panic, I jumped in the car, no joy for me in knowing that if I missed my flight because I was late, my company would make me pay the difference to reschedule. I could only hope it was a day that the line through security was easy.

I drove much faster than was safe (and I knew this too) and later found out I cut off a friend of mine in traffic. I pulled into the parking garage and drove up and around and around, Level 2, then Level 3, at which point, seeing no spaces at all, I said out loud 'screw it' and drove directly up to Level 5 and parked. Dragging my roller bag, I ran to the elevator and then waited until what seemed like my next birthday, for the doors to open. At Level 4 a guy stepped in and said smiling, "Where ya headed?" My blank stare caught him off guard. In that moment, I had to actually reach into my bag and look at my itinerary to remember ... I was going to San Diego. The cities had all become a blur.

As luck had it, I breezed through security and made it to the gate minutes before they shut the runway door. I had planned to stop and get my "breakfast of champions" — a Frappuccino and scone — on the way to the gate. Since I would have surely been late, I had nothing to eat before boarding my 4.5-hour flight. For the first half hour I kept looking down the aisle, willing the flight attendants to come by with my coveted Delta Biscoff cookies and something to drink. The smell of the cheese bagel from the guy next to me made me want to eat my own arm. Finally an announcement came on that the turbulence was too great and they would have to delay service. When it did resume, it would only be drinks. The airline had not received their delivery of

Biscoffs, and ... someone on the plane was allergic to peanuts, so no peanuts.

By the time I got off the plane at almost 1:00pm EST, I felt like someone had taken a hammer to my head while there was a wild animal eating its way out of my stomach, and, of course, I was supposed to drive directly to work at a site visit with my manager. It was in that moment I knew that if I was going to survive in this business, I had to get it together. My travel, my nutrition, my exercise, my sleep, and my work had to be very focused. There could be no more Marcey-induced spontaneity if I was going to have any hope to not end up a fat, frazzled business traveler that looked ten years older than I was, and burned out after two years on the road.

To understand why I believe health and productivity go together, it's important to understand my background, and to know that I've been where you may be right now, frazzled, tired and overwhelmed. I have a Bachelor's degree in Exercise Science and Wellness and Master's degree in Health Promotion and Exercise Management. Since 1993, I've been certified in group exercise, personal training, fitness nutrition, and integrative nutrition. For about 15 years, these certifications were all intended for me to become a better athlete. I worked in the Health and Wellness field for three years before entering the world of clinical research in pharmaceuticals, medical devices, and biotech.

My travel experiences began 2001 when I took a job for a large clinical research organization and immediately went on the road three-five days a week, which I did for the next ten years. I lived in Washington, D.C. at the time (in the district itself, not an hour away pretending I lived in D.C.) and travel was easy because it was pre-9/11. I could get to the airport minutes before my plane took off with no problem. After 9/11 the extra security increased my travel time at least 2 hours each trip. I took the Acela high-speed train as much as I could going north, yet could never, it seemed, get away from the new delays in air travel. This was also the time where you couldn't get out of your seat within 30 minutes of landing at DCA, which put the fear of God in me ... that I would have to go to the bathroom and end up peeing my pants. I shudder to remember ... Later I became an operations manager for global clinical trials and then moved into the clinical trainer role. I found my element! I got to teach people how to be clinical research associates, manage global trials, learn new systems and technologies, and write procedures and processes. I was able to unleash my inner geek. My favorite module was on *Travel Health and Work Hacking* that I developed and taught 'under the table.' I always received the best feedback on this course because it was practical *and* personal. When I had gone as high in the industry as I wanted to go, I knew that my belief that *you can't be healthy without being productive and you can't be productive without being healthy,* with both being more challenging as a routine traveler, was my *calling.* I wanted to teach people a better way to travel that didn't result in the Travel 20 (20 pounds of weight gain), Fear Of Missing Out (FOMO), broken relationships, stacked up laundry and feeling like the work is never done. I realized that even though I had many trials and errors, I was still able to do things that other travelers weren't able to.

My accomplishments while leading a life of heavy business travel include:

- 12+ marathons
- 30+ triathlons sprint to Iron distance
- 20+ adventure races of 6-30 hours in length (including 2 National Championship races)
- 4 ultra running races
- Umpteen road centuries of 100+ miles
- 10+ mountain bike races 6-12 hours, including three 100-milers
- Hiking the Grand Canyon rim to rim to rim

- Decluttering my home and downsizing to live next to a state park
- Shutting down with inbox zero every day for over five years

What's Kale to a Veggie-holic?

I grew up in a family that didn't eat vegetables and sugar was a major food group. Can you relate? We pretty much lived on nachos, Hormel chili bean burritos, deli meat, ice cream, and chili pizza. When we had vegetables it was corn, potatoes, and green beans. I never had a pepper, mushroom or anything green and leafy until I was in my twenties.

My senior year of high school, when I was tired of being chubby, I embraced the new fat-free fad. If it had more than two grams of fat ... it wouldn't touch my lips. I lost about 35 pounds, but my hair got thinner and my nail beds were blue. I remember one instance that I refused to buy a frozen yogurt because it was only 97% fat free. I almost passed out on the hour drive home because I was so hungry.

This continued into college where my diet consisted of Snackwell cookies, unlimited frozen yogurt at the dorm cafeteria, and late night trips to the Sunshine Café for biscuits and gravy. I put 10 pounds back on and started teaching aerobics to maintain at least some of my weight loss.

After college I became a vegetarian, which in hindsight was a carba-tarian or grainatarian because there still weren't very many veggies in my repertoire. It wasn't until my late twenties into my early thirties that I really branched out and learned to cook. I started eating bricks of tofu, soy products, and meat analogues. Analogues are processed non-meat products, the vegetarian equivalent of bologna and hot dogs. They aren't *healthy,* but are fine for eating occasionally out of con-venience. I was eating them daily.

I ate processed, refined carbohydrates and sugars. I was a Frappuccino addict who fooled herself by thinking that because I *got it Light without whip*, it was okay. I ate artificial sweeteners like Crystal Light and Diet Mountain Dew because I believed that artificial sweeteners weren't harmful. Now that I know how artificial sweeteners are one of the worst nutritional conspiracies in the history of history, I weaned myself off of those as well. If there is one change I would tell someone to make in their diet, it's to eliminate artificial sweeteners.

I was really just eating processed junk with ingredients I couldn't even pronounce. Traveling was horrendous and resulted in a steady diet of Auntie Anne's pretzels, frozen yogurt, Frappuccinos and Clif Builder Bars. I started to compete in marathons and became a gel-sucking, sports drink slurping runner that rewarded herself with a giant cookie the size of a small pancake from Eastern Market on Saturdays.

Looking back, I really can't believe I thought what I was doing was healthy in any way. But hey, I was a vegetarian and a marathoner, right? I was well educated. What I thought was healthy eating wasn't actually healthy at all. When you eat a bacon double cheeseburger you *know* it isn't the best choice. When I was eating frozen yogurt instead of ice cream or a soy burger instead of a hamburger I thought I was doing the right thing. It wasn't just ignorance because I followed nutrition heavily with continuing education for my certifications. Even the American Dietetic Association and the USDA pushed artificial sweeteners. Thankfully nutrition knowledge and research has grown exponentially in the last decade.

At business meetings or conferences it was challenging to eat the meals chosen for me. Fifteen years earlier, most people didn't consider vegetarians when they were planning a menu. In those circumstances, I didn't like to call attention to my diet and would end up eating things I didn't want to or eat bread and the dessert ... then feel bad about it later.

When I traveled internationally, I sometimes found it difficult to eat on my schedule because of the time of day people dined based on location. I used to be an early dinner eater, so when visiting Argentina, I would wander around trying to find something besides an empanada before 8pm. It was a window of about four hours, where if I didn't get a meal by 4pm, I wasn't going to get another one until after 8:00pm. I had a hard time because not all countries put the ingredients or nutritional information on their labels. I am a label-looker and would be anxious about what I was eating. I remember learning after three months in London, drinking hot chocolate daily, that it was so delicious because they used whole milk and Cadbury's! Now, wherever I am, I like to be adventurous and eat the local food. When my brother and I were in Beijing, we didn't always know what we were eating and thought it best not to ask. I still don't know what I ate.

My sugar addiction I got honestly ... from my family. I would eat protein bars, drink Frappuccinos, and get a cookie or brownie to take home and share with my husband ... sugar, sugar, sugar. I had to have a sweet treat every night. I stayed at the Doubletree Hotel just because of the cookies. Looking back, I can't believe I thought I was a healthy person. I was duped into thinking that at least diet junk was better than real junk. As long as it wasn't high in fat I was golden. Unfortunately some people still think this way.

I was always really fit, but never really lean. I was never able to see my abs until I changed my diet and cut out sugar, artificial sweeteners, and added a serious amount of vegetables. Abs are made in the kitchen.

In January of 2014, my world was rocked and I was diagnosed with Hashimoto's Disease, which changed my diet yet again. I was eating pretty healthy with lots of veggies, and less sugar and less processed vegetarian protein sources. My eating habits have changed quite a bit from pre-diagnosis vegetarian diet to now — more of a flexitarian diet. I don't eat gluten or soy and I'm picky about what kind of meat I consume. I also limit my servings of grains (corn, rice, quinoa, etc.) to about two servings a day and choose to get my carbs from vegetables, legumes, and fruits.

My biggest change was psychological. I identified with being a vegetarian. I thought that I might disappoint my vegan and vegetarian friends because I had advocated for so long that it was the healthiest diet for everyone and that I was letting myself down. I found myself embarrassed to say I was eating meat again. Then I started school at the Institute for Integrative Nutrition (IIN), where the philosophy is bio-individuality. What works for one person may not work for another. I realized I had put myself in an unnecessary and self-made box and it wasn't worth the stress to worry what other people thought of my diet. Not labeling myself as a vegetarian allowed me to eat my friend's Thanksgiving turkey that she spent hours preparing, one day a year, with zero guilt. It gave me freedom that my self-imposed label had never given me. My fear of being judged stemmed from *my* judgment of others when I wasn't eating meat. I had to say goodbye to Righteous Marcey.

Exercise has always been part of my life, but not by choice. Growing up I played group sports – volleyball, softball, basketball, and track. I absolutely hated basketball, and growing up in Indiana, there was only the choice 'to play.' I was chubby so track was hard. I went to the second smallest school in the state where I once went an entire season without participating in one winning basketball game and only two winning volleyball games. Talk about a self-esteem booster! The rule in my house was that if I didn't play the sport of the season, I was essentially grounded for those months and couldn't have friends over or go to sporting or social events at school. What would *you* have chosen? I suffered through the seasons and have never played those sports again as an adult.

All I wanted to do was dance. My senior year, when I got into the crazy fat-free phase, I also bought my first exercise tape by Jody Watley. That tape changed my life. I did those workouts at 5:30 am almost every morning before school, even when my dad made fun of my dancing. This led me to becoming certified to teach aerobics in college, which progressed into running my senior year.

Running 10ks turned into running marathons, qualifying for Boston, and then switching to triathlons. After competing in two Ironman Triathlons during my heaviest year ever of travel, I switched to dirt sports. My obsession with triathlons was starting to get to my head. I began to quantify everything, was up at 4:30 on Saturday mornings, would ride my bike around my cul-du-sac to get the last 45 seconds in of my scheduled 6-hour ride, and didn't go out at night on the weekends in order to be fresh for my long run.

Dirt sports started as mountain biking, then ultra-endurance mountain biking, ultra trail running, and Adventure Racing. I loved the freedom and that my *times* didn't mean as much on the dirt. The results of a 7-minute mile on the road doesn't mean the same thing as an 8-minute mile on a trail in the mountains over roots and rocks and running through streams. I also slowed down self-quantifying and participated in a 100-mile mountain bike race on a single speed bike with only my Timex watch. Not even a bike computer. That was big for me.

Adventure Racing was fun and helped me move further away from the clock-watching and a perfect training regime lifestyle, to one of flexibility, adaptation, and team work. I did over 30 adventure races from six to 30 hours and participated in the National Championships twice. Looking back, the stress of competing overnight in extreme temperatures did me no favors when it came to triggering my Hashimoto's Disease.

Hashimoto's Disease is a common autoimmune thyroid disease. I didn't cause it, yet I know when I triggered it, telling me *enough is enough*. One year I was traveling frequently, racing a lot, and had more work stress than I thought possible. I was doing the job of four people for almost nine months and basically stopped sleeping. For two years I saw different therapists and doctors and about $6,000 in copays and treatments, to figure out what was wrong with me. I only slept three to four hours a night, woke up with low blood sugar at 3 or 4am every morning, always felt super cold, would forget things, cried easily, had significant digestive issues for almost four years and was amenorrheic. Because I identified with being healthy, No one ... not even my closest friends, knew all of my symptoms. I had made myself a physical and psychological mess.

I finally received a correct diagnosis in January 2014. I had started my coaching business six months earlier and thought *"How will anyone trust a health coach that isn't healthy?"* It was a good question. I was also diagnosed with idiopathic hypothalamic hypogonadism (menopause caused by the hypothalamus), when I had been told that my lack of periods was my fault and was from training too much. Being in menopause at the age of 36 has its own risks and at the age of 40 I was put on hormones. I felt like an old woman.

With trepidation, I decided to write a 'coming out' article and the response was overwhelming. I began to tell the truth about what was happening with me and I received emails and even clients with Hashimoto's and other autoimmune diseases. After seeing six different doctors, I found a program that kept me healthy while allowing me to move forward with my busy life. I now see the disease as a true gift. I don't adventure race anymore and am still in the process of deciding if and how far I want to go with racing, yet it doesn't define me as before, for which I am grateful. I have lived five lifetimes when it comes to racing and competing. I have enough awareness of my body and disease state that I limit myself if needed.

My struggles with productivity were mostly internal. I've always been fast at typing, reading, and 'doing' of whatever task I was performing, but am very easily distracted and find I am still working on focus. I would get anxious if I couldn't check my email often enough. I had so many RSS feeds of articles, I always felt behind. It made me feel like I had much less time than I did because I had so much to read it seemed like a part-time job. I would be considered Type-A, although I hate that connotation. Not because I don't appreciate the characteristics associated with Type-A, but because it's rarely used as a compliment.

When I traveled I felt like I was always catching up because the time I spent en route wasn't subtracted from the amount of work I was given to do. I worked in the hotel at night addressing emails that I couldn't get to because I was on site all day. I answered emails on weekends, which resulted in teaching people I worked on weekends. It was a constant treadmill of work that felt like ... well it actually was 24/7/365!

My last corporate job required being on the phone and in meetings up to six hours a day. How companies think you can get anything done with that kind of schedule is beyond me, but, that was my life and is the same life of most of my corporate clients.

Thankfully, I have always worked from home when I wasn't traveling so I could throw in a load of laundry while listening to 50 minutes of a 60-minute call (often not relevant to my position anyway). *Upper Management, accept that people who work from home fold their laundry while on the call that doesn't apply to them, but are forced to attend. If they aren't, they're probably reading their email anyway like the people in the office.*

I've never tried to keep up with the Joneses (the pressure of anyone with the last name Jones!), yet when I got into expensive sports like triathlon and adventure racing, the equipment started to take over my garage. At one point, I had four bikes. I rode them all, but still...how many people need four bikes? You can only ride one at a time! I had books and CDs I didn't read or listen to, and clothes I didn't wear. I also lived in a house with a yard when both my husband and I abhor mowing. It caused friction between us and was never worth the energy of the argument. Who wants to argue about yard work?

And then there is the question of who does what chores. Me, because I'm gone all week and need to contribute to the house or my husband who is home all week and is the one there most of the time messing it up?

In 2009, I read *The Power of Less* by Leo Babauta and my life path was forever altered. I decided to make small changes in my life based on topics from the book. I started reading every minimalist and decluttering blog I could find, to the point of obsession, and started looking at myself from a different point of view. I decided on 100 things I wanted to change about myself and made a one-year plan on a white board. I decided on changing one habit at a time in productivity and one habit at a time in my health or personal growth. I also picked one room or area in the house to declutter. I did each habit and room for 4-8 weeks, depending on how hard it was to change, and put a little check on my whiteboard every day that I did it. Now there are great apps that can help you keep track of habit changes, like Coach.Me, but back then, there was just my whiteboard. What I would give to see that old list.

Some things were easy (adding more fruit!) and others weren't (checking email less often), but after two years I had made it through all of the habits on that white board.

Some of my habit changes, which I will also touch on in the book, were:

- Checking email 4 times per day (now I process once or twice)
- The Pomodoro Technique
- Turning off Instant Message
- Not checking email or working on the computer at least an hour before bed
- Increasing my fruit intake
- Increasing my vegetable intake
- Decreasing my sugar intake
- Eliminating artificial sweeteners

- Decreasing processed food intake
- Planning appropriately for work-related meals
- Decluttering every room in my house
- Decluttering my closet
- Downsizing my home
- Saving enough money to pay cash for a new car

My book, *Hack the Mobile Lifestyle: 6 Steps to Work Well and Play More!*™ was my first self-published book. It was an experiment to determine if there was a need for a book to explain how to be healthy and productive on the road. I've read books for the leisure traveler on how to have exotic vacations on a budget, for business travelers on how to get the most bang for your reward bucks, but never really found anything that addressed how to keep from gaining weight, losing sleep, getting a divorce, maintaining friendships and working 16-18 hours on a travel day. The feedback from the first book was positive enough that I knew people were hungry for this information.

That book was almost completely do-it-yourself. I self-published, had a friend edit and used fiverr for formatting and cover design. Looking back at that book, I am a little embarrassed after reading my run-on sentences, 1000 uses of 'so' and more than a few grammar errors. But here's the thing....a lot of people like the idea of being healthy, the idea of running a marathon, the idea of climbing the ladder or the idea of starting their own business, but they don't take action to actually do those things. When I was discussing my book with a client and friend, she pointed out to me that I acted on a dream and desire. I didn't just wish it or say 'someday'. I realized that what I had done was exactly what I coach my clients to do. It may not be pretty, but I did it.

If I had decided to wait for the perfect opportunity, I wouldn't have the business, clients or contracts I have now. I wouldn't be able to hire professionals to help me market, edit and launch this book. Almost everything sizeable that has come my way has been because I took action and wrote a book. Whatever first step you take could lead you to do something you never would have dreamed of.

Beyond Travel: A Road Warrior's Survival Guide, is a more comprehensive book on how to address the issues above and more. It's written as much for the employers of business travelers as the travelers themselves. There will be some repeat information from the first book, especially in the productivity section, in addition to updated hacks because of better technology and science. What I'm most excited about for this new book are the bonus pages. These bonus pages are online for easy linking for readers with the paper copy book or who have e-readers that aren't convenient to link from.

I'll be referring to business travelers, road warriors and mobile professionals as travelers throughout the book. My definition of traveler is "anyone working outside of a typical office more than 50% of the time." My clients have included C+level positions, clinical research associates, litigating attorneys, HR directors, outside sales reps, realtors and professional speakers.

How to Use This Book

I don't want you to *survive* travel. I want you to *thrive* travel — arriving home with enough energy left that you can spend time with the people you love and have time to play. After you have read the book, I recommend you go back and select a section that you want to incorporate into your travel regimen. Then, pick one or two habits to change in that section. Adding a behavior is typically much easier than removing one. By adding a behavior, you may end up removing another without much effort. For example, by adding more vegetables, I found myself automatically removing less healthy foods. Start with the simplest changes first, choosing only one at a time, and then after you have declared victory, and it's a permanent behavior change, find another one to tackle.

Special Bonus from Marcey Rader

Now that you have your copy of *Beyond Travel: The Road Warrior's Survival Guide*, you are on your way from the haggard, frazzled, caffeinated traveler to the calm, efficient and healthy traveler. You'll get loads of info and new habits to start incorporating into your life.

You'll also receive the special bonus I created to add to your productivity tool belt. Each chapter includes a bonus page online with links to all the references, companies, software, programs, and videos I mention. You'll get exercise videos, free webinars and discounts to products to help you further develop your arsenal of behavioral productivity tools.

There are books on being healthy, being productive, and travel, yet in this book I purposely covered all three to give you what you need in one place. When you finish this book, you'll be armed with the skills required to *travel like a boss.*

Go to http://www.beyondtravelbook.com/signup.html and login with your email address. You'll receive the password via email to access the page. With that access *you will automatically be added to my newsletter list. You may of course unsubscribe at any time.*

The sooner you know the *hacks* for air, hotel, auto, home, outsourcing, nutrition, exercise, and stress management, the sooner you'll feel in control again.

Let's do this.

Marcey Rader

Praise for BEYOND TRAVEL

Marcey confirms what we all suspected: work travel takes a unique toll on our bodies and our lives. It's not unusual to gain ~20lbs on the road. We lose almost an entire work day every time we travel. Marcey gets inside key issues for travelers (e.g., lack of renewal, accountability, decision fatigue, burnout, etc.). Her fact base will make you want to take action. Her practical suggestions will help you do so. I will recommend this book to everyone I know who is struggling to manage energy while living a mobile lifestyle."

— **Dana Bilsky Asher**, PhD, Senior Vice President of Organizational Transformation at The Energy Project

"Want to survive and thrive as a Road Warrior? Then Marcey Rader is your guide. Whether its nutrition, exercise or productivity, Marcey shows how business travel isn't just part of your job, it's a lifestyle that can be mastered. She shares the tips, tools and tricks to hack business travel. Buy this book now and get on the road to success."

— **Stan Phelps,** Author of Purple Goldfish, Green Goldfish, and Golden Goldfish, Founder, 9 INCH Marketing

As an airline pilot for a major US carrier, I can be on the road up to 18 days per month, crossing multiple time zones and ending up in various places. This book has given me a countless number of tools to help me lead a healthy, productive, fit, and rested lifestyle. It should be a travel companion and valuable resource for any traveler who is looking for a balanced experience in an easily unbalanced work environment. Thank you, Marcey, for giving me the tools to help me succeed in such a challenging lifestyle.

— **Matt Gheen, Airline Pilot**

Marcey's insight into the productivity, health, and lifestyle challenges of a road warrior coupled with her real-world experience in hurdling those obstacles make Beyond Travel: A Road Warrior's Survival Guide a must-read for any road warrior. After having finished the book several days ago, I got the best night's sleep I have had in ages. I wish I had read Marcey's words 300,000 air miles ago!

— **Brad D. Messner,** Eternal Road Warrior, Founder, Travel Development Group

"WOW!! Marcey really delivers! After 12 years in the productivity business, I've pretty much read it all but **Beyond Travel: A Road Warrior's Survival Guide** will inspire you to take control, quit whining or making excuses and start looking for opportunities and quite simply GSD!! Marcey gives you the tools and the push to change your life! Get reading and start on your GSD journey today!"

— **Dhawn Hansen,** Productivity Consultant, Speaker and Author, Organized for Productivity

In true, "GO, Marcey, GO!" style, Beyond Travel: A Road Warrior's Survival Guide, pulled me in. I got excited about getting organized, healthy and productive in my work and life overall. Marcey's writing is so real and sincere that it feels like she's talking only to you. Plus, this lady has major "walking the talk" cred! Whether it's beating stress, accomplishing goals, feeling better or playing more, Marcey asks key questions and presents kick-ass reframes that will have you looking at things in an entirely new (and totally doable!) way. This book is fun, dynamic, high-octane goodness that no on-the-go badass can do without!

— **Eyenie Schultz, The Technicolor Priestess, SoulStyle Alchemist and Client**

Wow! Marcey's new book, Beyond Travel: A Road Warrior's Survival Guide is chock full of tips, insights, cool tools, and information to help us "warriors" thrive on the road, stay energized, be healthier, and work smarter. I love the reminder to "surround yourself with people you can learn from that are better than you at whatever aspect of your life you are trying to improve. Life's too short to sit around on the bench." Trust me...You'll want her on your 'A-team'!

— **Diana M. Needham,** Author, speaker, CEO of Needham Business Consulting

Marcey Rader's prose is personal. I felt like I was having a meaningful conversation with her over coffee. Beyond Travel is a book I highly recommend as an avid business traveler and entrepreneur who strives to manage a balance between work and a healthy lifestyle. You will love reading every page of it!

— **Sophia Hyder,** Founder/CEO, Papilia

Marcey Rader gives you a glimpse into the road warrior lifestyle and looks good doing it. If you think you know it all when it comes to traveling, eating and working out smart while on the road for weeks at a time, you're wrong. Everyone from seasoned road warriors to newbies just starting need to read this book. Even non-road warriors can get something out of it. Even non-road warriors can get something from this book. There are new tips and tricks, apps to check out and videos to watch now for my travels. I'm already putting resistance bands in my carry on and looking into the Amazon Prime memberships. I have a renewed sense of GSD after reading this book. Thanks Marcey for lighting a fire again.

— **NIkki Dunn,** Senior Clinical Research Associate and Power Plan Client

Beyond Travel: A Road Warrior's Survival Guide is a complete business travel and productivity hack. A resource laden toolkit to help road warriors succeed and stay healthy while traveling.

— **Phil Hammer,** Business Travel Technology Entrepreneur

Table of Contents

1. The Current State of Business Travel

Am I doomed to be a fat business traveler?

The short answer is no, and ... it won't be easy. It's easy to tell
yourself that you deserve the pancake-sized cookie because you were
in meetings all day and now have to fly two legs to get home. It's
easy to tell yourself because the fitness center is humid, hot and has
equipment from 1973 that you can't work out today. Extended Stay
America did a survey of over 2000 people that reported 86% of
travelers gain three or more pounds during trips of fourteen days or
more. Travel weight is so prevalent there's a name for it — Pound
Packing. If you are a frequent traveler, it's no different than your first
year of college. The Freshman 15? Try the Travel 20!

It's not always a struggle on the road. It's a myth that travelers are
always stressed, fat, unhealthy and chronically tired. There are studies
showing business travel is stressful, yet there are also studies that say
it is less stressful than at home. When we travel, we experience a
different kind of stress. We don't have to deal with errands, chores,
and demands of our family members. I have clients that prefer travel-
ling because it's the only time they have to themselves, and they don't
have to clean up after anyone. On the flip side, if something does go
wrong, the immense guilt of not being at home overtakes any pleasure, and the rest of the trip is lost.

I agree it can be stressful and it can also be relaxing. A lot of the
stress is triggered by our response to things that are out of our control
(travel delays) or lack of planning (not buying snacks for the plane) or
self-care. You might feel like eating healthy is impossible given the
dismal choices in airports and hotels, but with proper planning you
can do it *most* of the time. Your exercise situation may not be perfect,
but you can adapt and find something to do to keep your energy and
strength up and your stress and weight down.

How Travel Affects our Health and Productivity

Much of my research on the impact of travel on human stress and productivity is from the Carlson Wagonlit Travel (CWT) and CWT Solutions Group Travel Stress Index published in 2013. No other study is as comprehensive as this one. It includes data from 15 million business trips booked by over 6,000 business travelers over a one-year period. Each trip was broken down into 22 activities pre-trip, during trip and post-trip and included such activities as booking the trip, traveling and completing expense reports. Each activity was calculated for "stress-free" and "lost" time.

The report disclosed that average lost-time per trip was **6.9 hours**. That's almost an entire workday! Flying economy class on medium and long haul flights and getting to and from the airport or train station caused the greatest loss of time. The financial equivalent upper limit was $662.00. For international trips, the lost time is 15.6 hours. This insight is important from a task and time management perspective.

It's important for companies to realize the ability to plan and be acutely aware as to how much work can get done on the road, which is largely influenced by the air travel industry, weather, traffic and other people's agendas. My rule is this: whatever I think I can get done on the road, I cut by 1/3. Yes, even though I'm going to be stuck in a hotel room three nights in a row on a solo trip, yet after a long day working onsite and possibly a drive or flight, the last thing I want to do is open up my computer. It's also the last thing I *should* do because it's not the amount of work you have to do that burns you out; it's the *lack of renewal*.

On the other hand, there are times when I get more done during times of travel. The time in the airport during my two-hour delay leaves me with nothing to do *but* work, interspersed with a few movement breaks. I consider a cross-country flight the perfect time to focus on a project. For a short trip like Raleigh-Durham to Charlotte Douglas, the 20-minute flight may mean no work because it's not even worth booting up. I'm lucky because I'm 5'2. A 6'4 guy isn't even going to entertain the thought of working on the plane if he's flying Economy. He's just trying not to eat his knees for two hours.

Traveler Stress Triggers

The main stressors found in the survey were:

- Lost or Delayed Baggage: Affects time, money (company won't reimburse for new clothes and airline won't reimburse if you receive returned bag within 24 hours *after* you've already had your meeting!). This category received the highest stress score among all factors for women and across all demographic segments.

- Poor Internet connection: Lost productivity and communication with colleagues and family. Internet connection was a significantly higher stressor for women. *I meet clients via Google Hangout, and hotels are notorious for having slow Internet. Sometimes we have to do the session via phone.*

- Flying economy on medium/long haul flights: Inability to work or rest. Economy flights are more stressful for men and older travelers.

- Delays: Affects time, routine, the stress of missing a meeting or prep time, and getting to a hotel late at night.

- What these resulted in:

- Lost time: The inability to work due to an Internet connection, cramped plane, excessive driving.

- Surprises: Includes losing baggage, airline delays, getting lost.

Routine Breakers: The inability to attend scheduled conference calls or meetings, eat a normal diet and continue an exercise routine.

Important differences to note

- Women experienced more travel stress than men, specifically in the areas of lost or delayed baggage, the inability to eat healthy and poor Internet connectivity.

- Not surprising, travelers who had over 30 trips per year experienced more of a cumulative effect of stress; however, they were more skilled at tackling *surprises*.

- Travelers with partners, whether they had children or not, had much higher stress when required to travel on weekends or more than three days at a time. Travelers with children and older travelers, however, have less issues with working long hours at their destination.

A study done by the National Institute of Health on international travelers reported that one-third of 498 respondents had high to very high levels of travel stress. Travelers were three times more likely to use health insurance for treatment of psychological disorders and have medical claims, than non-travelers. The more frequent the travel, the more frequent the claims.

The top three stressors for international travelers in this study were:

- Impact on family and sense of isolation,

- Health concerns of jet lag or worries about health and safety, and

- Workload upon return from travel.

- Most respondents thought it necessary to take a rest day after international travel, but rarely did it.

- Two-thirds reported that their managers rarely or never formally granted a rest day, yet 60% reported that approved time off would help them cope better. *If the workload is high when travelers return, they may feel even more overwhelmed by taking a day off.*

Frequent traveling can have benefits resulting in travelers being more adaptable, culturally-savvy and able to work the system as much as possible to get the benefits. When I first started traveling, I was so naïve. I used to teach a 3-5 week course to staff, most of which were new to business travel. I never took it for granted that they knew the ins and outs of travel, or even that they should tip the hotel maid. I loved teaching them the travel aspect of their job, as much I loved teaching them how to do clinical research.

How Companies Can Help the Traveler

Travelers can expect to have control over about one-third of lost time. Stress prevention can reduce expenses and increase productivity. An employee traveling cannot have the same workload as an employee who is office-based. A traveler not only needs to be given more support on the road, but may need additional allowances when they are back in the office, for example, a day prior to and after an international trip, or the ability to work from home. Having an extra one-two hours (depending on their work commute to and from the office) to do laundry, catch up on errands and be with their family, goes a long way toward a happy, healthy employee.

> *A Human Resources Director I know complains about how much money Clinical Research Associates (CRAs) earn, driving up all CRA salaries. This job entails being on the road 3-5 days per week. When you are paying a frequent traveler, you aren't just paying them to do the job, you're paying them to lose part of their life that other people often take for granted. They have very small windows to schedule doctor appointments, run errands and just hang out with their family in the evenings. They also sometimes have to travel on Sundays and don't get back until late on Friday evenings. Frequent travelers deserve every extra dollar they make.*

When companies cut costs by saving money and flying people economy on long flights, they cost themselves money. My former company flew people *internationally* economy class unless it was six hours or more. One trainer I know flew from Raleigh-Durham to Kobe, Japan in economy class. I never asked her how effective she was leading a class for three days upon arrival. I didn't need to.

Traveling less isn't necessarily the answer either, as some tasks can't be completed remotely, and important meetings don't always have the same impact as face-to-face meetings. Travel policies seem to be focused on money rather than the traveler, even though they ultimately spend more in lost productivity.

Ideas for companies to implement:

- Remote or home-based work before and after the trip.

- A compensation day for travel on the weekends. *This isn't just nice. It's fair.*

- Allowing travelers to have more convenient departure and arrival times. Options to fly in the night before to ease the stress of delays and be able to get their normal morning workout in or spend the night after a meeting rather than take a red-eye or get home in the wee hours.

- Convenient hotel locations.

- Reduce or eliminate last-minute trips as much as possible to alleviate the stress of planned events or daily routines with family/pets. *A study by the Centers for Disease Control noted this as a high stressor for travelers.*

- Concierge services to help with errands, pet sitting, etc.

- Reimbursement for Global Entry or TSA Pre-Check status.

- Dedicated administrative support to help with booking travel (total time-suck) and completing expense reports. This is something my clients, which are higher-level employees and business owners, consider a complete waste of their time and are often well behind in submission. Neither are stressful on their own; they are seen as low-priority.

- Seat upgrades to at least Priority seating for medium and long haul flights. Carlson Wagonlit Travel estimates that a company saving one million dollars a year in economy, loses three million dollars a year in lost productivity and traveler stress. The higher the position of the employee, the more impact on dollars lost during productive time.

- Direct flights even though they cost more. I'm always shocked how many companies make a traveler fly in multiple legs at savings of a couple hundred bucks, but don't think that it takes them three extra hours of lost time to get there.

- Realize that travelers are constantly trying to "catch-up" when they travel. They shouldn't be catching up because their workload accumulates when they travel because the travel is *part of their job*. Their workload either needs to be decreased during that time or more support provided.

Companies have the ability to decrease employee turnover, improve productivity and increase happiness and health by looking at the traveler as a whole person and what constitutes their lifestyle.

> *"Leaders inspire the highest performance by pushing those they lead beyond their comfort zones: challenging, stretching, exhorting, emboldening, and inspiring them to exceed their limits. Stress is the means by which we expand capacity, as long as it's balanced by intermittent renewal. That means leaders and organizations must also intentionally spend time encouraging, recognizing, appreciating, rewarding, and celebrating people's accomplishments..." Tony Schwartz, CEO The Energy Project, The Way We're Working Isn't Working.*

For links and references to this chapter visit http://www.beyondtravelbook.com/signup.html and login with your email address. Use the password provided in the follow-up email.

Marcey Rader

2. Behavioral Change

I would consider myself disciplined, methodical and systematic. I have had at least four different people, trying to describe me, put their hands in a position like they are holding a box and say, "You are very ..." and then move their hands three times to the right. In my head I would think, "they were saying 'You are very ordered, strict, neat, disciplined, rigid'." I didn't really know — and it used to bother me — until my orthopedist, Dr. Rob Jones, making these same hand gestures, said, "Systematic! You understand there is a process and you follow that process in a certain order." I'll take that. I like to say that those three small movements people make when describing me stands for "Gets Shit Done."

When I first started my massive self-improvement plan, I was very realistic and planned well (back to that methodical, systematic, ordered mentality). The first thing I did was documenting behaviors, habits or projects on my whiteboard and added to them as I thought of more. After about a month, I went through them and ordered them by importance, dividing them into two categories — Easy and Hard. I didn't want to do two to three hard changes at once since I was working on three different areas: Physical Clutter, Productivity and Mind/Body.

When people set goals they think of the outcome they want. They forget to focus on the trigger that causes the undesirable behavior that stops us in our tracks. The trigger is the key. Find the behavioral trigger and change it. Realize that changes don't happen overnight and they certainly won't in 21 days — the magical number that someone came up with for habit change. Plan in advance for vacations, travel, holidays and other events that you know might make you slip from the new behavior, before it even occurs. Then have a plan to get back on track.

9

An interesting study was done with parents driving through fast-food restaurants to pick up dinner. It only took a couple of interruptions to that schedule to change the behavior. *When the fast food restaurant closed, do you think that they changed to a different restaurant?* No! They went home and fixed dinner. This kind of information is helpful when considering your own triggers. If you stop and get a Grande Sugar Latte every morning, change the route you take to work, if you want to change that behavior. You may miss it at first, but eventually the trigger and automation of you pulling into the drive-through will disappear. If you normally eat dessert after every dinner, brush your teeth after you finish eating, before dessert ... or take a short walk, do a chore around the house; something that is different. Try to make it consistent and develop into a new habit. Make dinner a *trigger* for something else instead of dinner immediately followed by dessert.

Here are some examples of triggers and behavior changes my clients have experienced.

A.L. used to raid the kitchen cabinets when arriving home from work every day. He would be *starving* and eat a handful of nuts while looking for something else to eat until time for dinner. The change that we made was two-fold. 1) Eat a 200-calorie snack of fiber, fat and protein in the form of nuts, veggies and guacamole or Greek yogurt, *before* he left for his 45-minute commute. Then, (key step), he went into his house through the garage instead of the kitchen. The triggers of going through the kitchen and immediately going to the cabinet was eliminated.

M.S. didn't think she had time for exercise and didn't like it either. We needed to reframe her thinking. Instead of thinking of exercise in terms of putting on different clothes, getting sweaty and redoing hair and makeup, we framed it as *movement opportunities*. I gave her five 5-minute workouts she could do between client meetings, using what she already had in her workspace (including the Jetsetter Gym Kit), without getting sweaty, in a skirt. Every day she would have between one and five opportunities for this mini-workout. That was 5-25 minutes more exercise (sneaky!) every day that without this new regime she wouldn't have achieved ... and, she no longer thought of this as a *changing clothes event.* After a few months she sent a text saying "I think my butt's getting higher just from opportunities!" It's one of my favorite texts. Now she loves actual workouts and has a totally different outlook on exercise.

J.L is a high-powered attorney with three children who often felt like email controlled his life. He checked it in the morning before work, frequently during the day and then in the evening after dinner. He felt like he had to be available to his clients 24/7. When he gave himself permission to check email less by installing systems and tools to help him organize his inbox and processed rather than reacted to email, he quickly realized he actually had much less email than he thought and was then able to overcome the anxiety of the Fear Of Missing Out (FOMO). Gradually reducing checking email to only twice daily and informing his staff what his new process was, not only decreased his stress levels, but improved his productivity and focus immensely. One of the happiest messages I received from him was that he went to the beach and spent the whole weekend focused on his family when normally he would have been beside the pool checking his phone instead of in it playing with his son.

Steps for Behavioral Change

> *Unless you become aware of the hidden dangers that will sabotage you both professionally and personally, you have little opportunity to make actionable changes in your life. The process begins with awareness and the recognition that having low physical or mental vitality can diminish your effectiveness at work and impact your ability to maintain high velocity in this world of increasing blur—or cause you to sacrifice parts of your personal life that you will one day regret.*
> *– Gregory Florez, CEO V2 Performance*

Travelers who don't like to shop for groceries, wash, chop and cook fresh food, find it easier to eat more nutritious meals on the road. One client never ate fruit unless she was traveling because she could buy it already peeled, chopped or sliced. Mothers with young children often tell me travel is the only time they feel they can exercise. On the flip side, travel can make eating nutritious meals harder, especially when you eat your meals in airports, have a restricted diet, or have your meals chosen for you, such as business meetings or conferences.

From a productivity perspective, I have clients who love long plane trips because they can get more done on the plane than in the office. For others, particularly for men, they can't get anything done on a plane because they can't use their laptops due to the lack of personal space. Your new behaviors will need different triggers for travel versus at home.

The Fairy Tale

Most people are a little guilty of relying on *fairies* in at least one area of their life. I like to believe the Outlet Fairy will provide *working* outlets anywhere I need them in airports. The Security Line Fairy will allow me to keep on all my clothes, jewelry, and shoes, and walk right through the line. The Dishwasher Fairy will empty my dishwasher so the dirty dishes can go straight inside without sitting out on my counter or in my sink. You get the point!

People rely on fairies for their health and fitness without even realizing it. Here's an example using a couple of fictitious characters — Bonnie and Rick — which might put things into perspective.

Bonnie is a vegetarian who doesn't eat very well. Her diet is mostly refined carbohydrates, lots of sugar or artificially sweetened products, and very few fruit and vegetables. She participates in a bicycle spinning class three to four times each week. She is overweight and has a body fat of thirty-three percent.

Most of her friends are also overweight and don't exercise. Bonnie believes that because she *does* exercise, that the Diabetes Fairy is going to skip over her and wave her magic wand at one of her friends instead.

Rick's entire family has high cholesterol, and half of them have high blood pressure. Rick is a normal weight and doesn't exercise. His diet contains a lot of fatty, processed meat and fast food, which *for now,* isn't affecting his weight. Two of his three siblings are overweight, as are both of his parents. Rick believes that since he isn't fat he won't get high cholesterol or hypertension. The Heart Disease Fairy will just *skip right on over* Rick.

There are no fairies flying around seeing who is the *least bad.* We could all look around and compare ourselves to someone who is in a worse situation to make us feel better. We can do this with money, our jobs, and our weight. What we can't do is find someone who looks worse off than us and convince ourselves that the fairies will go for him or her first. There are many factors that determine whether or not a person will get a chronic disease, none of which involves fairies, praying or looking good in a bikini.

Don't compare downward, thinking you are automatically healthier than other people and then not take the steps necessary to move forward on *your* health journey. A study from Harvard showed that when you surround yourself with people who are overweight you are more than fifty-seven percent likely to be overweight and thirty-six percent more likely to smoke if your friends smoke. It might make you feel good to be the healthiest one of the bunch, but it isn't helping your habits in the long run unless you get the others on board.

We could go to the other extreme and compare ourselves to people who appear to have no faults. If we did this, we would never be happy with ourselves and feel doomed that the fairies were always chasing us down. Compare downward and you may end up diagnosed with a chronic disease due to thinking that you are healthier than you are. Compare upward and you feel depressed and disappointed in yourself for not being better. Believe in fairies and you end up fooling yourself either way.

When you are determining what changes to make, stick to one or two at a time and realize that it may take a while to get these habits into your groove. Ask yourself these questions:

1. What are Your Goals?

Goals are different than dreams. A dream is something that you don't plan for or try to make happen. It's often not realistic. A dream is winning the lottery when you don't buy tickets or playing with Prince on his next album when you have never picked up an instrument.

a. Who do you want to be?

b. How do you want to look?

c. What do you want to feel?

d. Why? The *why* is important. There needs to be a compelling reason to make a change. It's not "because everyone at work is doing it." Ask yourself *why* you want to do it, until you have drilled down as far as you can go and get to the real reason this goal is important to you.

Real-Life Client Example:

- I want to lose weight.
- Why? I want to feel better.
- Why? I'm tired all the time.
- Why? I'm a stress eater. I eat a lot of sugar all day and get jacked up on caffeine. I say I'm going to exercise in the evening, but at that point I don't have the energy and all I want to do sit on the couch.
- Why do you want to lose weight? I feel like I'm missing out on opportunities to have fun or do interesting things. I'm wor-

14

ried that my wife will find other people that can get out and do things, and I'll be waving at her from the couch.

See how that's so much more motivating than just 'losing weight?'

1. What's Your Whine?

Are you pretending that an excuse is a reason? Often people make excuses and state them as if they are reasons. If you planned to exercise in your room at 6:00pm when you arrived at the hotel, but your plane was delayed until 10:00pm, that's a reason not to exercise at 6:00. It's not an excuse not to find an opportunity to move at the airport and do some triceps dips or push-ups or walk around the terminal.

Who or what is standing in your way (or who/what do you *perceive* is standing in your way)?

2. What's your Win?

- What kind of resources do you have?
- Who can support or hold you accountable?

3. What's your Plan?

Coaching and Accountability

Are you someone who reads half a book, skipping through the exercises? Do you have a self-help library with so many styles and options that you just give up because you don't know which one will work best for you? We've all been there and done that. Even I skip through some of the exercises, and I'm highly self-motivated. A game changer for me was hiring a business coach, who gave me tasks and exercises that held me accountable, so I *had* to do them. Not only was I paying her to coach me, the exercises and strategies were critical to my business growth. My coach had four different coaches and was great at outsourcing, resulting in skyrocketing her career and business. I always have at least one coach and a mastermind group for whatever it is that I'm working on. I even hired a coach to help me market this book.

If you've already had a coach and need support for continued success or you know exactly what you need to change and how to change it, an accountability partner can be instrumental in keeping you focused on your goal. It's different than a mentorship because your partner is going through the same thing and has a similar goal. I used to think I didn't need one because I loved what I was doing, and I'm disciplined. I like my privacy and autonomy, yet I also like feedback and praise.

When I started my own business, I lost connection with people. Even though I worked from home for thirteen years and traveled solo for a decade, I still had a virtual team that I could bounce ideas off of, vent to when needed (probably more than they would have liked), and whine about the car rental of *Middle Earth* at DFW airport. I felt isolated and needed someone with whom to share all of my business updates and get feedback on my ideas, website, marketing, and packages when I didn't have access to my business coach. I realized what I needed was an Accountability Partner.

Four months after starting my business I found my business accountability partner. Still my partner to this day, she's also a productivity coach growing her business as well, yet we've never seen each other as competition. In some ways, we couldn't be more different, but certain aspects of our personalities are very much the same. We meet at least weekly by phone and every other week for lunch. We have an agenda and/or list of topics that we want to cover and provide feedback and information in support of one another. We share our struggles, tears, whines and wins. When one of us feels like giving up, the other person allows the vent and then says, "put on your entrepreneurial panties and hit it!"

My business coach said, "Your friends and family will support you, but they won't always *get* you." I totally get that now. Even though I am confident, capable, intelligent, energetic, persistent, determined, dedicated and unstoppable, it doesn't mean I don't have my moments. Having someone to lean on, text, call, email, and dine with is priceless when you are on a journey that is challenging and filled with the unknown.

Things to consider in an accountability partner:

- Your best friend is not a good choice. They won't be able to look at you with an outsider's lens and give you the right advice.

- Find someone that is brutally honest. You can cry on their shoulder, yet they still tell you when it's time to blow your nose and get to it.

- Consider someone outside your industry so you can help each other with your unique areas of strength.

- Set clear parameters on the arrangement, i.e. how often to be in touch, what topics you will cover, how long meetings will last and how much time each person is allotted.

- Have an accountability timeline of three months to one year and revisit the arrangement quarterly. That way, if one of you is moving forward faster than the other, you don't feel obligated to stay back while the other person catches up. This revisiting the agreement is important on the rare occasion that you are not resonating on all eight cylinders and you want a different partner.

- Celebrate your successes and consequences of failures. How will you reward yourself for big wins? If you fail to achieve your intended goal, will you donate money to an organization you *don't* like? Will you bet your accountability partner and pay up if you don't do what you say you are going to do?

Small Changes

When you are creating a new behavior, you have to treat the current behavior like a weak, atrophied, floppy muscle. To change it into a strong, fit, defined muscle, you have to work at it, right? You don't go from hiding your batwings in a short-sleeve shirt to sporting a tank top in a day or a week. Marathon plans to change behaviors take anywhere from three to six months. Your productivity habits and health behaviors also need plans that are continually increasing and building. Whatever the behavior you want to change, it didn't happen overnight, because overnight doesn't create behavior. It's just a one-off. Doing something repeatedly is what creates a new behavior or habit. The way you process email, what you order at Caribou Coffee, your knee-jerk response to a meeting request and the ginger ale you get every plane trip from the beverage cart is all a habit. Just like having a plan when you workout makes for a more successful session, having a plan for your behavioral change helps too.

I believe small changes create big results. I also believe in self-responsibility or discipline. Once you are diagnosed with a disease, disorder or syndrome, your options for baby steps may be over. You might have to take bold steps to get your health back on track. Say your doctor tells you that you have pre-diabetes. You say you're "going to *try* to cut down on sugar and lose weight." After neither of those things happens and a year later you end up with full-blown diabetes, you can see how baby steps may not be enough. Bold behavioral changes may have to occur. You had the chance to change, but you didn't or the changes weren't bold enough. It may sound harsh, I know. Please keep in mind that I wasn't able to take baby steps when I was diagnosed with Hashimoto's Disease. I couldn't *try* to control it on my own, I couldn't just 'cut back' on exercise until my hormones and adrenal glands were normalized, and I couldn't just eat *a little less* gluten to get my digestive system working properly. One of my favorite quotes is from Winston Churchill "When you're going through hell, keep going." Changing my life sucked for about four weeks, but now everything I do is my normal and I am completely happy and never feel deprived — for real. If you recognize and prepare that some of your changes may result in a grieving process of the old you, it will help you get through the challenging times.

Our behaviors are our choice. Yes, they are a process in our brain that snapping our fingers won't change, however we *can* first set the intention to make the change, start taking the necessary steps and ask ourselves when we slip, if the action or lack of action is an excuse or a reason. Then, we get back on the horse and keep riding. Remember, it may not look pretty, and it won't always be easy, but the more you practice the new behavior, the easier it will become and the longer your winning streak will continue.

One trick I play on myself is to refer to myself as whatever it is I am trying to become. When I first started my business, I would act as if I were already successful. When I was racing, I acted as if I was the one everyone was competing against. Refer to yourself as a healthy eater, good sleeper, intentional meeting maker and calm traveler. Make it all a decision and a choice. I could have chosen to cry about my diagnosis, but I gave myself a timeline — twenty-four hours — of how long I could cry about it (and it was a snotty, sobbing, ugly cry). Then I told myself that whatever happened was my choice.

When you're making excuses, handle or manage your choices and stop placing blame. Genetics doesn't play as big of a part in our health status as much as we think it does. Genes are bullets in the gun, but **you** pull the trigger. One of my family members blames her cholesterol and high blood pressure on our family history. I've had genetic testing, and we are at no more or less risk than the average person. Our family has these issues because of diet and lifestyle and it keeps getting passed on to the next generation. The last time I was home I saw four generations of people all eating the same and living the same lifestyle, and it wasn't moving in the right (healthy) direction on the health continuum.

Continually evaluate. When my goal of eating more vegetables got stuck on three servings a day, I looked at which days I wasn't able to break past three and why. I realized I needed to increase my support. Instead of chopping vegetables every day, I started washing, chopping, prepping, roasting, etc., on Sundays and Wednesdays. This made it easy for me to add them to whatever meal I was preparing. Now I regularly eat five to nine servings a day and I know when I don't do that Sunday prep time, the number of servings that week will drop.

> *"You hold the clicker. If you don't like it, change the channel." – Arianna Huffington*

Justin Case

I'm keeping my car insurance documents from three years ago ... Justin Case.

I'm going to check my email ... Justin Case.

I'm buying a box of cake mix ... Justin Case.

Justin Case is one popular dude. You know him. He keeps us from throwing away unnecessary papers, scanning and storing documents in the cloud, and canceling our unused gym membership. He encourages us to have sweets lying around in case unexpected guests stop by or continue getting Facebook notifications on our phone because someone might like the photo we just posted.

Stop blaming *Justin* for your fears and faults, and face the facts. You don't need your old insurance coverage information once it's expired. You don't need to check your email more than three times a day (unless you are in customer service). You don't need to always have desserts on hand in your house. You don't need to know immediately that someone has looked at your post.

How many items of clothing in your closet does *Justin* make you keep in case you lose the 20 pounds you've been trying to shed for 15 years? Justin has no sense of style or when fashion becomes outdated. Stop wasting your closet space and donate those items to someone who can benefit. Commit to breaking up your relationship with Justin Case. He is toxic and not helping you move forward in your life. Like all toxic relationships, we need to cut the ties, rip off the bandage and carry on.

The Willpower Bucket

You enter your kitchen after a long day and go straight to the refrigerator for the most convenient, processed food you can put in your mouth. There is no way you have the energy to even *think* about what to eat. *You stand at the ice cream/cupcake/bakery for several minutes before deciding on the flavor because the choice overload is too much. Then you get the same kind you always do in defeat.* You're asked to sign a contract that you are a little nervous about at 4:30pm on a Friday. You default to the status quo and just decide to decline the contract.

Every day we make thousands of decisions that affect our lives. Researchers at Cornell found that we make an average of 227 decisions daily about food alone. Willpower and discipline are not finite. Think about it like this ... you start the morning with a full bucket of Willpower Monkeys. Every decision you make causes one monkey (one monkey of will) to jump out of the bucket. At the end of the day, you have a lot fewer monkeys in your bucket. The ones left behind are the tired or lazy monkeys who didn't want to expend energy earlier. These are *not* the monkeys you want making decisions for you.

Some of the mundane decisions I have to make every day, within an hour of getting up:

What do I wear to exercise?

Do I start with strength training or cardio?

Do I eat breakfast now or wait until Kevin gets up?

Do I shower before or after breakfast?

What color of lipstick do I put on?

Even these decisions that may seem automatic, expend energy. When we are tired, depleted or have had most of our monkeys jump out of our bucket, we tend to ...

- procrastinate,
- defer to the status quo,
- make a fear-based decision, or
- take fewer risks.

How do you get around this? Keep as many monkeys in your bucket by planning as much as you can in advance and reducing your choices by automating your decisions. At some point, our brain and our willpower will become depleted, and no more decisions can be made. We cannot expend any more effort to decide. We raid the refrigerator and eat what we know won't make us feel good, but it's fast, convenient and requires no thought. We decide to skip the gym or our workout because we're tired, and the thought of changing clothes and doing anything other than sit on our couch is too much to bear. We argue with our kids, spouse or the TV because we don't have enough willpower left to make considerations.

We revert to status quo, automatic decisions. If an option is chosen *for* us, we take it because it's easier for our brain. Studies have shown the more boxes of cereal or jars of jelly we have to choose from, the less likely we will buy *anything,* and will often walk away. It's probably why my mind turns to mush when I walk into a department store. There's too much to choose from. It's a sensory overload. Just let me shop online where I can narrow it down to exactly what I'm looking for ... or a boutique where the options are far less.

It's called decision fatigue.

If we compare making decisions to a workout, it goes like this. If you start a three-mile run at a reasonable pace, you can probably sustain it and finish at the same speed. If you are running a marathon, maintaining the same pace for three to four hours takes a lot more work and energy. You may be able to keep pace, but it requires much more effort the last six miles than if you were keeping pace the last half mile of a three-mile run. Most people can't maintain the pace of their first half and end up slowing down in the end. It's the same with your brain. You start out every morning refreshed and a bucket full of decision-making abilities. The more strenuous your decisions, or the more decisions you have to make in volume, the more you will drag and slow down by the end of the day.

Inserting energy breaks into your day can help throw a few more decisions (or willpower monkeys) back into the bucket. When you take a break, whether it's a nap, exercise, meditation or simply just stopping whatever you are doing and going for a 10-minute walk, your odds of making smart decisions greatly increase. Need to look over a contract or job offer late in the afternoon? Be sure to take an energy break first.

Baba Shiv from the Stanford School of Business states that *morning is the best time to make difficult decisions because that's when your natural levels of serotonin and dopamine are high.* You are less risk-averse and can make hard decisions like whether or not to sign a contract or purchase a house. In the afternoon, your serotonin levels drop, so you are more likely to opt for the status quo bias or indecision.

- What else affects decision-making?
- Good quality sleep — Increases serotonin.
- Exercise — Releases a precursor to serotonin.
- Breakfast — Good quality and high protein help amino acids get across the blood brain barrier and sustains the serotonin release longer than a high-carb, high-sugar, low-quality breakfast.
- Short naps — Ten to twenty minutes of sleep can increase your energy levels.

- Hunger and thirst — Lead to making higher-risk choices.

- Full bladder — More likely to choose low-risk options and avoid impulsive decisions.

- Proper ventilation — The higher the CO_2, the more our cognitive abilities decrease. Open the windows or get outside for a quick break.

Some ways I automate my decisions:

- On Sundays, I plan my workouts for the week. The only thing that changes this is if my morning heart rate variability score is low on my *Sweetbeat App* or if the weather makes me have to flip around days.

- On Sundays and Wednesdays, I spend one-hour washing, chopping, prepping and cooking for the week. This way I don't have to make too many dinner decisions. I just throw together what's already cooked or ready.

- As I did as a child, I sometimes pick out all my outfits for the week on days I am leaving my house. Each outfit gets hung on one hanger and includes my jewelry. Weather or mood may change my mind on a specific outfit, but it's never a waste of time because that entire outfit is ready to go when I want to wear it. This is a major time-saver for me because otherwise I will stand in front of my closet for several minutes deciding what to wear.

- I'm not a condiment hoarder with an entire fridge door filled with different sauces. I have only a few and tend to eat pretty simply.

This may not seem like a big deal, but science tells us that it can help. Simplify what you can and make decisions in advance if possible. Make your important decisions earlier in the day or after you've done something that renews your energy, like exercising or eating a healthy meal.

Who's on Your A-Team?

If you made a list of the ten people in your personal and work life that you are around the most, would you rate them as **supportive, inspiring or have traits that you admire?** Or, are they **vampires,** sucking your energy and not encouraging you to grow as an individual?

Your friends, family, colleagues or workout buddies could be in a different place in their life than you. This could result in motivating you to do more or block your path and hold your head under water. At work, you may be career-oriented while someone else is focusing on the family. You may be ready to race a marathon while your running partner can't fathom anything more than a 10k. You want to cut off all Internet and email after 7pm, but your wife wants to spend an hour on Facebook. Rarely are you going to go through your life with the people around you moving at the same pace as you.

I've participated in several types of sports and trained with dozens of people over the years. Some became good friends, and others were just training buddies. As we progressed, regressed, changed sports, changed jobs or changed locations, I changed who I trained with. I never let a friend or training partner's choice dictate what I was doing or hold me back in any way. If I needed to move on or find someone else, I did.

The people I gravitate to are considered my 'A-Team.' In the 80s hit show the A-Team, each member had their specialty and was respected for what they did best. I like to surround myself with people who also have a specialty, preferably one that I don't own, so that I can learn from them. I didn't know how to paddle a few years ago and wanted a teammate that was a strong paddler. They took more of the load, and I learned from them. When I tried to learn to navigate, I looked for someone who had an easy teaching style and patience to deal with me.

Who's on your A-Team? Do you surround yourself with people you can learn from that are better than you at whatever aspect of your life you are trying to improve, i.e. business, finance, public speaking or health? Or, do *you* always like to be the best, no matter what, and surround yourself with the B-Team? If you're always hanging out with benchwarmers to make yourself feel better (and bigger), you're probably going to get stuck at the level of fabulous that you are right now ... until you are no longer fabulous.

I used to keep my toxic relationships a lot longer than I needed to and one thing about getting older is realizing I don't have to do that. If a friendship is exhausting — it's not a friendship, it's a chore. If it's a work colleague, minimizing time with them may be the only thing you can do. If it's a family member ... well, that might be a visit to a mental health counselor to prepare and debrief. One of my goals with every race was for people to want to race with me again. Not because I was the strongest physically, but because I was supportive, smart, fun and willing to make sacrifices for the team. I feel the same way about being on a team at work.

I have an A-Team for each area of my life: business, racing, finance, relationships, personal growth, etc. I have a lot of people that support me, but that doesn't necessarily mean they get me. Some people may not even realize that I'm looking to them to make myself a better person. They're secretly on my A-Team because they naturally inspire me. Start your A-Team roster. Life's too short to sit around on the bench.

If you find that you're struggling to create your behavioral change while reading this book, contact me at Marcey@marceyrader.com for a Strategy Session to determine if private coaching is right for you. If you are highly self-motivated, than this book may be all you need.

3. Productivity

'Mobile' can mean traveling by car, train or plane, across time zones or around your city. This chapter covers general productivity hacks (short cuts) that don't just apply to travelers and can be used even if you are an office-bound employee.

Telepressure

Have you ever made yourself busier than you need to be and somehow got satisfaction out of saying how busy you were? Why do people do this? Shouldn't we want to be productive so we can spend our time enjoying our life and playing more? We wear Busy like a badge. I can be busy all day tying and untying my shoes. It doesn't mean I'm productive or effective. I have a relative who is constantly talking about how busy her life is. I think she gets something out of it — some sort of payoff — because she fills her day up with meaningless tasks and then complains about her lack of time! Do you see yourself in her somewhere?

There's a new term, "telepressure," that describes the stress or need people feel to respond urgently to emails and texts. Telepressure is a significant problem because it leads to burnout. When people feel they are constantly working and don't have downtime, the treadmill of cognitive work overload weighs on their health and energy. Business travelers have this condition more intensely because they feel like they have to catch up all the time from traveling. The truth is that there is no catch-up when part of your job involves travel. That travel time should be considered part of your day and the amount of work you will be able to do.

Employees with a high level of telepressure sleep poorly and are more likely to miss work. They are also less productive because instead of focusing on tasks, they are just responding to the email drip. Fifty-two percent of Americans check their email before and after work, on sick days and during vacations. We've lost our boundaries and need to get them back. The issue with telepressure is more a workplace cultural problem than an employee problem.

Setting team or company policies can help people know what the expectations are on responding within certain timelines. Sometimes the pressure we impose on ourselves is much greater than reality. If someone chooses to work all hours of the night, it should be clear that they don't expect an answer, especially if that person sending the email is a manager or supervisor. Teams should be very careful using words like ASAP or URGENT because it has different meanings for people (and email is never urgent).

When everything is urgent, nothing is urgent.

One of my clients said she needed to be able to mark an email urgent for her client because he gets hundreds of emails, doesn't listen to voicemail and doesn't text. There isn't a way to do that with Gmail. He might have her as a Priority if his system is set up that way, but she can't mark it urgent. When I used Outlook I didn't even have the urgent setting turned on. If someone sent me an urgent email, it didn't show up any different than any other email. Why? Because most people don't understand what urgent is. Email is never urgent.

Attention Distraction Disorder

Attention Distraction Disorder is a disorder I made up. People loosely joke that they have Attention Deficit Disorder (ADD), but what they have are poor attention skills because they haven't trained their brains to be focused and have developed behaviors that encourage distraction. The people who suffer from ADD are in a different class and sometimes take more than behavioral change for them to be able to move forward.

Before we get into the nitty-gritty, it's important to understand why we do the things we do, even when they are self-defeating. Human brains have two kinds of attention: involuntary and voluntary.

Involuntary attention is triggered by outside stimuli and is used for survival. It's important if you're trying to run from an avalanche, but our brains have a hard time determining that the phone ringing, pinging or buzzing isn't an avalanche and takes our brain out of focus mode. Almost *all* individuals have a hard time ignoring loud noises and flashing lights. This can be dogs barking, airplane noise or an iPhone ringing in the background.

Voluntary attention is the ability to focus on a task ... like me writing this book or you reading it. While reading this book, have you put it down three times in the last 15 minutes to check something on the computer, get something to drink or answer the phone? Focused attention takes mental energy. It's a workout for your brain. You may run an extra five minutes or complete a few more reps when you are training your body, but no one considers training their mind. Forcing yourself to wait five more minutes before you check email *again* or committing to working for 30 minutes straight on a project or task is a workout for your brain. That's why it's hard at first.

> *"Developing greater control over your attention is perhaps the **single** most powerful way to reshape your brain and thus your mind. You can train and strength-en your attention just like any other mental ability."*
> *Buddha's Brain*

As we constantly undergo interruptions, *effortful control*, a part of the brain that regulates attention, declines. The more you check your messages, the more you feel the need to check them. It is truly an addiction or compulsion. It can take a long time to get over because it is a *process within your brain.* So far, most of my clients have been able to overcome it in about two weeks with the right steps.

Multitasking Myth

It's probably obvious when we are *multitasking* that we are not absorbing as much information as when we are focused, but yet we still do it. Whatever is learned while multitasking is less retrievable by the brain. Tasks requiring more attention like complex exercises are more adversely affected by multitasking during the learning process.

Procedural memory is how you ride a bike or tie your shoes. *Declarative memory* is remembering what you had for dinner last night or your friend's phone number. The part of the brain called the hippocampus manages demanding cognitive tasks and creates long-term memories. It's key for declarative memory. When you are multitasking or distracted, the hippocampus kicks the job down to the striatum, which handles mundane tasks. The striatum is the part of the brain that is damaged by diseases like Parkinson's Disease where people have trouble learning new motor skills, but no problem remembering things from their past. Sometimes, the mundane part of your brain is the one replying to the question on the conference call or writing a response in an email because <u>that part of the brain can't do two things at once</u>. The striatum is the brain's autopilot. Do you want your autopilot to send your client an email?

Statistics

Multitasking is not a behavior of a 'super-worker.' Science proves it's a sign of distraction. If a person is trying to read an email while talking on the phone, the brain is trying to perform language tasks that have to go through the same cognitive channel. His brain has to go back and forth between tasks, therefore slowing it down. Researchers at the University of Michigan found that productivity dropped as much as *40 percent* when subjects tried to do two or more things at once. One of the study's authors asserts that quality work and multitasking are incompatible.

In a study at the University of Minnesota, test workers who switch-tasked or multi-tasked took three to twenty-seven percent more time to complete the reading, counting or math problems. The harder the interrupted task, the harder it was to get back on track. A Microsoft study from the University of Illinois found it takes the typical worker

<u>fifteen minutes</u> to refocus on a serious mental task after an interruption such as responding to incoming email or Instant Messages. It was also easier for them to stray and browse personal websites after the interruption. A study at UC Irvine showed it took <u>twenty-five minutes</u> to get back on task!

> *To **truly** learn something your brain has to be focused 100%. - Rapt*

"How is your ability to multitask?" is a popular interview question. I had a trainee tell me they lied during an interview and said it was *"great"* but in reality, they knew that multitasking decreased productivity, and they tried to avoid it. They thought twice about taking the job at that company after knowing that it was so important that it was an interview question! If your company still states multitasking as a skill or job requirement, change it now or look completely outdated.

Multitasking in the workplace has reached epidemic proportions. A study by the Institute for the Future reported that the average employee sends and receives 178 messages a day and is interrupted an average of at least three times an hour. The estimated loss of productivity by multitaskers to the US economy is **$650** billion a year. A study by the McKinsey Global Institute estimates that employees spend thirteen hours a week or about 650 hours a year on email. I'm able to track mine using RescueTime, and I rarely exceed five hours per week.

Types of Tasking

These descriptions of tasking come from Dave Crenshaw's book, *The Myth of Multitasking: How "Doing It All" Gets Nothing Done.*

Multitasking

Only two percent of people can multitask effectively, and chances are, you aren't one of them. As people learn more about the decreased productivity contributed to multitasking, we can only hope it becomes more culturally unacceptable behavior. Multitasking can reduce productivity up to forty percent. I'm not suggesting to never multi-task, but remember that if you are truly trying to *learn* something, you need to have 100% attention.

Background Tasking

Not all types of *tasking* are bad and can sometimes even be beneficial. Background tasking can be efficient. Examples of background tasking are watching TV while exercising or listening to the radio while driving. Studies have shown that certain types of music can make people exercise harder. Personally, I catch up on podcasts while I'm cooking and cleaning and watch The Daily Show when I'm doing strength training indoors.

Hypertasking

Hypertasking is when work multitasking gets carried over into your personal life. This could be talking on the phone while driving (a very dangerous form of multitasking that is the equivalent to driving drunk) or working on a laptop while drinking coffee and talking to a friend. My girlfriend and I used to do this all the time. We would meet for lunch once a month at a coffee shop and spend two hours talking, eating, drinking coffee and working a little. We used it as collaborative time and to bounce ideas off of each other, as well as the normal office talkie-talk we didn't get from working remotely. Did we get more done than if we were at home? Absolutely not. It was more for the social engagement than for work, and we could and did stop talking when the other person was looking at their computer.

Switch-tasking

Switch-tasking is juggling two tasks by refocusing attention back and forth and losing time and progress in the switch. Switch-tasking is a serious cultural problem. We are switch-tasking more than we multitask because we can do it at such speed. We are under the illusion we are doing things simultaneously, but in reality, we aren't. If it's something that involves the same part of the brain, like writing an email and talking on the phone, you can't do them at the same time.

The average person spends three minutes working on something before they switch-task. Have you ever been able to tell when someone you are talking to on the phone isn't quite 100% listening to you? Their tone changes and there's usually a pause before their response. I've asked people if they want me to call them back after they're done writing their email. This usually gets their attention.

Now that we have some background on the statistics and research behind various levels and types of tasking, we can get started on working with some of our own issues surrounding tasking, as well as look at other areas of productivity that are difficult to manage.

Email

We love it and we hate it. It can make us happy, sad, confused, frustrated, laugh and it can make us cry. I can't think of another thing in today's society with which we have such a complicated relationship. When we get that pop-up or notification, the angel part of the email says, "Someone loves you. Someone needs you." The devil part says, "Here's another task. Here's a bill. Here's a complaint."

The philosophy and process in this section can be applied to all email, however, specific instructions will be for Gmail (my preferred personal email) and Google Apps for Work (my preferred for my business and my small business clients) and Microsoft Outlook.

Badges, Banners, and Pop-Ups

Slave: A person who is strongly influenced by and controlled by something. *Merriam-Webster*

The average person checks their phone 150 times a day. One of the first and easiest things you can do is disable any pop-ups, envelopes, badges or banner notifications. This includes notifications on your computer, tablet and phone. Remember earlier how every time your concentration is distracted you lose fifteen to twenty minutes? With those annoyances on all day, you are never focusing 100% on anything. According to a Basex Report, twenty-eight percent of a knowledge worker's day is spent on interruptions. Is email the core of your work? Does your job description say 'read and respond to email?' Doubtful. Stop letting it distract you from what is important. Every time we are interrupted by an email it takes an average of sixty-four seconds to recover.

- Twenty-two percent of people are expected to respond to email when they aren't at work.
- Fifty percent check work email on weekends.
- Forty-six percent check work email on sick days.
- Thirty-four percent check work email while on vacation.

Notifications create reactiveness. When we are constantly being alerted to this and that and who and what, we never have time to focus. It feels urgent, so we respond with urgency. Then we teach people that we respond urgently, and now it's expected. If you think you can tune out notifications, you're wrong. It affects everyone to varying degrees.

Badges are the numbers that show up on your phone to remind you how far behind you are on alert-driven tasks. Some badges, like texts and calls, may be important depending on how you use them. However, it doesn't mean you need the sound or vibrate activated. Most of the time, I have my phone set to Do Not Disturb (DND), so only people on a specific DND list on my phone can get through to me. Other times I just have it disabled so there isn't a distraction. If I'm on my laptop, I open up my messages app about once per hour to see if I have any new texts. I respond if I need to and close it out. I typically respond to texts on my phone if I'm out of the office. Additionally, my DND is automatically set from 8:00pm – 8:00am so only calls and texts from my special list can get through to me via sound or buzz. This is great if you go to bed early or work across time zones.

Turn off your social media, RSS feeds, and mail badges. You do NOT need to see how many blog posts or tweets are waiting for you to look at twenty-four hours a day. Just looking at seventy RSS feed updates to read makes my guts ache. Even if it isn't a necessity to read them, it can subconsciously cause anxiety. To turn off these badges, go into your settings > notifications and turn off any badges you don't need to see immediately. I promise that you will make it through the day without knowing that someone liked your photo of your lunch.

Turn off your Instant Message (IM) or Chat function for at least part of the day. My rule when I used to work for a company that used IM was to turn it off the first and last hour of each day. That way I wasn't interrupted during my first hour when I was trying to plan and start my day and not caught with a last minute 'quick question' when I was trying to wrap things up. I have very few people with which I use Google IM, and thankfully they don't abuse it and never use it for anything urgent.

Speaking of an instant message, let's give a universal pass to spelling and grammar errors on instant message and text. The vast majority of the time, I know what you are trying to say, so you don't need to cost me data or time by sending another text or IM correcting your spelling or grammar. If I make the mistake, please don't point it out to me. You have way too much time on your hands if you are going to be Officer of Corrections for IM and text.

Only Handle It Once! (OHIO)

Do you go out to your mailbox, open the letters, put them back in the mailbox, go back in your house and repeat the process 3-5 times a day? No? Then stop doing that with your email inbox.

Do you let your physical mail pile 6,000 deep on your desk in case you need it? One hundred deep? No. You file it, trash it or reply to it. Stop doing it with your inbox.

Do you have an inbox full of emails that you keep reading over and over and over again? Just like with paper documents, you should do your best to Only Handle It Once (OHIO). If you see an email that it is clear by the subject line that you can't respond or react to right away, skip it! If you can't do anything at the moment, then waiting until you have the time to respond will give you more time to focus on your response or think about the content of the email. However, you can *process* it correctly to avoid rereading it 20 times or clicking through it on a daily basis. We'll go into that later.

The average person checks their email 36 times an hour. Let's just say you check your email every 5 minutes. Then you're checking 12 times an hour, 8 hours a workday, 5 days a week, and 50 weeks a year (assuming you aren't checking your email while you're on vacation), which equals 24,000 times a year. If you work more than 8 hours or check email in the evenings, it's even more!

If you're checking your email 24,000 times a year, what are you sacrificing? What are you *not* working on during that time? Could you reduce your rate to every 15 minutes (a yearly total of 8,000) and be more productive with other aspects of your job? Think about that number for a minute. You automatically reduced it by *6,000* times a year just by checking 10 minutes less. Could you reduce it to once an hour or 2000 times a year? Three times a day for 750? I have found twice a day works perfectly for me for work email and once a day for personal email. In five years, I have yet to have someone hunt me down and say I did not answer an email promptly. If answering an email within 24 hours isn't timely enough, the sender should be picking up the phone anyway.

Many of my clients feel anxiety when I wean them off constant checking. One even said, "I feel like I'm going to vomit." There has never been a disaster, lost job or missed opportunity with any of my clients as a result of curtailing this behavior. After a couple of weeks, it's the number one thing people are thankful that we worked on, and they don't ever want to go back to their old behavior.

What about the people who call you to check to see *if* you received their email? Most of the time, you've *taught them that you respond immediately*. When you don't respond immediately, they think something is wrong. We teach people how we respond to email. If you're a slave to it, people will expect urgency. Once I got an email on a Saturday from a project manager asking me to do a task because she knew I would be working. I wanted to throw my Palm Pilot (yes, it was a long time ago) out the window. I was really angry with her for taking my Saturday. Then I realized that I had taught her that I worked on Saturdays because I was always sending her reports and email responses. From that moment on I only worked off-line on Saturdays and synced and sent Monday mornings.

Have you ever sent an email late at night or early in the morning to prove what a hard worker you are? STOP. STOP NOW. No one is impressed with that anymore. It's so easy to schedule emails to be sent at a certain time it doesn't even prove you were working late anyway. Go to bed.

Email Processing

Processing email in batches while working offline can decrease incorrect or inappropriate responses and just plain saves time. Processing email doesn't mean to open it, read it, close it and deal with it later. Processing email means to start at the top or in some other systematic way and start going through the threads. Processing email is no different than packaging chocolates from a conveyor belt. You have to do something with the chocolate as it moves past you on the belt. Otherwise, it will just pile up on the end. Maybe you package it, throw it away because it didn't pass quality control, move it to another belt that coats it in peanuts. Or maybe you even eat it, but you don't just let it get to the end of the belt and pile up because then the chocolates will eventually expire, melt or it could affect the worker on the peanut belt, waiting ...and now they can't do their job.

Email processing doesn't mean jumping around out of order, unless there is a real urgent requirement that needs your attention. Remember, this is your focused email processing time! Schedule it just like anything else. Set the intention 'I am going to process email for the next 25 minutes.' *Processing* emails rather than *responding* to or *checking* emails helps to change the mindset since every email requires one of five actions. Read the email and either Delete, Delegate, Reply, Archive or create a Task (DDRAT).

The order of email processing can change. I would suggest if you are coming back from a vacation or more than a couple of days away, start with the newest first. Why? Because the older ones may already have worked themselves out, and you don't want to waste any time working on something that is complete. If you use Outlook, make sure you have your settings to Conversation View to ensure you aren't reading outdated emails.

Delete: Quickly scan your email inbox to see which of your emails you can trash. These will be obvious ... emails that missed spam, are outdated, or forwards from friends/family/co-workers who send you jokes or junk. The first few days you work on processing, instead of just deleting, go in and unsubscribe so you don't have to keep performing the same step over and over or use *unroll.me* to roll up all your subscriptions into one email. Family members may forward emails that don't align with your values, yet you can't unsubscribe and don't want to read them. Create a filter. If an email comes from X and has FW: in the subject line, it automatically *skips my Inbox and goes straight to archives*. This works great for relatives who send me political, religious or sensationalized emails that have been regurgitated for the last fifteen years (and they don't check snopes.com before sending).

If you're afraid to delete emails, then just send them to Archive/All Mail in Gmail or create an Archive folder in Outlook and put everything in there. I rarely trash anything except spam. I archive it.

Delegate: See which emails you have to delegate, then forward with instructions so they can start their task.

Reply: For those that you can reply to in two minutes or less.

Archive: For the FYI-type of email. If you are only copied on an email and not in the 'to' box, it isn't your task, and it isn't a priority. At least, that is how people *should* use the cc: line. Get the information you need and archive.

Task: If the email requires research or action, create a new Task in your Task list. The point is to *move it out of your inbox*. Do NOT use the inbox as your to-do list. If you use Gmail and Google Tasks you can create a task directly from the email by going to *More* then *Add to Tasks*. If you use Outlook, you can simply drag the email to Tasks and assign a due date. Clients that just use flags, end up with one hundred flagged emails, doing them no good at all.

If this is your first time processing email, or you fell off the wagon and need to get back on, set a timer for twenty-five minutes. Go offline and perform the steps above as quickly as possible. You will be amazed how fast you can go through them by following this order. **Email is *another person's agenda* or task list.** Work offline as much as you can. Staying online and having more emails come in while you are processing the current ones is distracting.

What if your inbox currently has six thousand read and eight hundred unread emails? My recommendation is to create a new folder and drag every single one of them except for what has come in the last week into that folder. If you use Gmail, just archive them all into All Mail without creating a folder. If you're brave and feeling frisky, just drag in everything except the current day's emails. Don't panic. They're still there and searchable. If they were important to you, you would have responded or done something with them, right? You can name this folder whatever you want – archive, irrelevant, it doesn't matter. Most of them are probably outdated, and you don't need to do any-thing with them anyway. Start clean and work your way up from a week ago or even one day ago. Anything older is archived. Give yourself a fresh start. If you start with the old ones than the ones from today are already old by tomorrow. One of my mentors, Barbara

Hemphill of the Productive Environment Institute, says, "*Clutter is Postponed Decisions®*" and that includes email.

Working Off-Line and Pausing

I cannot sing more loudly the joys of working off-line or pausing your inbox. When using Outlook, I would work off-line, synchronizing only 2-3 times per day. It isn't helpful to have emails coming in while you're processing your inbox. It's like filling an already full pitcher. Stress levels increase when you are processing current emails. If new, unread mail drops in automatically; it can feel like you are getting nowhere. For Gmail, I use a system called Inbox Pause. This allows me to pause my inbox and only have emails pushed into my inbox at specified times during the day. I currently have it scheduled for twice daily for my work email and once daily for my personal email. The emails are in All Mail if I needed to see them, but looking at All Mail is an extra step and a reminder to ask myself "Should I be wasting time in my email or doing something more effective?" Most of the time, if I need to see a specific email, I type their name in the search field to check if there is new mail only from them.

Working offline and not responding to emails immediately, changes the conversation. Have you noticed that when you respond right away, and the recipient knows you are currently available, a conversation develops back and forth? It starts to become like an instant message, and you feel rude if you don't reply again right away because they know you are online.

When considering your processing, think about your schedule. Is it realistic to schedule at specific time intervals such as 10:00, 2:00 and 4:00pm? Or do you need triggers, i.e., after my first meeting, after lunch or two hours before I go home? Whatever time you choose, avoid the first or last thirty to sixty minutes of your day. Often people do the opposite and check first and last thing, yet the priority order is all wrong unless the most important part of your job and your highest value at your company is to be in your inbox. The absolute worst thing you can do is open your email as your first task. One little email can derail your whole routine and day.

The way I changed my behavior of being constantly online and checking email all day long, was working offline and downloading my emails every hour. I would work offline until I had Deleted, Delegated, Replied, Archived, or Tasked. The anxiety was pretty intense at first. I felt like I was missing something or I was doing something illegal or sneaky. I gradually decreased my syncing and sending until I was only doing it four times each day. My manager didn't realize until I told her that I had been doing it six months. She was so impressed that she later sent me screenshots of her zero inbox.

Trust me, when you start doing this, it will be perfectly normal for you to get that Fear of Missing Out (FOMO). However, once you realize that empires won't fall, people won't die and your world and your business will continue, you will start to feel better and even enjoy a sense of satisfaction on what you can accomplish.

Subject lines and Acronyms

Good subject lines are critical because they help to filter what is important, allow you to search and retrieve emails later and therefore provide a timely response. You already can tell the possible actions needed before opening it.

Writing 'Action Requested' or AR and the date in the subject line lets a person know that they need to respond or do something by a certain date. When I put this in an email, it tells the person that if they have more urgent needs they can get to my email later, or that mine is timely and needs to be prioritized. Writing NOT URGENT in the subject line tells the recipient that they can skip opening the email until they have more time. I like to use this when I know someone has been on vacation or is overwhelmed with their workload.

One of my pet peeves is the subject line *Quick Question.* If it's quick, put the entire question in the subject line. If you can't put it in the subject line, than it is not a quick question. If it's just a one-liner, type it in the subject line followed by EOM or End of Message. Then they don't have to open up the email. One of my clients did a search for *Quick Question,* and forty-seven emails came up. Not helpful for trying to find an archived email. *Hello* is another dumb subject line. Yeah, I said it. Dumb. Another client did a search and came up with seventeen emails with Hello, Hey or Hi as the subject.

If you send an email and you don't want a reply, you can always type NRN at the end for No Reply Necessary. This helps someone know that you don't expect a response, therefore avoiding the *thanks* or *OK* reply. If you email several people but only need a reply from one, just state "respond only to sender" at the end so they know they don't need to reply all, another often abused form of email laziness.

No Thank You to *Thank You*

One big timewaster is the 'Thanks' emails that people send as ac-knowledgments of receipt. If someone goes above and beyond, for example, stays late from work to get a required signature, I will email back and thank them. However, if someone is just doing his or her regular job, I usually don't respond back. Why? Because it's an email that they have to open and delete. When I used to be a manager I asked my staff not to respond with 'thanks' emails unless I did something above and beyond what I should be doing. If I didn't go out of my way to do whatever they were thanking me for, I wouldn't have even noticed if they didn't thank me!

How many people would actually notice if someone didn't write back a *thanks* email for routine things? Who has gone to bed at night thinking *'Gee, I sent that presentation to my manager to review, and they didn't reply back and say thanks. "* Most of the time, we don't even mean thank you. It's just a confirmation or acknowledgment that we received whatever they sent. Some clients may *need* a "thank you" but your spouse, sister or colleague may not. ***Key to remember, if it is***

just an acknowledgment, don't do it. I would use this with 'ok' too. The majority of the time, there is no need to acknowledge with 'ok.'

When I give corporate workshops, without fail, I get an email later that day like this ... "I know we aren't supposed to thank you, but that workshop was amazing! I learned how to process my email and prioritize my time so much better than before. I can already see the difference it will make." This IS the kind of thank you email to send! They are expressing how they feel and being genuine about how I helped them. They aren't just responding to a follow-up from me with an attachment or link I promised and acknowledging they received it.

No Email Fridays

Some companies have *No Email Fridays.* It's a movement where no email can be sent internally on Friday, or at a minimum, after noon on Friday. This may be challenging for many companies, but I'm sure people could call more and email less on Friday. This is a movement ... people don't want the Friday Dump. Receiving an email late in the day on Friday with a deliverable for Monday or anything that will make you shut down your computer and stress about it over the weekend ... is considered a 'dump.' Maybe it isn't realistic, but one thing to consider is *would you call a person and ask them to do something at the same time you are sending the email?* For example, would you call someone on Friday at 6:00pm or Saturday at 10:00am and request they create a new presentation for you? Probably not, but emailing it seems culturally acceptable. I think saving that email until the new workweek is more appropriate and lets people enjoy their weekend. If **you** want to work, that's fine, but you shouldn't expect others to work unless their job is to work on weekends. Save it in your drafts folder or schedule it to send on Monday.

Another reason companies have instituted a ban on Friday emails is that they want people to communicate with each other — by voice! At U.S. Cellular, No Email Fridays was initially met with resistance, but soon became not only acceptable, but appreciated. Employees got to know each other better and in one instance, two people who thought they were communicating across the country were on the same floor in the same building! Other companies banning Friday emails include PBD Worldwide Fulfillment, which dropped their email volume 75% and E-Verifile who only allows email on external communications on Fridays. They believe results show a happier workforce with better communication.

If you think that a phone call takes more time than an email, consider how long some threads are that could have been completed in one minute or less over the phone. Make a rule for yourself and start with your team. Try calling or physically speaking to a team member on Fridays. Then stretch this out to your department and later to the rest of your company. Who knows ... you may get your weekend back too!

No Email Weekends or Evenings

Awesome companies like Lovesocial and Vynamic have email guidelines for their employees. Employees are encouraged to *not* send emails in the evenings and on weekends. My business, and the businesses of my entrepreneurial clients aren't the typical nine to five set-up. Sometimes I work on Saturdays to spread out my work during the week or because I want to run errands or do 'Saturday Stuff' during the week. I also like the quiet of working a little on Saturday. When I remember, (because sometimes they sneak past me, and I don't realize until it's too late) I pause my outgoing emails to be sent on Monday morning. The fewer emails people have to read on the weekends, the better.

No Friday or evening emails makes no sense. My company is global!

I received this feedback from a workshop attendee at a large international corporation. If you are dealing with people overseas and their 10:00am is your 8:00pm, you're right, it may not matter. The point is to consider who is receiving the email and their respective time zone. Keep in mind that if you are in a hierarchical role, your subordinates may feel that if you send emails at nights and on weekends that they are compelled to respond at nights and on weekends. People will always use the excuse "If I'm not working at night with everyone else, I can't keep up, without realizing that they are actually a part of the problem. If you work a nine to five job, then your evening or early morning should be *your* time. I work in the evenings because I have private clients in the evenings, but I typically don't start until 9:00 or 10:00am and usually take a break in the afternoon. My schedule isn't a typical corporate schedule.

Folders and Filters

Stop making folders for everything! With most current email systems, like the newer versions of Outlook or Gmail, the search capability is so extraordinary that if you archive a file it's super quick to search for it. By using the search feature, you have just removed the act of determining which is the correct folder for the email (i.e., the receipt from your annual renewal for ACME Organization could go in *Receipts* or *Acme*), dragging it to a folder and then searching within that folder. If you must have multiple folders or labels, a good rule of thumb is to never have more messages than what it takes to scroll down. If there is any scrolling involved or it involves more than one click, you are over- or hyper-organizing.

I admit this was hard for me at first. A place for everything and everything in its place is my motto. This is hyper-organization, which is a form of procrastination. I've had clients with twenty to thirty folders and only two to three emails in more than half the folders. This causes them to scroll to find or drag to the folder. It's a waste of time. Have as few folders as possible and trust your search function. If you have less than ten emails or five documents on a subject, you don't need to create yet another folder for it.

I only have a few folders/labels because I use my search function. If I'm looking for an email, I type the subject and the person who sent it and any emails related to that search criteria pop up. I apply labels or filters that state *if a message from a specific email address arrives, it automatically gets sent to a certain folder before or after I open it* depending on the filter rule. It saves a step from opening and dragging an email or even opening altogether, if it isn't an email I need to read or is more of an FYI.

Filtering Gmail is the same as creating rules in Outlook. By simply filtering an email to bypass my inbox, it saves me from having to delete or archive when I don't need to look at it. I may want access to an email later but not need to see it every time I open my email program. This is why filtering is great. Emails can go automatically and directly to archive or to a specific folder.

Items you could filter include:

- Automatic responses or notifications.

- Receipts from online purchases. One of my clients is an interior designer, and the amount of receipts and invoices she gets is incredible. To be able to find them quickly, I created a filter for anything that says 'Invoice' 'Statement' or 'Receipt' in the subject to be labeled and filtered out of the inbox. She can see when something new comes in and goes straight to that label and can easily find it without searching through her inbox.

- Statements that you review within the bank website.

- Bills that have auto-pay.

- Mass emails from people who send from their personal account but you can't get off their list. Since there is no unsubscribe, you have to filter it out.

- Employee emails that don't pertain to you, i.e. company kickball information when you work remotely and aren't on the kickball team.

- To uber-filter, sign up for *Unroll.Me*. Unroll.Me rolls up all your newsletters, digests and notifications into one simple email delivered morning, afternoon or evening. You can determine which emails you want rolled up and which ones you want to stay in your inbox. It's the number one program I recommend to my clients. The only thing that bothers me about it is that it's free. It's too good. They could have made millions.

Canned Responses, Templates, and Snippets

If you write the same or similar email more than five times, stop rewriting and start using an email template. They are available as templates or signatures in Outlook and as canned responses in Gmail. You could also install Yesware or Streak, two programs that allow you to create templates or snippets on your own. You want consistency in your answers, and these programs help you do that. If you have staff managing responses, this method maintains consistency across your department. You can always personalize, but keep in mind, the less you have to write each time the better.

Items that should be *canned* include:

- Instructions to begin a project.
- Response to negative feedback or unhappy customers so you aren't emotionally charged when writing back.
- Appointment scheduling information.
- Instructions for completion of a task.
- Office hours, directions and logistics.
- Frequently Asked Questions.

A few items I have canned include:

- My Press Kit link.
- Instructions to share documents.
- Invoicing and scheduling instructions.
- Affiliate links.

- Testimonial requests.
- Instructions to complete the Health and Productivity Scorecard on marceyrader.com.
- Services.

Five Sentences

A movement called Five Sentences helps people with a personal policy against long emails. There are also three sentences and two sentences movements. If you want to share the message, at the bottom of your signature line simply state "*Why is this email five sentences or less?*" and list the link http://www.five.sentenc.es.

Fact: The longer the email, the less likely the recipient will read it.

Fact: The longer the email, the longer the recipient will feel the need to respond.

Fact: The longer the email, the longer they will take to respond (if they respond).

If you require action by the recipient, be very clear and direct in your email. If something is easy to address, the person will respond. The more complex your email seems, the less likely you will get what you need, even if it's important. Cut out excessive details, but don't cut out praise. If someone went above and beyond for you, let them know it! I'm not saying we should be completely cold-hearted and omit "*Hi, how's it going*".... but at the same time, if I know the person and there is *no greeting* in the email to me, I am not offended and don't think twice about it. I also don't need to be greeted after the first email of the thread. Say what you need to say and move on. Once the conversation is started, I don't need to address you by name each time because I wouldn't do it if we were talking.

Reverse Office Hours

If you work as a team where you are expected to answer emails immediately, one thing you could try is reverse office hours. Every team member has scheduled time during the day where they are not online, so they have focused time to perform and take action on their tasks.

Apps

I usually check email on my phone twice a day if I'm traveling, but only when I can't use my laptop. I find processing emails on the phone ineffective unless I am deleting, archiving or have a quick reply. I can't OHIO (only handle it once) my emails effectively on the phone, so I opt not to check it unless absolutely necessary. Most of the time, we check our email out of boredom.

One app I highly recommend if you have Gmail is the free app *Mailbox*. It lets you archive, delete and delay emails. If you want to read an email at 2:20pm to remind you of the call-in information for your 2:30pm meeting or because that's when you are processing email, you can have it re-sent then. If it's a blog post you want to read for pleasure, you can delay it until the weekend or when you're on vacation. If you have travel plans booked, you can delay your itinerary until the day before you leave so it can pop up when you need it.

Gmail also has the *Boomerang* service, which can boomerang emails back to you at a specified time, delay send and remind you to follow up. It's free for ten emails per month and then $4.99 per month for unlimited personal or $14.99 per month for professional accounts. There is also Boomerang for Microsoft Outlook for $29.95. *RightInbox* is free software that allows you to 'send now,' 'send later' and 'remind me.' I use *Streak* for all of these things, which I'll discuss later in Client Relationship Management.

AwayFind enables you to flag specific email threads, senders, and domains to make sure that those get to you as a notification through the app without seeing the emails you haven't marked to be alerted to. This way, you're only interrupted by the important emails that need attention while you are traveling. It also alerts you if someone emails you from an email address that is on an upcoming meeting invitation. This is the best app for email management on a smartphone, especially if you can't get past that email isn't urgent.

Sharing Documents

It isn't efficient to send documents back and forth over email all the time. First, it clogs up the inbox and slows you down because you have to download the attachment rather than view it in the cloud. Second, you may not know who has the latest version of the working document. Storing documents in the Cloud allows access from any device, at any time, from any location. Storage is free up to a point, and then there is a minimal storage fee. It is worth it. Some people sign up using different email addresses to hack Cloud storage fees, but I find too many accounts confusing. I just bite the bullet and pay when I need to. Cloud storage saves space on your phone, computer or tablet and syncs your files over all your devices.

Many people are afraid of using Cloud storage and are worried about security. Cloud storage is more secure than email. If you are worried that your document will just go 'poof' think about if your hard drive went 'poof.' How often do you back up your hard drive? Isn't it better to have it on a server backed up by another server than just sitting on your hard drive at home? There are many different services, and I'll share the ones I use and am most familiar with.

I like to share files and notes using Dropbox, Evernote or Google Drive, and ideas via *WorkFlowy* or the mind mapping software *Coggle*. There are so many applications for sharing beyond just documents; contracts, client files, policies and procedures, project plans, inventory and task lists. You can upload family documents and share as well. Here is a brief comparison and how I use them.

Dropbox gives you 2GB of free storage plus 500MB of extra space for every person you refer. You can also get *Pro Dropbox* and upgrade your storage. A negative for Dropbox is that it does not allow collaboration in real-time for live documents being revised and edited by several people. A recent upgrade now allows edits to be made within the application without downloading the document. This will encourage me to use it more frequently with documents. I like to be able to send a link to a document to allow people to download the latest version onto their computer. Dropbox has a two-step verification feature when logging in to your account through the web or link to a new device, with a security code sent to your mobile phone. When using the app, you need to punch in a four-digit passcode.

Many people are afraid of Dropbox because their account was hacked at some point. This gives me confidence because they are probably the most secure sharing app available. Just like you don't fire the employee who made a thousand-dollar mistake, as they will never make it again, Dropbox is now hyper-vigilant as a result of a past hack. At least I'm crossing my fingers that's the case!

How I use Dropbox:

- Photo Storage
- Client agreements and documents to upload for signature
- Workshop Flyers
- Press Kit
- PDFs and MP3s of workshops I've attended

Google Drive is available for those with a Gmail or Google for Work accounts and starts with 5GB of free storage and more available to purchase. It has capabilities for documents, spreadsheets, presentations and forms and can upload and download into Microsoft Office, sometimes requiring minor edits. If you haven't tried it in a couple of years, give it another shot. It's greatly enhanced than the previous versions. It also integrates with *Hello Sign* and *Hello Fax* (for those companies still living in the 80s who require faxing), which allows you to indicate your signature on a document, without printing. *Drive* also has a two-step verification feature when logging in to your account through the web or when linking to a new device, by sending a security code to your mobile phone or you can opt in to use the *Google Authenticator App.*

I love this for real-time work with other people because the changes are seen immediately. I'm the President of our Home Owners Association, and if we all have our laptops open, we can make changes and adjustments on our own Drive and the others see it immediately.

How I use Google Drive:

- Client Strategy spreadsheets documenting each session.
- Real time work for collaboration.
- Google Forms for my client scorecards and surveys. When a potential client completes a scorecard, it alerts me via email. I can enter Drive to see the responses in spreadsheet format.
- Documents or folders I want to give specific permissions for, i.e. view only, comment only and edit rights.

Evernote captures screen shots, web pages, ideas, audio, notes and emails ... basically anything you can think of! You can record an audio file, snap a photo of a handwritten note or business card and upload it via your phone. The Optical Character Recognition (OCR) search mechanism is extraordinary. We took photos of my husband's sheet music and filed the hard copies in a cabinet. By tagging the photos with words like 'marimba,' 'solo,' 'ensemble,' etc., he can do a search in Evernote for particular pieces, glance through them and then go directly to the hard-copy file based on how they were tagged. It works perfectly. The search even works with handwritten notes, and you don't even have to have great penmanship! *Evernote* can also be shared by the document, entire folders or by link if the recipient doesn't have Evernote. The *Evernote Skitch App* allows you to easily mark up a screenshot, PDF or document.

How I use Evernote:

- Scan certifications, passport, driver's license and any other important documents to have them on hand if my wallet is stolen and I need to provide proof.
- Store downloadable eBooks.
- Download online manuals for electronic devices or equipment.
- Save entire web pages of information that I want to review or use for marketing.
- Checklists for packing.
- Checklists for client procedures.
- Recipe folder for any recipe I find online or when I take a photo of a recipe from a magazine. There is nothing better for snipping recipes online than Evernote. Have sweet potatoes on hand? Type in 'sweet potatoes' and every recipe you have stored with sweet potatoes is highlighted.
- Snipping workouts online that I want to try. Instead of bookmarking, I just use the Evernote browser extension to snip 'n save.
- Recording thoughts or memos. This works well for sending information to an assistant.
- Taking photos of business cards.

Workflowy is one of my favorite programs for writing speeches and outlining content for workshops and presentations. It's very simple to use as a list-making program and it's searchable by hashtags. I can share entire categories or just one section of a list with someone else to keep what they don't need to see private.

You may not need all of these programs or may find that you can do everything within one system. I like some better than others for certain tasks and don't feel overwhelmed with four storage places. I know exactly where everything is and what I use them for. That's the key for your system.

What should I store?

Do you store everything, then go looking at your list of files and have no clue what half of them are? Do you also have an attic full of yearbooks from Kindergarten to twelfth grade and the crumpled Kleenex you used at your senior prom? We often store much more than we need, thinking with good intentions that we will have time 'someday' to go back and review the files. Or maybe, our good old friend *Justin Case* will knock on our door and say he needs a document or photo from the year 2004. What's the likelihood?

Questions to ask before storing a document:

- Do I have immediate benefit from storing this?
- Do I need it or could I easily search for this and find it within five seconds online?
- How relevant or critical is this to my goals or my life?
- How am I going to use it?
- If I don't review this within six months, will I feel like it's another task on my plate?

Time Management

Calendar management can be extremely challenging as a business traveler. Your schedule isn't always your own due to travel or traffic delays. On the other hand, I sometimes am at my most productive when I am traveling because I don't have the distractions of an office or household chores, and I am up in the air with no access to the internet. I'm someone who likes when Wi-Fi isn't available on planes. I can get focused without distraction.

Determine if the calendar you are using is working for you. If not, it may be because you haven't mastered the basics and/or shortcuts. I always recommend taking five to ten minutes to watch the tutorials and learn how to maximize program capabilities. Other people want to be electronic, but their heart is really with paper. They feel outdated and sometimes embarrassed to admit this. Use what will work for **you**. There are streamlined electronic calendars, and there are beautiful, functional paper calendars. It's all very individual, however, most people send electronic invites to meetings and I can almost guarantee unless you seriously keep up with the paper, an event will be missed.

Scheduling

Most people find it difficult to figure out how much time to schedule for specific tasks or meetings. Think about how much time you are working on a project. People tend to grossly overestimate or underestimate until they start tracking their time. If we stop switch-tasking and multi-tasking, we'll get things done a lot quicker. There's no way to know how long a project or task takes if we are always working on multiple projects. We tend to spend our time on menial tasks that can be done quickly instead of the things that are really important. This is why email is a great way to procrastinate when we have a project to work on. We can delete the email and reply and feel like we are getting somewhere when, in fact, we are just delaying the inevitable.

One of the best things I have done for my schedule is to have one day every week as my Get Shit Done Day (GSD Day). This is a day where I don't schedule anything. I save my most intense work for this day, i.e., writing, creating content or presentations, and proposals. If you can't have an entire GSD Day, at least schedule three to four hours of GSD chunks of time. Everyone needs an entire morning, afternoon or evening (if you set your schedule and work in the evenings, not if you've been working all day in a typical nine to five job) to be able to focus without interruption. Decide ahead of time what your most intense tasks are for that week and schedule to work on them that day.

Meeting Planning

As a former manager, I was instructed that I needed to have one-hour meetings with my direct reports at least every two weeks (ideally, weekly) but the high achievers didn't need this. Our meetings would last 15-30 minutes and were just quick check-ins. I didn't try to stretch it out just because it was on my calendar. Since all of them traveled it sometimes became a nuisance part of their day. It was much better when I just checked in when I needed to, and they did the same.

First and foremost, stop defaulting to *accept* and scheduling 30 or 60-minute meetings. Don't invite people or accept invitations to meetings unless it's necessary to attend. If you aren't sure, ask the person how important it is for you to be there. Can you just read the minutes? Can you attend only part of the call and drop off when you are no longer needed? I'm sure everyone has been in a teleconference that lasted an hour, but only five minutes was relevant. *Atlassian* states that an average of 31 hours are spent in unproductive meetings per month, and 73% of people do other work during the meetings. When asked what the #1 timewaster was in the office, 47% stated meetings. If time equals money than we are seriously burning some cash.

NO! to Mindless Accept Syndrome (MAS)

Companies like U.S. Cellular have not only adopted No Email Fridays, they also instituted No Meeting Fridays. I think this is fabulous. It allows people to GSD before the weekend.

Here's what effective companies do:

- Stop scheduling recurring meetings when they are no longer necessary.
- Stop defaulting meeting times to an hour. If you schedule a fifteen-minute meeting, people won't mess around.

- If it's just to touch base, schedule a meeting for ten to fifteen minutes or forget the meeting altogether and ask for an email summary.

- End meetings at 1:50pm, 2:50pm, etc. This gives people a chance to stand up, take a biology break and get a drink of water. It also keeps you from waiting for five minutes for people to join a call because they are trying to get off the last one or they are doing one of the tasks mentioned above.

- Only invite people to the meeting that need to be there. The Rule of 7 states that everyone in a meeting over seven people reduces your ability to make decisions by ten percent.

- Tell people you have a hard stop at a specific time. I do this as soon as I get on a client call particularly when they are late joining the meeting.

- Conduct standing or walking meetings.

- Don't allow laptops or phones in meetings except for a note taker or researcher. This creates better engagement and focus.

- If you have non-urgent questions before a one-to-one meeting, keep your inbox(es) clean by starting a list and saving them for the meeting. I used to ask my staff to come to me with a list of non-urgent questions before every meeting instead of emailing me every thought that popped into their head.

- Use a service like Attentiv to create an agenda, automatic minutes and get anonymous feedback.

- Have an agenda or goal for every meeting. If the goal is to just 'catch up' then that can be done over email.

- Put time limits on each topic on the agenda.

Controlling Your Calendar

To be the master of your calendar, take a look at it a month out and look first at your recurring meetings. Determine which ones are truly mandatory. If you are the person running them, see if they can be done less frequently or if they can be done in a shorter time frame. People tend just to keep going with the same frequency and time of meetings even when they don't need to. Can a meeting be done once a week for fifteen minutes instead of thirty? Can it be changed to every two weeks instead of weekly as the project is progressing?

Block out (schedule no appointments) your calendar in the mornings for thirty to sixty minutes after you arrive and again before you go home. This gives you time to get settled and ease into your day and wind down and transition to leaving without worrying about a first or last appointment. If others have access to your calendar, it's very important you keep it current. If you're traveling, block it out. I don't know how many times I tried to schedule meetings with people based on their availability in their calendars, and they wrote back and said "sorry, I'm flying at that time." If you have shared calendars, you're wasting other people's time by not keeping your calendar up to date.

Block out at least two hours in your day, every day, to have focused time to perform your tasks. If you are someone who is in meetings all day, this may be that first and last hour of each day. Ideally, it should be your most productive time. In the corporate world, I had meetings almost every day that started at 9:00am. This was unfortunate from a productivity perspective because it was shortly after I started my business day and had the most energy to perform. My clients that have scattered meetings all day with 30 minute intervals (if that) in between, never really get to work on the projects effectively because the short intervals are filled with timewasters or quick tasks that usually don't amount to much.

Clubs and Networking Groups

If you belong to clubs or networking groups, give yourself 1-12 months to determine if the group works for you. If not, stop going, or at least be honest with yourself that you are there for social reasons and not to build your business. When you consider the value of your time in dollars, ask if the event or club is worth the money you're spending on the membership, gas, follow up, and lost time socializing when you could be producing income. I belonged to Business Networking International (BNI) for a year. I truly enjoyed it and made very good friends. It taught me how to run a business and surrounded me with other entrepreneurs, which I desperately needed at the time. However, it wasn't a good fit for my business. It was a heart-wrenching decision, but when I calculated my time in money, it didn't make sense for my business. I still refer to members of the group and hang out with some of them because they're my friends. Not every club or event is going to work for you or *your business*. Find one that does.

Meet with people by phone first before taking time out of your schedule to meet face to face. Entrepreneurs and some career positions do a lot of 'meeting over coffee.' I find that coffee meetings often result in lost money and time. I know I have offended people by saying I don't meet face to face first, but if I met with everyone for coffee that asked me, I wouldn't be able to build my business. Not every opportunity is fruitful. If you feel 'meh' about it, start with a phone call. People have no problem doing a 30-minute call, but feel like they need to schedule an hour for a coffee meeting.

Derek Sivers says that if something doesn't make you say "Hell Yeah!" Then the answer is No. Sometimes it's even Hell No. I say stop wasting your time on meh and do what excites you. That lunch or coffee you are going to do out of feelings of obligation may keep you from a Hell Yeah! invitation.

Standing and Walking Meetings

If you want to be one of the cool kids, perform standing or walking meetings. When people have to stand in a room for a meeting, meetings go much faster because most people don't want to stand around for an hour. Making participants slightly uncomfortable physically, combined with not being amenable to electronics, makes for a much more efficient meeting. A study from Washington University found that standing meetings boosted excitement around the creative process and reduced people's defensiveness.

Walking meetings are great between two and three people. This doesn't mean power walking and getting sweaty. You can stroll along and talk. Getting out of your normal office environment and walking can improve creativity and encourage more openness in the conversation. Walking also decreases intimidation and the hierarchy that comes with sitting across from someone at a desk.

Guidelines for walking meetings:

- Make sure it's an area you know. This is not the time for exploring or getting lost.

- Consider the time of day and weather.

- Ask the person ahead of time if they are okay with walking. Don't surprise them with a walking meeting when they are wearing a three-piece suit or three-inch heels. *I once did a walking meeting with a chiropractor who forgot his sneakers. He walked three miles in soccer cleats, the only thing he had in his car other than the dress shoes on his feet, because he was so happy to be doing something other than 'coffee.'*

- Keep it short. This is not the time to show your physical prowess or prove how fast you can walk a mile. Check in with them about the pace to ensure they aren't dying inside while you are skipping along.

- Two of my clients are a manager and his direct report. They live in different cities and are trying walking meetings outside while talking on the phone wearing headsets.

- Ideal walking meetings are with friends, one on ones with your manager, meetings with referral partners or sales calls if you know the person is interested in their health. If you want to be memorable, you'll do something besides coffee, lunch or drinks.

Airport Meetings

I try very hard to avoid meeting in an airport. The announcements over the loudspeakers can be distracting to say the least. You could also be speaking about something that is confidential and not know who may be listening. Also, most people are annoying by talking too loud on their cell phones. Cell phones are sensitive and if your reception is poor, talking louder isn't going to help you be understood the same way yelling isn't going to help a non-English speaker understand you. If you are sitting on the tarmac waiting to take off, please be considerate of others and talk softly. I can almost promise the person you are speaking to on the other end will hear you. No one thinks your conversation is as important as you do, even if you are a CEO, a celebrity or a Chicago Bull.

Scheduling Systems

There are many scheduling systems on the market that allow people to see available blocks on your calendar and request an appointment. If you spend your time doing the email dance to schedule a simple appointment, start using a system. Having a simple link saves about twelve minutes for each meeting scheduled. After five meetings, you've saved yourself about an hour.

Check out systems like *Schedule Once* (my preferred), *TimeTrade* or *YouCanBookMe*. Schedule Once allows the creation of different lengths of meetings as well as syncs with Google and Outlook calendars so you never have to post your availability. Besides your calendar, it also syncs with *GoToMeeting, InfusionSoft*, and *Cisco WebEx*. In my set-up, you can choose from three different meetings with me – a twenty-five minute Strategy Session, a twenty-five minute coaching session, and a fifty minute coaching session. I have my link in every email in my signature line, as well as on my website. Here is an example of an email with my scheduling link in the content.

Hi Jim,

It was great to meet you on Thursday. I would appreciate a quick chat on the phone to talk about the project you requested. Please use my scheduling link http://meetme.so/MarceyRader to cut down on the email thread.

Another great tool, that happens to be free, is *Assistant.to*. It allows you to embed your availability directly into the email. You can choose from different lengths of meetings, locations and if by phone, web conference or face to face. The email recipient can choose a time that works for them without ever closing the email. The downside is it only lets you pick times for three different days. I use Assistant.to for one-off meetings or meetings within the next couple of weeks. If a person takes too long to get back to your email, the times you allocated to them may already be gone. Right now, it only works with Gmail and Google Apps for Work calendars.

Virtual Meetings

I love the use of web conferencing to do virtual meetings. It's much better than phone because you can see the person's expressions and it prevents both parties from multi-tasking and checking email. I use Google Hangout for all of my client sessions. It's super-functional because we can share desktops. I can look at their email set-up, their calendars and tasks for the week. I can also show them my desktop as an example. I've used it for up to four people without any technology issues and have recorded several travel seminars on *Hangouts On Air*. Besides Hangouts, you can use *Skype* (I find it clunky), *Facetime* for Mac and iPhone, *oVoo* (up to 12 people), *Anymeeting* (up to 6 people); *join.me, GoToMeeting, WebEx*, and *freeconferencing.com*.

If you are part of a virtual meeting, please take the following steps to prepare, so people aren't waiting for you:

- Sign in a few minutes ahead of time because you may have to install software or an extension.

- Ensure your camera and microphone are on.
- Use a headset if you have a lot of external noise around you.
- Try not to have the angle of the camera looking directly up your nose.
- Learn where the chat function is if you lose the volume or need to interject.

Apps

If you're someone who constantly checks their phone during meetings or repeatedly gets interrupted and you have an Android device, consider installing the *Silent Time* app. This allows you to automatically turn your phone notifications off during scheduled meetings and set times of the day when you don't get calls or texts. It also allows you to set a group of people (partner or parents) that can get through to you in an emergency.

AwayFind syncs with your calendar and will forward urgent emails to you through the app for anyone who you have an appointment with within the next specified block of time. This way, if someone is running 15 minutes late, you know you have time to spare, and you aren't sitting there twiddling your thumbs or fuming about how irresponsible they are.

Task Management

Some people see it as a point of pride to keep all their to-dos in their head. They point to their noggin and say "I keep it all in here." I already have enough in my brain space. Anything I can remove to make room for more is better for me. I listicize everything.

Your inbox is the last place to have a task list. It's hard to keep in priority order and there may be multiple tasks with multiple dates within one email. There's also the time wasted rereading that email or clicking through it ten times a day. Instead, pull out the tasks within the email and enter them in your task list. In Outlook, you can simply drag the email to Tasks (*not To-Do*) and then when the window pops up, assign a date to it. I keep it simple and recommend only adding a start or due date and changing the subject line if it's not apparent the nature of the task is within the email. Then, you have the full email within the task if you need it and can move the email out of your Inbox. If you categorize by date, you can see which tasks are a priority. If you use Gmail, just assign emails to tasks in your menu bar by clicking More > Add to Tasks. The email can then be archived because the link is now automatically in your Task list, which also shows up in your calendar and email view (if you check the box in your settings).

An advantage of an electronic list is documenting repeated tasks. For example, I write my newsletter on Thursdays. If I check it off my task list today, it automatically moves forward to next Thursday because I've marked it as *repeating*.

Ideas for recurring tasks that you shouldn't keep entering into your electronic task list include:

- Completing time sheets and expense reports.
- Recurring project deadlines.
- House work or chores.
- Paying quarterly taxes.

Some things that I recur on my task list include:

- Writing and newsletter creation.
- Medication reminders that aren't daily.
- Social Media (yes, it's a task, not a default go-to when I want to procrastinate).
- End of month reviews of analytics, website, community list, profiles and press kit.

If you're a paper person, you may not need to have an electronic task list. If paper works for you, stick with it. Something as simple as writing your tasks on an index card every day can be gratifying, crossing off tasks and then throwing it away when you are finished. However, it is unrealistic to task your *emails* on paper. You can have a hybrid system and task your emails electronically and your daily to-dos on paper. You also can't share all information with a Virtual Assistant, family member or colleague if you only task by paper. I have a minimal hybrid system where my stream-of-consciousness thoughts go on a piece of paper beside me at my desk. I don't interrupt what I'm doing to put it on my e-list which would be a distraction. These thoughts are typically taken care of that day, but if not, they go on my electronic list.

Ideas to listicize:

- Travel checklist. I have separate ones for business travel, camping, and racing.
- Shopping staples.
- Items you need or want for the home.
- Places you want to visit.
- • Questions to ask your doctor.
- All the health and productivity behaviors you want to adopt!

Batching

Batching your tasks is a huge timesaver. Instead of opening up my website every time I want to add something, I save that for Thursdays. I have a running list of what I need to add in the notes section of my recurring task for Website Maintenance. Consider batching tasks like running errands or making cookies. Doing all of your errands in one chunk each week in an order that saves you time and money is like saving up your project work to tackle on Monday and Wednesday GSD times. You wouldn't get all the ingredients measured and laid out to make one cookie each day, right? You would do it all at once to save time and cleanup. Your tasks are the same way. You can get in the right brain space to work on the task without distraction.

Top Three Priorities and Tasks

On the first day of each month, I jot down my *Top Three Priorities* on the whiteboard beside my desk and also make it my desktop wallpaper. This helps me determine what's important for me to work on each month and can be very broad. On Fridays or Saturdays (depending on which is my last day of work for the week), I look at my calendar and determine my top three priorities for the week. Why only three? We really can't have more than three top tasks. Then it becomes just one more task list that can go on forever. If you have monthly or weekly meetings with your manager, ask them to share what they think your top three priorities for the week should be. You may find that you have placed high regard on something that they don't consider important. It also helps to stop procrastination because even your boss didn't include "answer all your email" as one of the top three priorities for the week. Sometimes asking them if a certain email is a top task may have them think about all their urgent requests via email and if they should be concerned that you respond within minutes.

Each evening during my transition from work mode to personal mode, I schedule my top three tasks for the next day. This could also be done first thing in the morning. I like to end my day knowing exactly what I need to do tomorrow. Either method works. Then I drop and drag my tasks around to schedule them according to my energy level or my appointments for the day. I try to abide by Brian Tracy's rule to *Eat That Frog* in his book named the same. I do my most important task (the one I will most likely avoid) first or at a time that I know I will have uninterrupted focus time. If I know I am going to be working during a layover or while waiting for a client, I'll do things that I can quickly cross off my list with minimal focus required. If it's writing or creating, I know I will need completely silent, non-distracted time and will wait until I am on the plane with no Wi-Fi, in my hotel room or after my husband leaves for work when I'm working from home.

Causes of procrastination can be not liking the task, fear of doing a bad job, fear of doing a good job (and getting rewarded with more work), or fear of not knowing how to do it. Procrastination can also be selfish. If someone is expecting something, you might unconsciously wield your control by withholding what they need. If there is something you find is a frequent task that doesn't get done, evaluate why and get down to the bottom of it.

Eisenhower Method for Priority Order

- Urgent and Important. Tasks must be taken care of immediately. Either there is a crisis, or you have procrastinated too long and it needs to be done now.

- Urgent but Not Important. Tasks are things that need to be done quickly and are associated or assigned by someone else. Tasks, where other people are waiting for you to do something, may be a high priority, so you aren't the bottleneck.

- Not Urgent but Important. These tasks help you move toward your goals and should be scheduled appropriately. If, however, you procrastinate, they can quickly move to Urgent and Important.

- Not Important or Urgent. These tasks can be sent to the bottom of the list. These are things that are 'nice to have' or can be done during a light day during the week. They are activities that are distractions and probably can be discarded altogether.

Think of your tasks in terms of whether they are urgent or important. If they are both, then it will be obvious which are most important, even if it means shutting down your email and completely focusing. If you know you have a flight in the evening and can work uninterrupted, postpone focus work until later when you know you will be able to maximize that time on the plane.

ABCDE

What if you have more than three tasks? Of course, you do! The important thing is the priority order of those tasks and to look at your day in terms of "If these three things don't get done, there could be a negative impact, possibly affecting the rest of my week or other scheduled tasks." When looking at all your tasks, indicate your top three as Task A, Task B and Task C. Then see if there are any you can D (delegate) and/or E (eliminate). Are there any tasks you have repeatedly pushed forward to the next day, over and over again? If so, they probably don't need to be done. Chuck 'em. It's good practice to evaluate your tasks now and then to determine if they are even still a priority. Arianna Huffington states that one way she completes her tasks is to decide not to do them. She kept saying she wanted to learn German but couldn't find the time. She decided to complete the task by getting rid of the goal altogether! Box checked!

$10.00 Tasks

Are all your tasks value-added? Will each task impact you tomorrow, a month from now or six months from now? Will it make a difference in your business or to a client? Would they pay you for what you are doing or is it a 'nice to have?' If your boss or client wouldn't pay you for spending twenty minutes formatting a spreadsheet to perfection, don't spend more than a couple of minutes on it making it fancy. If what you are doing is so menial that if you told them it was part of their fee your client would say, "Forget that part, I don't need it," then reconsider.

How much time is spent on $10 an hour tasks? If your time is worth $50, $100 or $200 an hour, at what point would you pay someone to do this for you? I have a client who bills $250 an hour for her time as a consultant. She was spending about six hours a week on tasks that she could pay a VA service $20-$35 an hour. She ended up engaging them 20 hours per month. After six months, she could consistently see that she was able to bill about eight more hours a month $2000(!) and started taking a martial arts class for six hours a month. For the price of a VA at $400 per month she improved her health and made out with an average of $1600 more income each month. She gave herself a raise, increased her confidence and strength and gave someone else a job.

Reflect at the end of each day and look to see if there were any time wasters. What did you achieve? If you didn't achieve what you needed or wanted, can you see where you might have been able to be more productive? I can easily get sucked into the rabbit hole of the Internet and sometimes I will distract myself with household tasks. While writing this book I often went to the State Park next to my house, sans phone, where I didn't have Wi-Fi access and could write in silence. I also went to coffee shops and hotel lobbies to work. Having people I don't know around me isn't as distracting as being in my home office with all of the things I could be doing around my house. I know I am typically distracted when my husband is home, so I do my minimal-focus work until he leaves. When you look at your day, don't just focus on what you didn't get done, look at what you were able to achieve and why.

The bottom line: If you can't decide which task should be first, think about which task will have the biggest impact on your day, your job or your life. Then choose that one.

Busywork

Stop being busy and start working! **Busy isn't work**. Busy isn't creating. Busy is a waste of your time. People become martyrs and braggarts about how busy they are. I am irritated with myself when I catch myself saying I'm 'busy' when someone asks me about my week or day. I have had people take their voice down to a whisper to tell me they only work about thirty-five to forty hours a week because they either feel guilty, or they know that more work will get piled on them. It is too bad salaried people don't get incentivized for being efficient. One reason I didn't tell my former manager right away about how much time I was saving by processing email and working offline was because I was afraid I would just get more work added to my already full load. Sometimes being productive can feel like a punishment.

Why Am I Doing This? (WAIDT)

How often do you evaluate a task or meeting to ask yourself "why am I doing this?" I have a random reminder on my daily task list that says WAIDT? Every task in your day should be started with this question. If you can't answer why, evaluate by asking:

- Am I doing it solely because I've always done it?
- Do I still need to do it or can it be delegated or eliminated?
- Is it value-added or just nice to have? If it's just 'nice to have' stop doing it.
- Is there a better way to do this or could it be outsourced?
- Do I still need to account this much time to this task?
- Here are some examples of tasks I've changed by asking myself WAIDT?
- Allowing sixty minutes for website and newsletter work on Mondays. Now I only need twenty-five at most and it works better on Thursdays.
- Daily check-ins with some of my private client coaching logs. Now I do this twice each week, in addition to their scheduled meeting with me.

The Pomodoro Technique and Timecapping your Timesuck

Because I am easily distracted, I had to learn to work in intervals. I highly recommend interval work to give you energy breaks. Make a deal with yourself and work for forty-five minutes and then give yourself five to ten minutes of time to check your personal email, social media, get a drink, or stand up and move around. We are not robots. Everyone needs a break. Initially I felt guilty for taking these frequent breaks. Then I realized I got so much more done because I was time capping and able to focus more effectively. My brain wasn't so tired or distracted. You will undoubtedly take as much time as you give yourself, so cap it, focus and do it in less time when you can.

Depending on what the task is, I sometimes use the *Pomodoro or Tomato Technique*. The most basic way to describe it is to set a timer for twenty-five minutes and work completely focused on one thing followed by a five-minute break. It's best if this break involves getting up, moving a little bit and looking away from the computer. Then when the timer goes off, go through another twenty-five minute round. After four rounds, take a longer break of fifteen to twenty minutes. If you think you won't get as much done, you're wrong. Unless you are someone who can get lost in your work or project (and I envy you) these intervals of short focus and short breaks will make you much more efficient. I was surprised to find that even twenty-five minutes of focused work is sometimes hard for me. When a thought enters my mind, or I want to click on a new link, I jot it down on a piece of paper beside me and come back to it later. When I first started with the technique, I put a tick mark on paper every time I got distracted during that round. I realized after a few weeks what my good times of day were and the behaviors that easily pulled my mind off task.

The Pomodoro Technique also helps to train you how long a project or task will take. Estimating how many Pomodoros it takes to complete the email campaign and realizing it took me twice as long, was helpful for planning my next campaign. I use an app called *Focus Booster* that not only runs a countdown timer on my screen, it keeps track of my assigned 'clients' or tasks that I'm working on and I can run a report showing how much time I worked on specific tasks each week. I know how much time I spent to write this book under the client *Kindle* or how long it took me to create a workshop under the client *Workshop Creation*. It also keeps track of money earned if I assign a dollar value to each client.

The twenty-five minute time limit not only works if you are trying to stay focused, it keeps you from staying on other tasks too long (I'm talking to you Facebook and Twitter!) and works as a reward to complete even the tasks that you don't like.

Items I typically Pomodoro include:

- Housework
- Food Prep for the week
- Social Media
- Email
- Internet Surfing

The Absolute No List

When you are looking at your tasks and meetings for the month, week or day, determine if there are any that are timewasters or tasks you really dislike that you can toss. Are there any tasks that are not value-added? Networking events that you dread attending and leave you with nothing? Red-eye flights that you repeatedly take thinking it will save you time yet you end up dog-tired the day you arrive anyway? Make an *Absolute No List*. These are the things you won't do again. Ever. Absolutely Not.

Concentration and Focus Programs

There are several programs and apps to help you focus. *RescueTime* allows blocking out of distracting websites during focus time. You can categorize websites, apps and programs from very distracting to very productive and see at the end of the day or week how productive you were in managing distractions. I set goals and work to stay within those parameters every day. RescueTime is free for the Basic Service, but the paid premium is worth the investment.

Freedom lets you schedule blocks of time to prohibit opening all or allowing a few specific sites to open. If you absolutely must go back online, you have to restart your computer. I used Freedom to keep me focused when writing this book.

ChromeNanny lets you block sites at specific times of the day. If you want to make sure you don't check Facebook or Twitter at work, set it up to block access during your workday. Successful and efficient people aren't always more disciplined; they just set themselves up better and prepare for success. Making it difficult to continue with a behavior, or even to think twice about that behavior, can be enough for behavioral change.

Facebook News Feed Eradicator is an extension that replaces your newsfeed with an inspiring quote.

Focus@Will is a music productivity app that runs in the background. I seriously dig this app. I set it for a prescribed amount of time, type of music and the intensity depending on my energy level. At the end of my session, it asks me how productive I was and then 'learns' what makes me productive and adjusts accordingly. If I'm using Freedom and can't be online, I use the Deep Focus playlist on *Spotify*.

Relate, Create, Research™ (RCR)

Depending on what kind of work you do, you may be able to incorporate something I call Relate, Create, Research. Ask yourself the following questions:

- Who do I need to **Relate** to today? Who do I need to contact or reach out to?

- What do I need to **Create**? A presentation? A training plan? An email campaign?

- What do I need to learn about? What information do I need to **Research** to perform my job or a task better?

You may find that you can have specific days that are assigned to relating, creating, and researching.

An example of an RCR schedule:

Monday: **Relate** by hosting client sessions, calling prospects and JV Partners. **Create** client plans.

Tuesday: **Relate** by hosting client sessions, calling prospects and JV Partners. **Create** client plans and workshops.

Wednesday: **Relate** by going to Toastmasters, meet with my accountability partner Melissa, and errands

Thursday: **Create** as a GSD Day. Write, website work, design presentations and workshops. Research content for writing and presentations.

Friday: **Relate** by hosting client sessions, meeting 1:1 with referral partners.

Saturday: **Research** by reading articles saved for marketing swipes or latest studies on health and productivity.

Sunday: I keep Sundays screen free.

Energy Scheduling

No one can maintain the same level of energy all day long. Save the more mundane tasks like filing, timesheets, or expense reports for the time of day when you are tired. Your heavy decisions should be scheduled for the morning. This is when your natural levels of serotonin are highest, so you are going to make a more rational decision than later in the day or evening when they are lower. Decisions made in the afternoon are more likely to be made as status quo, postponed or not decided at all.

If you don't get a good deep sleep, your serotonin levels will be low and you are more likely to make decisions out of fear. Exercise is a precursor to serotonin and can help in your decision-making. Moving your butt in the morning or at lunch can give you a boost mid-day or afternoon to fight off postponing a decision. It doesn't have to be a sweat session; even a ten to fifteen minute brisk walk can help. Eating breakfast with high protein can also give you a boost a little later mid-day, so your ability to make important decisions lasts a little longer.

Apps

There are a million and one apps for Tasking. Some of my clients like *Remember the Milk, Asana, Wunderlist,* and *Calengoo.* I just use the native task application within Gmail because I love tasking straight from my emails and seeing my task list whether I am in email or on the calendar screen. The app I use is *GoTasks.* If you have an Android, the same app is called GTasks. It allows me to have different lists, assign dates, make recurring events, and drag to prioritize on my phone. Evernote is also great for listicizing and is easy to copy, manipulate and share information. There are a plethora of task apps out there. Pick the simplest one for you.

Miscellaneous

Clean Up

I have a reminder on my computer for the first day of every month to do a clean sweep. I use *Easy Duplicate Finder* to help find and eliminate duplicates on my computer. I was amazed the first time I used it to see how many duplicate files and photos I had. I also get rid of all my .dmg files, downloads and any documents in my Temporary folder that are no longer needed. Your computer isn't infinite space. Clear up some of that hard drive and let your computer run more efficiently. If you do this regularly, like once per month, it saves time down the road. Clean out your trash while you're at it. On a Mac, iPhoto has a separate trash bin so remember to empty both.

While you're doing this, clean up your desktop. Having a million files and folders on your desktop slows down your system. Besides, wouldn't you rather see the photo of your daughter at the beach without your spreadsheets covering her smile?

Passwords

Remembering a million passwords is difficult and using the same password over and over is dangerous. A password program will save time and brainpower. Password programs like *LastPass* and *Dashlane* are recommended and have a free and premium feature. Dashlane will remember your passwords, alert you when they aren't strong enough and will generate strong passwords for you. It also allows the storage of credit cards, so that information is available automatically when you purchase online. It has a sharing feature that allows you to send a username and password to someone else via email that expires after a certain amount of time. This is great when I want my VA to have access to a website temporarily. I can also store my clients' usernames and passwords for the ones who want me to 'accountability check' their inbox or set them up with Google Apps for Work. A feature that will help your loved ones is what I call the 'death setting.' If something were to happen to me, there are two people who have access to all my usernames and passwords. They simply contact Dashlane and if I don't respond to Dashlane's request after a specified amount of time, they have limited or full rights access.

If you are worried about keeping all your passwords in password software, note that security experts recommend password protectors over the passwords that people typically use, which can easily be hacked. Typing in a name using 3 for E and ! for 1 isn't all that hard to figure out anymore.

e-Signature

I dislike printing so much it takes me at least a year to go through one ream of paper. There are too many steps required and it feels wasteful. Printing, signing, and scanning is tedious. Instead, I import anything I need to sign, like agreements or contracts, directly into *Hello Sign*. I also use Hello Sign to send documents to my clients for signature. It emails them directly, alerts me when they sign it and automatically stores it in a Hello Sign folder within my Google Drive.

If you do need to scan documents check out portable scanners like the *Doxie, Neat Receipts* or *Scansnap*. I prefer to take a photo with my phone and store it in Evernote.

Forms and Surveys

I use *Google Drive* to create surveys, questionnaires, and polls. It's super easy to do, and all the responses get uploaded directly to my Drive. I can also choose to be notified every time a questionnaire is completed. I even used this to poll my guests for our annual Holiday Party to determine which date worked best for them.

Survey Monkey is another easy tool to use to create surveys and questionnaires. If you have to send an email asking for a multitude of responses it will be faster to complete a form in Drive or Survey Monkey.

Smart Phones

Your phone needs to be cleaned and evaluated every month just like your computer (physically cleaning the screen should regularly occur of course!). Think you need to upgrade because your phone doesn't have enough storage? Try deleting the apps you haven't used and remove the photos you don't care about. If you like to text photos but don't want to have them stored on your phone, sucking up your memory, use an app like *SnapChat* that removes it after sending. I regularly review my phone and look at the last used date of all my apps. If it's been awhile or I don't need it right then, I remove it. If I'm not flying for a couple of months, there's no need to have *iFlyPro* downloaded. When I need it, I reinstall it.

I also recommend organizing your apps in a way that makes sense and feels natural to you. Your most used apps shouldn't take two swipes and a tap for you to get to. However, if you are trying to cut down on social media or email take those apps off your home screen and create multiple steps to get to them or keep them off your phone altogether.

If you're someone who downloads every new app you hear about, you're probably going to have a hard time finding one that works for you. I've often heard from people "that app doesn't work for me" only to find out they tried it for two days. You have to give the app a chance. On the other hand, if something *is* working for you, don't fix what isn't broken! I know there are dozens of apps with more depth and breadth than my *GoTasks*, but I don't need those and am satisfied with what I have.

Don't download an app because a celebrity, friend or even I say it's the best one, unless you're looking for a problem to solve. Apps are free or cheap to download but will cost you a lot in productivity by constantly switching back and forth. A couple of my clients specifically stated an app I recommended wouldn't work for them and within a month both of them loved it. It all comes down to taking the time to learn it and using what solves your problem and no more than that. Complexity, bells and whistles doesn't always equate to more productivity.

Podcasts and Books

I am a big fan of listening to podcasts and books on tape in the background when I'm driving, cleaning, taking a walk or cooking. I use the *Downcast* app and subscribe to no more than five podcasts at a time so I don't feel overwhelmed or behind when I can't listen often. I also use the *Overdrive Library* through the Public Library System, which allows you to download both eBooks and audio books to your device. If you find you don't have enough time to read or don't like to read, try podcasts or audio books instead.

If you do like to read books, I highly recommend signing up for *Goodreads*. It's the world's largest site for readers and book recommendations. You can track books you're reading, have read or want to read. If your friends or colleagues that read are on this site, you can see their feed and reviews as well. I have a queue of over ninety books recommended by friends, websites, mentors, etc., and before Goodreads, I didn't have a good way of keeping track of them. It has an app so I can add books on the go when I hear about them. If you have a Kindle, the Send to Kindle extension in Chrome will upload articles or eBooks for quick reads in line or on the plane.

Social Media

Social Media can easily be a time-suck for people if they don't time-cap or limit the number of days they check their accounts. Before they know it they have five tabs open, three sets of photos, a video playing of a monkey riding on a pig and an hour has passed!

Like many business owners, I consider much of social media a time-suck, but necessary to communicate with my community and the companies I like. There are so many social media channels I can't even keep up with them all. When I started my company I narrowed it down to five channels – YouTube, Google+, Facebook, Twitter and LinkedIn. Every year I evaluate and determine if these channels still work for me. If not, I spend very little time there or delete the account completely. Set guidelines for yourself on how many social media platforms you will join, how often you will visit them and how much time you will spend on each.

I've mentioned the Fear of Missing Out (FOMO) earlier. FOMO is that anxious or nagging feeling you get when you don't check your email, Facebook page or Twitter feed every hour. A couple of my clients who had FOMO would sleep with their phone and check Facebook before they even got out of bed in the morning. I don't check social media daily for my business or my personal use, and I haven't lost any friends or clients because of it. I wasn't surprised to read a study that showed social media can lead to more negative emotions following use; jealousy, social tension, isolation, and depression. People are putting their best foot forward in social media, so you don't see the bumps in their roads. If social media overwhelms you and you're using it for personal use only, it might be worth it to delete that account and set up a new one. Now you can be choosier about who you allow into your circle or list of friends. Before I had my business, I used a fake name so I couldn't be found. If the people or businesses you like don't add any value than you shouldn't waste your eyeball's time reading them. My rules for my personal friends on social media are:

- Over 18.

- No coworkers or business peers unless I would have them over for dinner.

- I would have them over to dinner if they were in town (this includes family because I have a big extended family).

- Appropriate posts (I had to unfriend family members who do not know the meaning of privacy. I didn't know whether to feel sorry or embarrassed for them).

- Business Pages of people I support and am interested in their product or service.

- A maximum of twenty people on Facebook as I won't invest any more time than that requires. It makes me think carefully if I just want to be a voyeur in their life or if I care about them.

- Check the last few posts of a person on Twitter before following them. If they weren't relevant to me, they probably wouldn't be moving forward.

I have established these rules for myself, so it's easy for me to explain why, when someone asks to friend me, I click *ignore*. I have a rule that I only check social media three times per week. I set a Pomodoro to timecap it at twenty-five minutes. This also includes any links or videos that I visit while on social media.

My favorite social media outlet is Twitter. I use this to contact businesses when I have a one-liner question and need a quick response. I also like LinkedIn for business contacts.

"Life is for living, not tweeting." –Louis C.K.

Financials and Receipt Tracking

CWT's "Travel Stress Index" found that frequent fliers (thirty or more trips per year) get a high level of stress from lost time related to the reimbursement of expenses. One statistic I found stated that business travelers spend approximately two to three hours per trip on the task of expenses and reimbursement. That's unacceptable.

I'm a huge fan of *Shoeboxed*. The days of keeping your receipts and taping them to a sheet of paper to scan and fax or email them to accounting should be over. With the Shoeboxed app for smartphones and iPads, simply snap a photo of your receipt, check if it is *reimbursable, deductible* or *I don't know* and submit. You have photo documentation of your receipt, and after it has processed, you can see your receipt categorized just like it would be on a credit card. For example, if you went to the BP to get gas and snapped a photo of your receipt, you would see your receipt, BP, and it would automatically be categorized into Fuel. You can create your own categories and set rules that receipts from specific companies automatically get tagged to GO THERE. A PDF of all the receipts related to a single trip can be emailed to your accounting department.

If you have a lot of paper receipts, all you have to do is mail them in the Shoeboxed-provided envelope. You can also just scan them using your desktop scanner. One feature I love is the browser extension so I can clip and upload all of my electronic receipts that go to my inbox. For receipts that are emailed to me on a regular basis, I provide my Shoeboxed email address to bypass my Inbox and go straight to my Shoeboxed account, or I create a Gmail filter to make an automatic forward.

The app also comes with a mileage tracker calculating your reimbursement based on government rates. You simply press start to track your mileage. You stop it by dropping a pin in the app. They also have a feature called Speedy Reimbursement so you can email the expense to be reimbursed directly from the app. A great feature for businesses is account sharing, allowing your account to be shared with a bookkeeper, assistant or spouse. At any time, you can run a report or import it into financial software like Quickbooks or Xero. The savings in time for you, accounting, and your personal accountant will be invaluable!

I like the Shoeboxed staff so much I became an Ambassador for them in 2014. They are socially conscious and employ people from the TEACCH (Teaching, Expanding, Appreciating, Collaborating and Cooperating Holistic) Autism program to help with their scanning.

Financial

It's easy to stay up to date on your finances on the road. Besides Shoeboxed, you can use almost any financial software on your computer and as an app on your phone. For business accounts, *QuickBooks* and *Xero* work well. For smaller, personal accounts, I like *YNAB* or *You Need A Budget.* I've used *Quicken, Mint,* and *Moneywell* and prefer YNAB to all of them. They have excellent free tutorials, and their customer support is fantastic. I still use YNAB for both mine and my husband's business account by setting up separate budgets in the program.

On a personal note, I don't use the time-saving feature of automatically importing my statements. When I make a purchase, I enter the transaction into the mobile app or computer so I always know my account balance. By entering it manually, it makes me accountable and keeps my budget front and center. If I'm just letting the computer enter in everything, it's easy to overlook expenditures until it's too late, and I've gone over my budget.

Paying bills and transferring money via bank apps or websites is pretty standard now, and all bills should be electronic. There are differing schools of thought on setting up to pay bills automatically or manually. It's a huge timesaver to have them paid directly by your bank, but if you tend to overdraw your account or not pay attention to your statements, you should do it manually so you aren't surprised. I have most of mine on automatic bill pay, but I reconcile my accounts one or two times per week. I knew pretty quickly when I was getting charged an extra $7 for a bogus Internet charge and $5 for a bogus phone charge. One client of mine didn't know for a year he was being charged for Sirius radio (which he does not even own anymore) until he had to start reconciling his accounts!

File This Fetch is a program that fetches all of your financial statements and bills. Every time a new statement comes in it gets uploaded to Evernote, Dropbox or Google Drive (your choice). It has the highest security available in modern browsers and encrypts all the data communication between File This Fetch and your accounts. I like having all of my statements and bills in one place, especially during tax season.

Paperless or Less Paper?

Do you dream of having a paperless office? How about reframing to a *less paper* office? Eighty percent of what people keep they never use, and the more they keep, the less they use. Think about your papers and how often you rifle through them. Both my husband and I are self-employed and we have one two-drawer file cabinet. That is enough to hold all of the physical paper we need. One of the drawers contains mostly electronic peripherals — no paper there!

Most papers can be scanned and stored electronically via services like Dropbox, Google Drive or Evernote. When people say they are afraid to store things in the cloud on a giant server that is backed up by several other servers, I ask them if they back up their paper with paper copies stored somewhere off-site from their office or house since a fire or flood would render them useless. Sometimes, the excuses are more just fear than logic. For more help or guidelines with paper, check out the book *Taming the Paper Tiger©* by Barbara Hemphill, Founder of the Productive Environment Institute.

Portable Scanners can save a lot of time and are super light for travel. They have great Optical Character Recognition (OCR) so you can just do a keyword search after you have uploaded the file to your computer. The portable *Doxie* can scan directly to Google Drive, Evernote, Flickr and others. It only weighs 10.9 ounces to fit easily in your carry-on. *NeatReceipts* is another mobile scanner that weighs 10.6 ounces and uploads to the NeatCloud. Fujitsu ScanSnap weighs twelve ounces and has capabilities for scanning to PDF, editable Word or Excel file, business card scanning and the ability to upload to Evernote, Google Drive, Salesforce, SugarSync or SharePoint. If you have a smartphone, you can download DocScan and snap photos, organize them into a folder and then email the documents. This way you can completely bypass the old scan and fax method. I scan almost everything to Evernote by just taking a photo.

Faxing

When someone asks me to fax something, I wonder if they still have a rotary phone. A fax machine is about as 1980s as it gets, minus jelly shoes and neon pink. It also requires each person to be physically somewhere specific to get the document with the risk that other people could see the document. Eliminate the paper by using an eFax service like the afore-mentioned Hello Sign and its partner, Hello Fax.

SwiftFile ᵀᴹ

If you use paper files, I highly recommend a tickler file system, called the *SwiftFile*. It's a mobile filing system to remind you of bills due, birthdays, invitations and appointments as well as to hold your specific paper documents for the exact day you need them. It has thirty-one unique folders for the day of the month and twelve taller month folders. After purchase, you can watch tutorials on how to maximize use.

Client Relationship Management (CRM) and Contacts

A good CRM program helps manage client relationships in an organized database or marketing campaign and can track customers or campaigns over multiple channels such as email, search, social media and direct mail. For smaller businesses and solopreneurs, it may be a simple contact manager system that integrates emails, documents, and scheduling.

Streak is my preferred CRM for email and works with Gmail and Google Apps for Work. I create Pipelines, place clients, and email threads into Boxes and assign steps within the process of my Pipelines. I use Streak to create my Snippets (canned responses), snooze emails to come back to me on a specific day and time, set reminders to follow-up with someone and assign emails to be sent at a specific day and time. It also has a 'big brother' option where you can see if a person has opened your email and how many times. I do not enable this option.

Examples of how I use Streak:

- Pipelines: Prospects, clients, corporate clients, networking and miscellaneous.

- Boxes: Each person or company within a pipeline is a box. For corporate clients, I categorize them as Initial Contact, Interested, Scheduled, Not Interested and Completed.

- Snooze: If I work on Saturdays, I snooze my emails to be sent on Monday. If someone asks me to follow up with them at a later date, I go ahead and write the email and snooze it to be sent then.

- Reminder: If I email a prospect I immediately set a reminder to follow-up on a certain date if I haven't heard from them.

- Snippets: My canned responses to FAQs and instructions.

Scrubly is a program that cleans up your address book by removing duplicates and merging matching contacts. It works with Outlook, Mac, and Gmail. It can also add social data. I have two Gmail accounts, and it looks through both of them to find similar names and asks if I want to merge them.

Rapportive is a browser extension that can be customized with Gmail, *Klout, Crunchbase, GitHub, MailChimp, Aweber* and more. I have Rapportive installed in my Gmail so every time I send an email, it gives me information on the right hand side of my screen that includes the recipient's profile photo, LinkedIn profile, Location (if they have this enabled), latest Facebook, Google+ and Twitter posts, and a spot for me to write a note if I need to. You can even ask a person to connect with you via LinkedIn without leaving the page. Since it's coming from an email, there isn't a permission step as if you were requesting directly from the site. I love being able to learn more about people and instantly see their photo, especially if they have a gender-neutral name.

SendOut Cards is a wonderful tool to use for customer relationships and is super convenient when on the road. You can send hard copy cards through the mail, right from your computer. The cost is cheaper than buying one from the drugstore, customizable with your photos and you can schedule entire campaigns around marketing efforts or holidays. They also have an online gift catalog and gift cards available to purchase. I've heard people say it isn't personal because you aren't writing on it. When I've used them, I personalized it with their photo and wrote something fun inside. I use this for my family and friends cards with photos from holidays, parties, etc. If you are a business, you could show before and after photos or them with their new product. It may keep them from chucking it into the trash so quickly and works better as a long-term advertisement.

Digital Detox and Vacations

Email and social media can be true addictions. The way we respond to them becomes a process or behavior imprinted in our brain. This is why when we are without phone or unable to check email, we become anxious, feel ill, are afraid we're going to be caught and have the FOMO.

When you are weaning yourself from checking email as often or trying to limit your social media visits, remember that email is never urgent and unless your job is in social media, it isn't going to wreck your career or social life not to know every time someone likes your post.

Ideas for digital detoxing:

- Start with the bed. If you use your phone as your alarm and you have enough discipline in bed, put your phone in airplane mode. Ideally, it will be out of the room altogether, but at least start here.
- Stop checking email/texts before breakfast and after dinner.
- Stop checking email/texts during dinner, coffee dates or entertainment events. I can't believe people will pay $70 for a concert ticket and check their email during a show!
- Stop checking email and texting in your car!
- Stop checking email during meetings.

Have a screen-free day. Start with once a month, then once a week. I try to have a screen free day on Sundays. I still use my phone because I call my family, and I listen to music, but I don't check email and limit my searching and surfing, if at all.

Vacations and holidays are separate categories that need to be consciously planned to enjoy and not take work with you. Once I was on a conference call with a guy who was on a Mediterranean cruise with his family. He was wearing the "I'm So Important" badge that he was calling in from the ship! I thought it was sad and pitied him. Especially since his loyalty didn't matter as he left the company six months later.

According to Marketplace, Americans carry over or lose about nine days of vacation a year. Why? Are they scared that they won't be seen as committed? Feel like it isn't worth it for the amount work they will come back to? The company doesn't promote reenergizing? Or, they feel like they are so important or haven't delegated appropriately, that certainly the company would fall apart if they weren't available for a week.

Vow to have at least one day of every vacation (ideally the whole vacation, but let's start slow) that you are completely screen free. The other days, schedule the times you are going to work or check and stick to those times. Ask your vacation mates or family to hold you accountable, even if it's just surfing the web. It's called vacation for a reason. Can't you surf the web at home? Why would you want to do it in Fiji?

When my husband and I were on a vacation in San Francisco for a week, I made a clear plan on when and how I would work since I was a solopreneur at the time and was doing my own VA work. I worked on the plane going and returning because it was too much valuable time to waste flying cross-country, and I can be productive en route. For three days I worked one Pomodoro in the morning and one in the evening. When that timer went off, I shut down completely. I kept my phone on DND the entire day. I'd have my husband check my texts to see if there was anything I needed to address urgently. I only engaged in social media once, on my birthday, because I wanted to respond to some of the messages. I didn't get behind on work and really felt I had 'gotten away.'

To prepare for vacations:

Plan ahead. I tell my clients to "treat every day like you are leaving for vacation tomorrow." Why? Because people Get Shit Done when they are leaving for vacation. They prioritize and wrap stuff up, don't let themselves get distracted and focus on what matters. Have a solid plan in place and decide if you are going to work when you're gone and when those work hours will be.

- Stick to your plan. When a client asks you to meet with them on your vacation, unless it is a major 'make or break' deal, ask someone else to do it or postpone the meeting.

- Save your pennies. If you're a Solopreneur, Contractor or Small Business Owner there are no paid vacations. Put money back into a 'deferred payment' bucket for the weeks that you won't be making income. This way it isn't as painful when you go on vacay because you can take what you would have made that week out of that bucket.

- Lean on someone. Ask a virtual assistant, personal assistant, co-worker or friend to cover for you. Set them up with every-thing they need and then trust them to do it. Tell the people you are going on vacation and about your digital detox and make them hold you accountable.

- Ease back in. Don't schedule meetings the day you get back. If you work from home, put the Out of Office Message on for one day after you are back in the office. Work off-line the en-tire day, answer all your emails and then sync them on your first 'official' day back. Of course, clear it with your manager first since your OOO won't line up with your time off. If you work from an office, at least block out your calendar.

Information Vacations

I take 'Information Vacations' for one week each quarter. I started this because, as an entrepreneur, I had a lot to learn about areas I wasn't familiar with, like marketing and web design. I was constantly reading reference and business books or listening to podcasts to improve my skill set. Even though I enjoy reading and listening to learn, I know sometimes I need to just chill out and read fiction and listen to music. I also have friends with businesses who spend more time learning about their business than they spend working on or in their business. It's a great form of procrastination that doesn't always result in revenue. Some days, you just have to *ready, fire, aim* and learn by experience.

Information Vacations are scheduled for one week, typically when I'm on vacation or during Christmas holidays. I don't learn

ANYTHING! I just watch fun movies, listen to music and read only fiction. I focus on what I already know and put it into practice. It gives my brain a break and reduces a lot of screen time. It's not as strict as a digital detox because I'm still working, if it's not during a vacation. I'm just not focused on research. This may not be an issue for you, especially if you are cruising in your career and aren't a big reader. For those high achievers out there, give your brain a break every once in a while and soak up the awesomeness of who you already are.

For links and references to this chapter visit http://www.beyondtravelbook.com/signup.html and login with your email address. Use the password provided in the email to access the page.

4. Outsourcing

I firmly believe in outsourcing the things you don't like doing and that you can afford. There are so many ways to outsource now that will free up your time, save money in the long run, and you don't have to be fancy or rich to do it. The first thing to consider is how much your time is worth. This is an estimate of course because money is never worth as much as time, unless you are in dire straits to pay your bills and buy food.

Not sure how to calculate how much your time is worth? There are a couple of different ways to do it. The easiest way is to determine how much you want to make this year or how much you currently make per hour. Divide by 12. Divide that by the number of weeks per year you work. Divide again by the number of hours you want to work per day = Bingo. This is how much your time is worth. If you're worth $96 per hour than hiring a VA for $30 per hour for eight hours a month will let you focus your time on what matters most and save you money in the long run.

I also recommend using the Personal Earnings Goal or PEG method to determine how much it costs you or your family to live per hour. I've included the website link in the bonus chapter. This takes a little more time, but it helped me determine how much I need to make to live, my yearly goals for my business and what type of assistant was most important for me.

Virtual Assistants (VAs)

Virtual Assistants can do everything from scheduling, answering email, customer service, email campaigns, travel arrangements, and social media. The list could go on depending on what type of VA you hire. There are many services like *Zirtual, Fancy Hands, Ruby Receptionist, oDesk* and *Get Friday*. I use *Essistant Pro*. Some companies are set up to be task-oriented. You pay for a specific amount of tasks per month, and any VA could be assigned to do that task. Plans with Fancy Hands are by task instead of by the hour. You don't get a dedicated VA this way, but paying by a task can sometimes work in your favor. Don't have time to be on hold for twenty minutes with tech support? Fancy Hands will hold for you and patch you in when they join. Need some research for your summer vacay? Get Friday can research it for you.

Other services give you a dedicated VA for a set number of hours per month. You may also have a local Virtual Assistant that works from home but can pick up marketing materials at a printer and deliver them to a venue or run your business errands.

Overwhelmed and need a VA but don't know where to start or how to use one? First, write down everything you do on a daily basis that is personal and work-related. This may take some time and works best over the course of a week or even a month since some time-suckers aren't done daily. Look carefully at that list. If you consider what you earn per hour, how much money are you wasting doing tasks you shouldn't be? Are you doing $10.00 an hour tasks? Fifty dollar an hour tasks or $100.00 an hour tasks? My guess is you are doing a lot of $10.00/hr. tasks. Why? Because they are usually quicker tasks like scheduling, social media posts, researching flights, etc. that make us feel good to tick off the list but aren't revenue producing.

Track your time to find out how long you are spending on $10.00 an hour tasks and assign those first. Note that Virtual Assistants are not $10/hour. The point is the tasks that you shouldn't be doing because they aren't in your line of genius. Consider the type of assistant you need. Do you need admin work? Travel arrangements? Scheduling? Hire a Virtual Assistant. Need help with social media? Hire a Digital Assistant. Want someone to grocery shop, run errands and chop your vegetables? Hire a Personal Assistant. After you've decided the tasks to assign, start writing down clear instructions for each task, or better yet, record yourself doing them online using a program like Jing or Screencast.

Using a VA helps budget your money because you don't have to employ them all year, and you may be able to change your hourly needs each month depending on the service. My service doesn't require a contract, and I can hire a VA to work more during busy months if required and they are available.

If you know someone using a VA, get a referral or recommendation. Many people opt to go the cheap route and hire a student, friend or family member. Know that many VAs have owned their own businesses or have business degrees and are very experienced and skilled. They choose to work from home and make their own hours, so they opt for a VA position. Sometimes you get what you pay for and if you want to pay minimum wage you might get someone that you spend two to three times as long teaching your tasks. I know there are great VA services that use international VAs, and the Philippines are known for excellent work, but I don't know enough to recommend a specific service.

Things I have used a VA for include:

- Social media posting
- Scheduling
- Travel arrangements
- Edits and updates to my website
- Finding photos online
- Writing emails
- Tasks my clients have used non-dedicated, task-oriented VA services for include:
- Research on vacation rental homes.
- Research on wedding caterers – how much, reviews, types of food and setting up the appointments.

- Finding skin care products that were ranked high on Beautipedia and the Environmental Working Group and putting them in their cart on Amazon.
- Specific fit, color and style of a suit online and narrowing it down to three.
- Research for companies they were interviewing for.
- Client and family gifts.

Procrastinate creatively. Give a VA all those tasks you don't like doing, yet must get done. Spend your time in your line of genius.

Fiverr

I've used *Fiverr* for book formatting and cover design of my first book, graphics and press releases. If there is a task to be done, there is someone on Fiverr willing to do it. Some tasks do cost $5 per task or gig in Fiverr-speak, but many worth hiring charge multiple gigs for one task. It's helpful to get recommendations and always look at the reviews and ratings for each person. Need to do market research? Hire someone from Fiverr instead. Want to compile a collage or video of your family holiday photos? Take your pick. One client had her entire website done for $30.00, and it looks fantastic.

Personal Assistants (PAs)

Personal Assistants can sometimes overlap with virtual assistants and housecleaning services. If you aren't sure what you need, this might be a way to start. Some people feel embarrassed by hiring a Personal Assistant. Either they think that only wealthy people should use them or that they should be able to get the tasks done themselves. It goes back to the question, "how much is your time worth?" Would you rather be catching up on errands and chores or going to the TEDx event or play in your company softball game? Your company may have an agreement with a concierge service and provide a discounted service. Check with your benefits department first.

Concierge and personal assistant services describe the tasks of their PAs to include:

- Laundry and ironing.
- Light or detailed cleaning.
- Errands such as grocery shopping, shipping/mailing, dry cleaning drop off/pick up.
- Food prep.
- Accept home deliveries or be there for home maintenance services.
- Perform research.
- Manage vehicle maintenance.
- Manage household projects.
- Help with party planning and hosting services.
- Serve as a house manager.

By using a website like www.care.com, you can put all your specific requirements in a job posting and even do background checks of the people who respond to your request.

Housecleaning Services

If you are a traveler, this is the number one outsourcing I recommend. When you are traveling the last thing you want to do when you are home are chores. It may eliminate the arguments of who should be cleaning – the one who is home messing it up or the one traveling because they aren't participating in the other household tasks. If your relationship with your partner or roommate is in trouble, hire a housecleaner first. You may be able to forgo the U-Haul. You can have them come in as often as once weekly or once monthly. At the very least, arrange for someone to come in quarterly for deep cleaning.

Laundry Service

If you don't like doing your laundry, don't have time to do it or don't have a washer and dryer in your residence, in which case the *time* to do it can really be costly, consider dropping off your laundry twice monthly to a local Laundromat. Make it a line item in your budget. The bonus is that they won't be delivered with all the wrinkles you have from doing them on your own and leaving them in the dryer while you're on the next train to meetingville.

Lawn Maintenance

When we bought our second home, we were on .2 acres. We thought it was a step up. It didn't take long for us to realize that we liked the *idea* of having a yard, but neither of us wanted to do the work to make it look nice. Now that we live in a townhome and have landscapers, I can enjoy my yard with the occasional planting of a flower or two. General lawn care can be cheap. If you are getting warning letters from the city saying your grass is too high, or you just don't want to be mowing in one hundred degrees in July ... outsource.

Personal Chef or Chef Service

Personal chef services can vary in price, but if you are someone who eats out often, you could end up saving money. Chef services range from someone coming to your house with a list of pre-approved menus, then prepping, cooking and storing your food for the week in the freezer. It may also be a service that makes specific meals for the week and drops them off at each home. For my clients who don't mind cooking but want everything they need for a meal to be delivered to their door, Blue Apron or Hello Fresh fits the bill. Everything is seasonal, measured and pre-portioned with meals typically between five hundred to eight hundred calories. A two-person plan for three meals a week is $60-$70 or $10-$12 a meal. See how this saves money rather than eating out? You'd spend at least that and it probably wouldn't be as good for you.

Grocery Delivery or Community Supported Agriculture (CSA)

If you live in a fifth floor walk-up, use public transportation or simply don't like going to the grocery, use a delivery service or a CSA. My Community Supported Agriculture service, Papa Spuds, Inc., delivers fresh produce, mushrooms, fish, meats, cheeses, eggs, dairy ... almost everything fresh I need, right to my door every Wednesday, year round. I also have the benefit of choosing what is delivered, although many CSAs don't offer this option. They have recently started making recipe kits with everything pre-measured and instructions included.

While I am a huge proponent of CSAs, I also understand if people are traveling and there isn't anyone to pick up their box (not all CSAs deliver) or take it inside their home to refrigerate, this might not be a good idea. Cleaning, peeling, chopping and prepping vegetables requires a lot of time. If time is of the essence, buy it ready to fix. Pre-washed salads and pre-washed and chopped vegetables and fruit will help you to eat healthier. I always buy giant bags of frozen berries, so I have them on hand for breakfast and smoothies. When it comes to veggies and fruits, buy them however you will eat it, whether it's fresh, frozen, or pre-chopped, but please try not to buy it loaded with salt or sugar.

For grocery delivery, some of my clients use *Peapod, Lowes Foods to Go* or *Green Polka Dot Box*. You simply shop online and they deliver to your door, or you can pick them up at the store. The first time you make your grocery list may take a long time, but after that it's just adding or subtracting here and there. You're also less likely to snag that box of granola bars or processed deli meat if you aren't in the store looking at it. If you're traveling, have it delivered or ready for pick-up the day after you get back. The last thing you want to do when you get home is put away groceries, but you also don't want to go too long without having real food in the house.

Amazon Subscribe and Save

I LOVE Amazon Subscribe and Save! If you are a Prime Member, it's included, if you aren't a Prime Member, the $99 you spend a year will blow your Costco and BJ's membership out of the water. Plus, products are delivered to your door and it feels like Christmas! With Amazon S&S, you get your order delivered on a flexible schedule that you choose – monthly, every three months, every six months, etc., which can also be changed by moving up or skipping a month. I buy almost all my dry goods, paper products, makeup ... Anything I would go to Target or Wal-Mart to purchase, on Amazon S&S. If you have more than five things in the order, then you get 15% off the already low price.

Examples of things I buy on a schedule on Amazon S&S so I'm never without and don't have to do the big box store errand run:

- Raw nuts
- Bob's Red Mill products
- Salsa and mustard
- Sandwich and trash bags
- Teeccino and coffee
- Toothpaste
- Vitamins and supplements
- Coconut and MCT oil
- Mascara
- Cleaning products
- Tahini
- Toilet paper and facial tissue

Clothing/Accessory/Skin Care Delivery

Think you can't afford a personal shopper? Think again. My clients have had mad success with clothing delivery services. After setting preferences, getting very specific with style and size and picking out looks that you like from the site, these services deliver a box to your door every month with clothing curated especially for you. Some services are for purchase only and need to be returned within seventy-two hours, and others are more like rentals; where you receive a new shipment when they receive your clothes.

These types of services are ideal for people who don't have good style, don't like to shop, don't have time to shop or just want to break out of their comfort zone. Two of my clients have been shocked at how well the clothing fit and made them feel like a walking magazine cover. When you look good, you feel good. When you feel good, you take better care of yourself and have more confidence. A list of men's and women's clothing delivery services can be found in the bonus chapter.

Birch Box is a beauty and grooming subscription that surprises you each month with supplies like makeup, shaving accessories, and shampoo and comes in both men's and women's boxes. I subscribe to *Dollar Shave Club* and get blades delivered to my door on a set schedule. It is way cheaper than retail, the quality is great and their marketing is hilarious. These types of subscription services also make great gifts.

Driving

If you have a long commute or drive, it might be worthwhile to have a driver or use a service like Uber. You can work stress-free in the car, giving you back all that time you would otherwise be wasting staring at the road. One of my clients determined that using Uber to make a twice-weekly two-hour round trip commute to a client's office made him an extra $100 per trip. He calculated his time per hour, his ability to get through tasks uninterrupted or make calls he wouldn't (shouldn't) be doing while driving and how much he would have to pay the car service. In the end, he saved two hours of extra work a day while also generating a little more revenue for his business.

There you go. Several ways to outsource to free up your time to make more money, have more time and work and live in your line of genius. If you are self-employed, you can typically have more options to outsource. If you work in corporate, you may be limited on what you can use for your work, so focusing on outsourcing the personal tasks makes sense.

For links and references to this chapter visit http://www.beyondtravelbook.com/signup.html and login with your email address. Use the password provided in the email to access to the bonus page.

Special Bonus from Marcey Rader

Now that you have your copy of *Beyond Travel: The Road Warrior's Survival Guide*, you are on your way from the haggard, frazzled, caffeinated traveler to the calm, efficient and healthy traveler. You'll get loads of info and new habits to start incorporating into your life.

You'll also receive the special bonus I created to add to your productivity tool belt. Each chapter includes a bonus page online with links to all the references, companies, software, programs, and videos I mention. You'll get exercise videos, free webinars and discounts to products to help you further develop your arsenal of behavioral productivity tools.

There are books on being healthy, being productive, and travel, yet in this book I purposely covered all three to give you what you need in one place. When you finish this book, you'll be armed with the skills required to *travel like a boss*.

Go to http://www.beyondtravelbook.com/signup.html and login with your email address. You'll receive the password via email to access the page. With that access *you will automatically be added to my newsletter list. You may of course unsubscribe at any time.*

The sooner you know the *hacks* for air, hotel, auto, home, outsourcing, nutrition, exercise, and stress management, the sooner you'll feel in control again.

Let's do this.

Marcey Rader

Marcey Rader

5. Mobile Office Nutrition

When I first became a vegetarian at nineteen, and it really seemed like there wasn't anything for me to eat, I solved this by skipping the meat and eating twice the dessert or bread. Sometimes you have to ask yourself if your food rules need to be flexible enough to eat *healthier* options. Food rules determine what you will or won't eat. For example, after needing to change my diet after my diagnosis, I now eat beef if it's grass-fed, chicken if it's antibiotic and hormone free, wild game and wild fish. I eat sweets only on the weekends and holidays, very few fried foods and avoid artificial flavors and sweeteners.

If you are choosing to eat a certain way for ethical reasons, you may not be as flexible. If you are vegetarian for health reasons and the options are eat nothing but bread or dessert all day or eat soup made with chicken broth, you may question which is the healthier option for you.

Does a cookie at the airport on business count?

How many times have you said, *"I'm on vacation." "I've been really good all week." "My company is paying for this."* I used to justify treating myself with that cookie, fooling myself by using these excuses. I'm not against the occasional treat and I don't have the perfect diet every day. To me, the perfect diet doesn't exist because it's always evolving. Depending on my lifestyle, health issues, and the latest research, what is great for me this year may be different next year. However, some people will give themselves way too much leeway by constantly making up excuses and justifications as to why they are eating a particular food or a particular way. At some point, they may even be telling themselves that every day.

When you are looking at a giant, pancake-sized cookie after you've had a long workout, do you think that cookie knows or cares that you sweated for an hour? No. It will still metabolize the same. The Cookie Fairy will **not** say *"Hey good job Marcey! You deserve for NONE of* *these calories to affect your recovery, stimulate an insulin response or make you crave more sugar later. You rock, Girlfriend!"*

When you are on your third glass of wine at your company dinner, do you think that wine knows that this is a special occasion? No. It will metabolize the same. The Wine Fairy will not say *"Hey AJ, you deserve for NONE of these calories to be metabolized into sugar, affect your sleep and make you wake up dehydrated with a headache. High Fives!"*

Moderation is key, but how many people abuse this concept? If I snorted cocaine, would it be okay as long as it was in moderation? If I drove 70mph down the winding, hilly road by my house, but only did it once or twice each week, would it be okay since I'm not doing it every day? Your body doesn't know you are on vacation. It doesn't know or care that you have a $75 a day per Diem. *Don't eat your per Diem!*™ It doesn't even know that it's your birthday! (Yes, for real, it doesn't recognize birthdays.)

If you want to have something, have it. Tricking yourself into think-ing that the effects will somehow bypass whatever the effects are in a normal situation is not going to help you. As a frequent traveler, remember that being on the road is your 'normal.'

Eating for Energy

People eat food for many reasons and emotions — hunger, anger, anxiety, overwhelm, loneliness, tiredness, sadness, happiness, social pressure, etc. Most people don't focus on eating for energy. I would say seventy-five percent of what goes in my mouth is a calculated decision as far as timing and nutrient composition because I eat for energy. The other twenty-five percent would be because I'm at a party or friend's house, it's Saturday night movie night with my husband or it's a holiday. Sometimes I don't have a choice, like at a small region-al airport or a catered meal. Eating for energy means eating foods that are stimulating in the morning and calming in the evening. It means eating often enough that you don't let your blood sugar get too low, but not so often that your body never knows the feeling of true hunger.

Caffeine: The most vilified and loved stimulant on the planet. The coffee haters like to showcase the addictive nature. The coffee lovers like to showcase the health benefits. I think both are great arguments. If someone *needs* coffee in the morning, I think this is an issue where weaning off is recommended, until it becomes more of a pleasurable habit rather than a true need to function. Contrary to how it's normally used, coffee is best used when you are relaxed, healthy and calm. Adding a stimulant onto an already stressed and fatigued person makes them more stressed and fatigued and leads to a vicious cycle. It makes the adrenal glands work harder, promotes greater blood sugar swings and can and often disrupts sleep.

Coffee has very significant health benefits for some people. It has been shown to reduce the incidence of Parkinson's Disease, non-malignant melanoma, lower risk of early death, lower risk of diabetes and cardiovascular disease and have cognitive benefits that increase alertness. However, citing studies that show benefits or risks doesn't necessarily show the whole picture. Coffee consumption is different for each of us and like many things should be enjoyed in moderation. Drinking six cups a day is going to stress out your kidneys and adrenal glands regardless of how healthy you are. There's also a gene that determines if you metabolize caffeine fast or slow. Depending on that gene, coffee can make you more or less at risk of heart attack. Thankfully, because I've had genetic testing, I know I'm in the beneficial category, at least for heart attack risk.

If you drink coffee in the morning, and then you feel like you need some later in the day or it makes you jittery and feel over-stimulated, you need to wean yourself off and then stick to one or two cups a day max. I call that feeling wired and tired or jacked and crashed. Using it as a little bit of a stimulant or brain booster early in the day works well for most people. Just be cautious of adding too much sweetener and making it a dessert drink.

Water and tea: If you frequently get headaches, often the problem is a lack of water or fluids. Soft drinks are America's number one source of sugar. I don't advocate any soft drinks, especially artificially-sweetened ones. I cringe when I remember that I used to drink Diet Mountain Dew. Drink plain water with lemon, lime, basil, cucumber, blueberries or raspberries or unsweetened hot or cold tea. Stay clear of adding powders like Crystal Light or drinking flavored enhanced waters. Most of them have chemicals in them that you don't need. I'm a huge fan of Kombucha tea and started brewing my own a couple of years ago. I even bought a continuous brewer through Kombucha Kamp to brew a gallon a week. Kombucha is a fermented tea that may have many health benefits. I drink about eight ounces daily.

I always start my day with warm water, lemon, and cayenne pepper. It ensures I drink water right away since I haven't had anything all night, and the lemon and cayenne are stimulating for digestion. This has become a daily habit for me between waking up and working out. If I'm on the road, I seriously miss it and try to substitute with just warm water and lemon slices, but I miss the cayenne kick.

In the afternoon, I like to drink the coffee-alternative Teeccino. It's caffeine-free and made with dandelion root. Dandelion root may help to balance blood sugar, have a beneficial effect on the liver and stimulate digestion. Teeccino also has carob, chicory, dates, and figs. I like to add a nut or coconut milk to mine.

Avoid or minimize sweets: This is obvious and also hard for many people. When I significantly decreased my sweets and started having them only on the weekends, my already high energy levels soared. I usually get my sweet fix using vegetables like sweet potatoes, beets or steamed carrots or fruit. As you start to decrease your sugar intake, you'll crave it less. I promise. Don't think you're tricking your brain by using artificial sweeteners. You'll still release insulin because your brain thinks it's eating sugar. If you are used to having a treat every night after dinner, try a new habit or trigger. Brush your teeth right away, take a quick five-minute walk or eat a half an ounce of cheese or a few nuts.

Animal products: Just like coffee....we're going to have two very different camps. This answer is going to irritate some and make others rejoice. I truly believe in bio-individuality. I believe that some people feel better eating meat, and some people feel better not eating meat. I believe that it can change depending on your age, where you are in your life, disease process (if you have one) and so on. You can be a healthy vegan and a healthy Paleo. You can also be a horrible vegan and horrible Paleo. Take off your Righteous Hat (I used to be one, so I'm speaking from experience). Many studies that have been done on nutrition look at meat versus non-meat eaters, but they don't take into account the quality of food of the meat-eaters or other lifestyle factors. If you're going to eliminate animal products, don't replace it with a bunch of processed products because that's not healthy either. If you're going to eat meat, don't fill your plate with meat treated with a bunch of fillers, antibiotics, hormones and items that are processed.

Superfoods: Using natural sources of energy that have both established and anecdotal benefits is the way I choose to get some of my immunity and energy boosters. The reason the benefits are sometimes only anecdotal is because there isn't a lot of money in natural foods or companies, universities, and hospitals fighting to research them.

What I use and how:

- Chia seeds – smoothies, yogurt, soup, puddings. I usually only eat these during the day because they are a natural energy booster. Chia seeds gel up and act like a thickener and can even be used as natural sports nutrition.

- Cacao nibs or powder – this is not cocoa powder. Cacao is raw and made by cold-pressing unroasted cocoa beans. This protects the living enzymes and removes the fat. Cocoa powder is raw cacao that has been roasted at high temperatures. I use cacao in smoothies, coffee, yogurt or cereal.

- Seaweed or Nori – torn into pieces for soup, stir-fry or used as a wrap for veggies

- Hemp seeds, hearts or powder – I sprinkle the hemp seeds and hearts on just about any dish. The powder I stir into soups or more savory dishes. Hemp is related to marijuana but doesn't contain any traces of the psychoactive ingredient of their cousin.

- Kombucha tea - This tea doesn't *cure* anything and isn't a panacea, but it does help bring your body back into balance to heal itself naturally. It is a natural probiotic and adaptogen and may help with digestion. There are many reported anecdotal benefits but not enough scientific research to make claims. It contains three to six times the Vitamin C as store-bought orange juice without the sugar rush. I drink it daily.

- Kefir – Plain, unsweetened fermented milk high in probiotics. It's similar to yogurt, but runnier. I use it in smoothies or in place of yogurt.

- Nutritional yeast – Daily staple for me! If you are vegan, this is one of the best sources of Vitamin B-12, mostly found in meat and dairy products. I use nutritional yeast as I would Parmesan cheese. It's delicious on vegetables, pizza, eggs or made into gravy.

- Sauerkraut – Loads of good bacteria in here! Be careful what you buy. The ingredients should just be cabbage and salt.

Weekly Food Prep and Planning

Eating for health and energy does take planning and prepping, but not as much as you think if you time chunk it. Sundays are my days to prep and make food for the week. If I'm home during the week, I also do this on Wednesdays when my fruits and veggies are delivered from the CSA. I set the timer for one hour and do as much as I can during that time. It might include washing and prepping veggies and fruit, cooking some grain like rice, buckwheat or quinoa, throwing dried and soaked beans in the crockpot, boiling eggs or grilling meat. I also make baggies of Marcey's Muesli Mix to make a quick breakfast or pack for travel.

Marcey's Muesli Mix includes:

- 15 grams muesli (I use gluten-free Bob's Red Mill - no added sugar)
- .5 Tablespoons of chia seeds and/or 1 Tablespoon of flax meal
- .5 ounce of nuts
- 1 Tablespoon of hemp hearts
- .5 scoop Vega or Deep 30 Protein Powder

If I'm going to be eating it the next morning, I'll empty a baggie of muesli mix in a bowl with three quarters of a cup of frozen berries or other fruit and four to five ounces of unsweetened almond or coconut milk and stick it in the fridge. By the morning, the fruit has thawed, and the muesli has thickened. It's great to travel with to add to yogurt or milk and fruit at a hotel.

Business Travel Nutrition

How do you survive when your meals and when to eat are decided for you? What do you do to eliminate pound packing? Remember, you aren't on vacation and the more parties, conferences and meeting meals you have, the more you have to plan and prepare.

Portion Distortion

Twenty years ago a serving of soda was considered 6.5 ounces. A bottle of Coke was sold to serve three people, whereas now a twenty-ounce serving is the norm. A buck can buy you a burger at McDonald's, but it costs $5 for a salad. Do you want meat that is so cheap that you can get a whole sandwich for a buck? I say if a restaurant serves a lot of *quantity*, it's because they can't serve *quality*. How can you trick yourself in this super-size world and overcome portion distortion?

- Eat from small plates and bowls when you can. Restaurant dishes now are the size of serving platters. At home, use smaller sizes to fill up the dish and trick the brain into thinking it's more.

- A taller glass looks like more to the eye. I used to pour our Kombucha tea into a tumbler. When I poured the same amount into a tall glass, my husband thought it was too much and couldn't drink it. All a trick of the eye. When people drink alcohol out of a short glass, they tend to drink twenty to thirty percent more. Is that wine glass you're drinking out of really a bowl?

- Ask for the take home container when you get your meal. If you know you won't take it with you because your hotel doesn't have a fridge, then physically separate your food on your plate to eat only the amount you want. If you're someone who picks at his or her food as long as it's there, place a napkin over it or pour salt or water over what's left so it doesn't tempt you if you can't leave right away.

Martyr Syndrome

"I didn't have time to eat."

"I'm so busy I forget to eat."

As a traveler, we've all been in the situation where we think we will have time to grab something from the airport in between connections, but our first flight was delayed and now we're running to catch the next one. Or, we arrive at the hotel thinking they will have a restaurant, but it's closed and the pantry consists of Advil, toothpaste, Diet Coke and sugary granola bars. These things happen, but are you the person who goes all day without eating and wears it like some badge to tell people how you are so busy you can't possibly eat?

I worked in an industry where I would see this all the time. The person would show up around 8:00am and work all day until 5:00pm without stopping to eat lunch or even eat while they were working. If someone was with them, they might actually try to make them feel guilty for wanting to get something to eat and act proud about how they just work through lunch. Truthfully, I used to eat lunch while I was working or ran out to get something and brought it back to eat, but I never went all day long without fueling my brain and body.

That's what you're doing folks ... you are fueling your brain and body. Whether your work is tedious or physical, you still need to eat something. I was with a woman once who had oatmeal for breakfast (about one hundred, fifty calories) and about four ounces of OJ (about fifty calories). She didn't eat anything else until 4:15pm. How focused do you think her brain was by 2:00pm? This poor woman said she sometimes felt dizzy at the end of the day and ended up hitting the drive thru for a bacon double-cheeseburger at first chance.

Stop being a martyr. Eating helps stabilize your blood sugar and leads to better decision making. There's a reason we make unhealthy choices when we let ourselves get too hungry.

The Business Breakfast Meeting

Breakfast can be one of the hardest meetings to deal with because you either have too many options or too few. Business meetings or conferences tend to feed you into a coma. It starts out with breakfast, typically consisting of sugar-laden, refined carbohydrates like bagels, donuts, and muffins. These bagels and muffins are two to four times larger than a normal serving. If you're lucky, they may offer fruit, yogurt, and hard-boiled eggs. Unfortunately most yogurts at these types of events are sweetened or filled with chemicals. I always take a small bag of nuts or eat something in my room *before* the breakfast meeting just in case they won't have anything healthy. If you know you're going to eat something no matter what and you must have a bagel or muffin, eat only half and try to balance it with some healthy fat like nut butter. Unfortunately, the peanut butter offered probably

111

isn't natural and is filled with trans fats and sugars so you would have to bring your nut butter packets.

Coffee, tea, soda, and juice are typically served all day long at meetings. Be careful with drinking your calories and 'caffeinating' yourself to death. If you know you will drink coffee all day, try to make every other cup decaf tea or water. Drinking tea or water all day will keep your hands busy and possibly keep you from mindless eating. To cut back on calories in juice, dilute it with some water. It will last longer, you won't get as much of a rush from the fruit sugar and if you drink less of it, you've saved yourself much needed calories for the rest of the day.

The Business Lunch

If the business lunch is served buffet style, you may have so many options you can easily overdo it. If the meal is catered with only a few choices, you may panic that there isn't anything for you to eat. Who among my vegetarian readers has survived on nothing but salad or bread for days during business conferences?

If your lunch or dinner is buffet style, I recommend fixing a big salad first, paying careful attention to the amount of cheese and croutons you add. Place your dressing on the side and dip your fork in the dressing BEFORE picking up your food. I prefer just using vinegar and oil or just straight balsamic vinegar or lemon juice since most prepared dressings are full of sugar, sodium and fillers. A plate of straight-up raw vegetables is even better.

Most people are going to take a second trip to the buffet. If you know you will, having a salad, some raw veggies or a cup of soup *first* may help you make a smarter choice on the second round than if you just went through and started loading up your plate the first time without a conscious plan. You'll be able to see what is there and consider where you want to focus your calories.

A recent study showed that thinner people scope out the salad bar or buffet first and then go back and fix their plate. Overweight or obese people tend to just get in line without determining how much food is on the buffet or what they want to choose.

Business Sugar Coma

A business meeting or meal doesn't usually occur without some coma-inducing, calorie-infested, high-fat dessert. If they have cheesecake and you want it, go for it — but note to yourself you'll have to cut back somewhere. Since all you are doing is sitting in meetings, I don't recommend having any sugar at lunchtime because you'll crash in the afternoon. In my former company, it was common to order heavy desserts or at least cookies and brownies at lunch. As a corporate trainer, I switched to having a fruit salad for the afternoon break. Only twice did I receive complaints that I didn't offer sweets and for those two; I reminded them how tired people were in the afternoon!

Sometimes it's important to splurge. When I was in New Orleans for the first time, I happened to be with a friend and mentor and had to try a beignet (French cousin of the donut). I didn't know if I would ever be back; it was something special we shared together, and that was something I couldn't get back home. Bonus that I was there on a Saturday, so I still kept my food rule of sweets only on the weekends or holidays! I also had to eat Alfajores dulce de leche (shortbread cookie sandwiches with a sweet filling) every time I went to Argentina.

The Business Dinner

How many people have been in a situation where there are eight to ten people at dinner and they insist on ordering eight appetizers, individual meals and then a few desserts for the table? I love *(insert sarcasm here)* to get pressured to eat the dessert by the person who ordered it, so they feel better for eating it themselves. When you are surrounded by food choices, take small bites of the things you really like and you wouldn't get at home. It isn't realistic for most people to say they will be able to refuse to take something when several plates are being passed around. Instead, think 'what are my favorite things here?' If you only think egg rolls are 'okay' but you would trade your iPhone for some crispy green beans, have a few crispy green beans and pass on the egg rolls. This way the attention isn't drawn to you because you passed on everything, and you are still enjoying your meal and socializing.

The Office Birthday Cake

One week I was working out of a corporate office with an audit team and received an email inviting me to celebrate a team member's birthday with cake. I didn't know him well but wanted to show my team spirit. Here was the scenario…

There are ten of us in the meeting room and Birthday Guy comes in as we break into *Happy Birthday*. A team member cuts the cake and starts to divvy it up. The Birthday Guy asks for a very small piece. I can't remember now if I saw him take one small bite and throw it away or just throw it away. Later I asked him if he liked cake. He quietly said he was on a 'no sugar' diet and didn't want it. I could tell he felt guilty for even saying that. The worst part of this whole party was that several people *knew* he was on a no-sugar diet! *Even the woman who bought the cake!* It was one of the most insensitive acts I can think of to do at a birthday. When I mentioned his no-sugar diet to her, she said that everyone else would eat it.

We were not celebrating this guy at all. The office just used his birthday as an excuse to buy and eat cake. Maybe what this guy wanted was just an acknowledgment with something that he *liked* to eat, or maybe nothing at all. I used to teach a class and the students knew that I didn't eat the catered in cookies and brownies and that I always had a fruit salad in the afternoon instead. After the three-week class was over, they bought me an edible fruit bouquet. It was one of the most thoughtful and practical gifts I have ever received — as opposed to a bottle of wine someone gifted me at our housewarming that said 'I know you don't like wine, but here you go.' Uh … *thanks*?

I have always worked remotely and being part of that birthday scene made me glad I was remote on so many levels. No one should feel guilty on his or her birthday for not eating something. If you are someone who pressures people to eat the dessert or drink the wine to make yourself feel better, take an emotional inventory. If you want those things, have them and enjoy!! The whole table doesn't have to join you to make sure you feel good about yourself.

I've been in countless situations where I felt obligated to share the dessert or appetizer. Later I would ask myself why. It's not that I don't ever eat these things, but I don't eat them all the time and the question was more 'Why did I eat them? Was it to fit in or decrease someone else's guilt rather than because I actually wanted them?'

Restaurant Bombs

There are many restaurants where you can get good quality food, however, more often than not, it's the issue of the *quantity* of food on the plate. Restaurants serve way too much. Most people would never eat as much at home as they do in a restaurant. It's also part of our culture not to waste food. How many people have eaten past being satisfied because they couldn't take what's left back to their hotel, and they felt bad about not finishing it? Guess what? The meal costs the same whether it ends up in the trash, on your butt or your belly. If you're traveling for business, your meal is reimbursable or deductible so leave it. Personally, I think that a lot of restaurants serve *quantity* because they can't serve *quality*.

Let's look at some examples, keeping in mind the average recommended calorie intake of 1800-2200 calories and less than 1500mg of sodium a day. I'm not fat-phobic by any means, but it's important to note that the majority of the fat is *not* coming from a healthy source.

- Cheesecake Factory pasta Carbonara with chicken has 2500 calories and 1630 mg of sodium. More than an entire day's worth of sodium in one meal! They now have a Skinnylicious menu with reasonably sized options.

- PF Chang's chicken lo mein has 2050 mg of sodium, 1240 calories and 25 grams of fat.

- Applebee's pecan crusted chicken salad is a nutritional nightmare at 1360 calories and a whopping 80 grams of fat! It also has 2640 mg of sodium, which will make you swell up and bloat until you need to buy a new pair of elastic waist pants.

- A Smoothie King Cranberry Supreme has 1108 calories and 192 grams of sugar. Considering a daily limit of sugar is about 30 grams, this is over six times what you should have in one day. You just drank almost a week's worth of sugar. Was it worth it?

- Lastly, we have the Ruby Tuesday avocado turkey burger. Think you are eating healthy because it's a turkey burger? This artery monstrosity has 1313 calories, 73 grams of fat and 3221 grams of sodium. You just ate two days worth of sodium. Still want fries with that?

One website and book I like is *Eat This, Not That.* Men's Health put this out a few years ago and gives the better choices at restaurants.

Fast Casual

Some restaurant chains that make it easy to eat healthy and are also inexpensive, made-to-order and quick, are *fast casual restaurants.* I've added some information below for common food rules of vegetarian, Paleo, non-GMO, hormone-free meat, gluten-free or organic. I've only included the largest chains. However, there are several on the rise that will soon be more common due to their healthy, more sustainable options, and focus on fresh foods.

- Chipotle was named one of the best gluten-free friendly restaurants and have recently made changes to offer healthier and more sustainable options. They are now also 100% GMO-free. Get a burrito bowl or salad and load up on the veggies. Ask for half or no cheese and sour cream.

- Panera Bread has some healthy soups and salads if you don't load up on the dressings. You can order half sizes or Pick Twos to get more of a variety. Panera has recently vowed to cut out artificial flavors, colors, preservatives and sweeteners by 2016.

- Au Bon Pain has 'small plates' and a kiosk to look up nutritional information before you order.

- Jason's Deli and Atlanta Bread Company have several organic, gluten-free and Paleo options as well as smaller sizes.

- Noodles & Company has lean, hormone and antibiotic free meats, organic tofu and gluten-free and Paleo options.

- Zoe's Kitchen has several healthy items that are vegetarian, gluten-free or Paleo that are fresh with reasonable portions.

- Mongolian Grill is great to be able to choose your ingredients and load up on veggies to add to your bowl.

- McAlister's Deli has gluten-free, vegetarian and Paleo options. Be careful ordering a giant baked potato loaded with toppings.

- Zpizza offers pizza by the slice as well as 100% whole wheat and gluten-free crusts.

- Starbucks has a new entrée that's great to grab when you get your fix in the morning and aren't able to take off at lunch. The Hearty Veggie and Brown Rice Salad Bowl is packed with brown rice, kale, and veggies.

Breakfast Bombs

Muffin and a latte? The breakfast of champions? Yes ... if you want to win at 'crashing' and making poor decisions later in the day. These muffin sugar bombs are about 450 calories and will make you crash faster than a toddler after an afternoon at Chuckie Cheese. Would you eat a cupcake for breakfast? Muffins are cupcakes without icing.

There are ways to make muffins healthy, but I bet the ones you are buying aren't.

Beware of items that are seemingly healthy, like the Dunkin Donuts egg white veggie flatbread. I used to eat these all the time when traveling, only to find out that besides being highly processed and having over thirty percent of the daily max for sodium; they contain azodicarbonamide as a dough conditioner. This is banned in Europe due to studies showing it can cause asthma or allergic reactions. A Subway egg white flatbread isn't quite as bad but is very high in sodium. A McDonald's egg white delight or egg McMuffin, which somehow always ends up on a 'not so bad to eat list' has trans-fats, over 30% of your daily max for sodium, plus a dose of nitrites and nitrates. When nitrates and nitrites are broken down in the stomach, they've been shown to cause cancer in young children and pregnant women.

The use of azodicarbonamide in food carries a hefty fine up to $450,000 or a 15-year jail sentence in Singapore. Why it's still allowed in the US is a mystery.

If eating in the hotel restaurant, try hard boiled-eggs, veggie omelets, whole grain toast, cottage cheese, fruit, and oatmeal. Steer clear of the pancakes and waffles. The sugar crash will bring you down quickly since it's basically like eating cake and icing for breakfast. These should just be eaten as treats, not something to start your day when you need energy.

General Restaurant Guidelines:

- Skip the bread basket and chips. Seriously, would you eat an entire bowl of chips or half a loaf of bread before dinner at home? Who cares if it's free?
- Choose roasted or steamed vegetables over mashed potatoes or French fries.

- A serving of grains is a half of a cup. Practice portion control if you are going to order any starch like pasta or rice. Better yet, get your carbs from starchy vegetables like sweet potato, yams, squashes, beets and carrots.

- Skip fried foods or at a minimum, ask the server when the last time their oil was changed. Restaurants don't change their oil often, and your food could be cooked in something that is rancid. Most restaurants use vegetable oil too, which isn't a healthy cooking oil. Stick with coconut, olive or sesame oil, and grass-fed butter or ghee.

- Box up half the entrée when it gets to your table, so you aren't tempted to keep picking at it.

- Share your entrée if you're there with someone willing.

- Ask for any dressings or sauces on the side. Most restaurants use commercial dressings, which are high in sugar, artificial flavors, and colors.

The Forgotten Choice

People forget about grocery stores when they travel. When I mention it in workshops or to my clients, I see the light bulb above their head and an "oh yeah, a grocery store"! I highly recommend staying at a hotel with a kitchen if you are going to be anywhere for more than two days. Extended Stay America has full kitchens and is a reason I partner with them. It's one of the top three things I look for if I'm staying anywhere for more than two nights. Extended Stay America recently moved to washing and sanitizing the dishes outside of the room and bringing the kitchen kit to the room upon request. This makes me feel more confident they have been cleaned, rather than trusting that the person staying in the room before me didn't eat off a plate, thought it looked clean enough and put it back (I knew someone who did this and thought it was acceptable because it saved water, and the plate didn't look dirty!). Even if you don't have a kitchen, take advantage of the mini-fridge or microwave. I'm not a huge fan of microwaving, but it's nice to have one when you don't have a stove or oven.

When I used to travel to Florida frequently, I ate almost all my dinners from a Publix grocery store. I would get a big prepared fruit salad, edamame, grape tomatoes, salad, hummus, and nuts. None of these needed to be prepared or heated. If you eat meat, it's easy to get grilled chicken or salmon. If you're lucky enough to be near a Whole Foods, Earth Fare or Trader Joe's, you can pick up prepared food from their deli/restaurant areas. I would eat these over most restaurant choices any day!

If you are staying somewhere for a few days, take a trip to the grocery. I often hear people say they feel like they may waste food because they won't be able to eat it all. If you buy a bag of tortillas for $2.99 and you eat three of the six and have to throw the rest away, do you really think that you would have spent less than $1.50 if you ate out for three meals? It's not rational. Go to the grocery store. I asked a housekeeper once what they did with the food that was left behind. She said they were supposed to throw it away, but if it was unopened or something like fruit they could wash, they appreciated when guests left food. *Note about corporate meal policies — some make it hard to stock up on groceries because they won't let you spend beyond your per diem allowance for one day, even though you are buying for four to five days. Get permission first or be a risk-taker and ask for forgiveness later.*

Apps

Apps can be a real savior on the road. These are my most frequently used pocket friends:

- *Fooducate* gives food a grade from A – F and rates them according to their food category. That way, when you crave a muffin, it will at least tell you which one is more healthy. They also have a premium service for gluten-free and diabetic offerings. I can quickly see if an item is GF by the green asterisk beside the item. It has scanning capability, so I don't even have to enter it by hand.

- My Fitness Pal has an enormous food database that includes many restaurants. It is a nutrient and exercise tracker. Lose It is a similar app.
- Find Me Gluten Free locates gluten free restaurants in your area.
- Happy Cow locates vegetarian restaurants

#1 Biggest Mistake

What's do you think is the number one biggest mistake you can make as a traveler when it comes to food?

Eating every meal like you're on vacation or out for dinner!

Do you try to eat based on your per diem? If you get $75.00 per day, do you feel like you have to spend it? If you've only spent $30.00 so far on food, do you end up ordering a couple of drinks, an appetizer and a dessert with your dinner? When you're eating three meals a day plus snacks on someone else's dime, you *can't see every meal as a treat*. I used to treat myself with a Frappuccino every day when I traveled. Then I switched to Frappuccino Light. Later I realized that because I was traveling two to four days per week, I was taking in an enormous amount of sugar and that Frappuccino was a dessert I was drinking at 10:00am! It was no longer a treat because I was doing it almost every day.

On the flip side, I've seen people almost starve themselves or eat very low-quality food because they get to keep the dollars they don't spend. When I had a job like this, I ended up paying a lot more attention to what I bought. However, I ended up going to grocery stores more so I could save my money and spend it on other things.

Questions to ask when eating on per diem are:

- Would I buy this much food if I were paying for it myself?
- Am I buying this food because I'm hungry or because I feel like I'm burning a hole in my pocket?

When you frequently travel for business, you are *not* on vacation, and it is *not* a treat. Eat like you would eat at home. *Don't eat your per Diem!*™

This book isn't a book on nutrition or a specific diet plan because there are many different appropriate and good plans depending on the person. However, I will share some of the more common mistakes among business travelers besides eating every meal like you're on vacation.

- Eating too much sugar. I don't think I need to go into too much detail here. Sugar is inflammatory, creates energy highs and lows, provides empty calories and is nutritionally devoid of benefits.

- *Eating too many processed foods.* Convenience tends to win out for a majority of travelers. Are you committed to being healthy and having more energy? If you are, you'll be able to find a way with the tips I've shared, at least seventy-five percent of the time.

- *Not eating enough vegetables.* Get them in when you can. Remember that your meal in the airport may not have any vegetables, so if you have to load up earlier in the day, do so. Your meals may not all be balanced but over the course of the day your overall nutrition can be.

- *Caffeinating to death.* Much like sugar, caffeine can create energy highs and lows. Use it in a way that is smart. If you know you will need it or want it, wait until you do need it and if you drink a lot of it, try alternating with tea. For me, it's more about the hot beverage in my hand and the comfort of it than the actual caffeine. I drink one cup in the morning and a Teeccino in the afternoon. In the summer months, I do the same, but drink them iced.

Airport Nutrition (is that an oxymoron?)

The airport is a land of fast food, giant-sized bags of trail mix, protein bars, and little variety. Even a large airport doesn't guarantee a healthy meal. I've walked miles up and down terminals trying to figure out what is the 'least bad' thing I can find.

A few years ago the Physician's Committee for Responsible Medicine (PCRM) started rating major airports for healthy meal choices. The criteria were that the airport had to offer *one* low-fat, high-fiber, cholesterol-free vegetarian entrée. This is not *per terminal* but *airport*! This is abysmal. Offering only one should be given a big fat **F** in my book. In 2014, 75% of 23 of the top 30 airports met the criteria.

The top five airports for healthy choices, according to PCRM are

- Baltimore Washington International: More than ninety percent of BWI's restaurants fit criteria.
- Seattle-Tacoma International: Ninety percent meet criteria. This is their first year on the list.
- Los Angeles International: Eighty-eight percent meet criteria.
- Ronald Reagan International.
- Newark Liberty: Tied with BWI for most improved. All-vegetarian and vegan restaurant expected to open in 2015.
- While Hartsfield-Jackson Atlanta Airport has been rated the worst for four years running (at least they are consistent) with only fifty-two percent of restaurants meeting criteria, they have improved somewhat. Having connected there many times, I am not surprised they are ranked the worst. C'mon Atlanta!

Help! What can I eat?

First, look for foods that are the *least processed*. No matter what nutrition plan you are following: Paleo, vegetarian, low-sodium, gluten-free, low-fat, 40/30/30, the one common denominator is the lack of processed foods. Show me a healthy nutrition plan that tells you to eat more processed food and I will show you a unicorn brushing its teeth. If your food is minimally processed, more often than not it will be naturally low in sodium. The air pressure on the plane combined with being sedentary for so long causes you to retain fluids. Sodium exacerbates that. How many people have experienced a little constipation after flying? There lies the one result of this problem. It happens to the best of us.

Most flights don't offer meals unless it is an international flight or long haul in first class. It's important to know that you can choose low-sodium, vegetarian, low-fat and low-calorie meals as long as you choose at least twenty-four hours in advance via the airline's website. The typical airline meal has 950 calories, which is half an average woman's daily caloric intake. Think about it ... if you are eating a meal served on an airplane, then you are probably on a very long flight and not expending many calories that day. You just ate half of them in one not-so-tasty meal!

Did you know that altitude affects our taste buds? Airlines have to add more salt to the food for it to taste good. This means you are taking in an excessive amount of sodium, which when combined with a lack of movement, will make your body retain water in your blood vessels. This is why your ankles swell and your pants feel too tight. Altitude also affects your digestive system causing gasses to expand by as much as 30 percent. Another reason not to have carbonated beverages on board. Forget Food Baby. Think Plane Baby.

Humidity falls to about twenty percent in a cabin as opposed to forty to seventy percent in a typical environment. You may not get dehydrated much on a short flight but if you've ever experienced dry eyes, nose or throat or saw blood in your tissue when you blew your noggin, this is due to the dry air in the cabin. The last thing you want is a high-sodium meal making you retain fluids, worsening the problem.

Buy plain water or decaf coffee or tea. Try to avoid having caffeine on the plane or make sure you drink a lot of water as well. The carbonated, sugary or artificially sweetened sodas they serve on the plane will exacerbate swelling and gasses in your stomach.

It's much safer to purchase your water, coffee or tea *before* you board. Aircraft have been under scrutiny for testing positive for e-Coli in the coffee, unbottled water, and ice. A little poo with your beverage?

Grab and Go Coolers

Be careful when purchasing food from the grab and go coolers, especially if you're buying a meat product. Inspections records for almost eight hundred restaurants at ten airports found a variety of violations. A review of thirty-five restaurants at Reagan National Airport, which is probably representative of most airports, revealed that seventy-seven percent of the restaurants had at least one CRITICAL health violation. Critical violations included: Meat stored at low temperatures; raw meat contaminating ready-to-eat food; rodent droppings (there's that poo again), kitchen's lacking soap (poo on hands). Yuck.

If you are purchasing from a grab and go cooler, be sure to eat the food right away and not let it sit in your bag for an hour to eat on the plane. Consider that your items with ingredients such as mayonnaise, eggs or meat may have already been at a low temperature. I've heard people complain that they ate something bad from the airport. In reality, it may have been okay but they bought it 20 minutes before boarding and then didn't start eating it until after they had taken off, and the beverage cart had passed by. Their tuna salad sandwich that was 'bad' was sitting in room temperature conditions for over an hour before they ate it!

Foods to Avoid

When I first started traveling fifteen years ago and was a bad vegetarian, I lived on soft pretzels, protein bars, frozen yogurt and Frappuccinos when I had to eat in airports. Besides the Grab and Go Coolers, there are a few things you should avoid or consider as treats only.

- Soft pretzels are 400-500 calories of refined carbs with very little fiber. Since it's a simple carbohydrate, you may as well treat it like a muffin. It will digest quickly and not do anything to make you feel full or give you energy. Plus, you're usually getting it coated in butter or dipping it into some sugary sauce. Ask for it with no salt to combat plane bloat.

- Frozen Yogurt is one of the most processed foods you can eat and comes in a bag in liquid form. Don't let the brands that masquerade as 'healthy' fool you either. They either have a ton of sugar or are artificially sweetened. Pinkberry frozen yogurt's second ingredient is sugar, and it has around twenty-three ingredients, one of which is artificial flavoring. How can something that is marketed as healthy have so many ingredients? If you need a treat, just get a single scoop of real ice cream.

- Sugary coffee drinks have a quadruple whammy of sugar, caffeine, calories and sodium. A Grande Mocha Cookie Crumble Frappuccino with whip is 470 calories. It's dessert and should be treated like a milkshake. When I see people drinking them for breakfast, I wonder if they would have a bowl of ice cream before 9:00am?

- Sauce-laden foods at Chinese restaurants may be high in sodium and probably sugar, adding a lot of calories as well. I've traveled to China, and I can promise you that what we get here is completely bastardized and not Chinese at all. Typically the only thing worth eating at these types of places are the steamed mixed vegetables.

- Raw fish sushi may not be stored properly. Be careful if it's in a grab and go cooler. Otherwise, sushi can be healthy, just make sure it's prepared fresh and avoid fancy rolls covered in sauces or tempura.

- Processed meats like deli meats and hot dogs will be very high in sodium. It's common for one typical airport sandwich to have an entire day's amount of sodium in it. Remember how sodium+dehydration+lack of movement = your reading an entire section of The USA Today in the bathroom?

- Lastly, the giant muffins, scones, and cookies are usually three to four servings a piece! I like that some restaurants are starting to offer human-sized versions, as opposed to the ones for Jack in the Beanstalk.

Options to Choose

If you have tight food rules, airports can be challenging. If you're vegetarian, you may get lucky and be in an airport with great salads that you can add beans, hummus, fruit, and nuts to. Meat eaters who aren't picky have it the easiest at airports. However, I've never seen antibiotic or hormone-free meats at an airport. Depending on your food rules, you may have to opt for plant-based meals. I'm picky about my meat, so I opt for plants or taking my own food at airports.

Ideas to buy or pack:

- Hummus
- Edamame
- Salads (careful with dressings, meats, and eggs unless fresh)
- Steamed mixed vegetables
- Non-meat or freshly-prepared sushi
- Fish (wild is preferable over farmed)
- Chicken (ideally hormone and antibiotic free)

Gluten-Free

After being diagnosed with Hashimoto's Disease among other things, I went on a very strict gluten-free, soy-free diet. It works for me and symptoms I had for at least four years went away after a few months with this food plan. Airport chains that have gluten-free options include California Pizza Kitchen, Chili's, and Wolfgang Puck Express. Always double check with the staff even if you are ordering a salad or vegetables because they may have been cooked in a sauce with gluten or be contaminated in some other way.

Cheap Airport Packing

I am cheap at the airport if I'm going on a personal trip and business isn't paying for it. I refuse to pay $9.00 for a crudité cup or $6.00 for a small fruit cup. When I'm traveling on my dime, I plan ahead and make sure I pack a meal and 'Hangry' snacks. I also take my reusable coffee mug so that my drink stays hot, and I'm less likely to spill it.

Other ideas for taking on the plane:

- Grape Tomatoes
- Single-serving packs of hummus and Wholly Guacamole. Freeze them the night before and put them in your liquids bag.
- Pre-cooked individual bowls of quinoa or brown rice
- Canned wild salmon or sardines (eat this in the airport, not on the plane, to alleviate the stink eye from fellow passengers due to the smell).
- Pre-cut vegetables.
- Nuts and seeds.
- Kind, Exo or Lara bars.

- Tasty Bite lentils or chickpeas. They don't require heating. Just tear the bag open and eat out of the bag or pour into a cup.
- High-quality protein powder to mix with yogurt, coffee, milk, water or sprinkled over fruit.

Apps

My favorite airplane app to help plan my meals is *iFly Pro*. It has a wealth of information, which includes restaurants and cafes in each terminal. If you have this app, you can check ahead of time and know if there is something for you to eat during your connection. If not, you may need to get something at your first airport, on your way to the airport or even take something with you from home if it is your first leg.

How to Eat Healthy in a Hotel

Remember the biggest mistake of a business traveler? Eating every meal like they are on vacation! Extended Stay America polled their travelers and found that the average weight gain from two weeks on the road is three pounds. The majority of respondents stated that staying in a hotel with a kitchen helped them continue their nutrition routine.

I can't emphasize this enough. If you are a frequent traveler, your body cannot afford to eat every meal out. The portions are almost always going to be bigger than what you serve at home with a lot more sugar, fat, and salt. Stay in a hotel with a kitchen, or at the very least, a mini refrigerator, to store half your restaurant meal to save for later.

I always keep my suitcase stocked with a few things to make sure I'm never desperate enough to go through a drive-through. Because I'm not always sure I'll get a good protein source in an airport or work meal, I keep baggies of protein powder to mix into yogurt, over fruit, into iced coffee, nut milks, etc. You can also buy single-serving packets or put three servings into an infant formula container. I use

Vega or *Deep30* brands, but there are several good ones on the market. Check consumerlab.com or consumer reports to make sure your brand is high quality. It should be free of refined sugars and artificial sweeteners. If you get unflavored hemp, it can be mixed into soups and sauces. It may seem as if I'm a big proponent of powder and gobble up serving upon serving every day since I've mentioned it a few times, however I usually only have one half to one serving total during a day, if I have it at all. I also keep single serving bags of nuts, Wild Planet canned sardines or salmon, a Minsley cooked quinoa bowl and possibly a Tasty Bite lentil bag in my luggage. If you like bars, look for minimally processed with low sugar added to it and no sugar alcohols. Lara, Exo and most Kind bars fit this bill. These suitcase items will keep for a long time, so I don't have to worry, and I always make sure I restock. Hotel pantries tend to be filled with junk food so I need to have something in my arsenal when I get there at 11:00pm and my only choices are a Luna bar, Dinty Moore Beef Stew, and Lance crackers.

To prepare meals in your hotel room, it's helpful to do a little thievery. I find that there is always something small I'm missing that keeps me from being able to prepare a dish easily. Be on the lookout for packets of honey, salt, pepper, and butter when you go to a restaurant to use later in your room. Head to the grocery when you get to your destination where most of these packets are offered for free in the deli section. Pack a few sandwich bags to be able to store your leftovers.

Items to purchase at a grocery include:

- Soup or low-sodium broth in aseptic boxed containers. These are nice because you can pour as much as you need and continue to store it in the container. Cooking vegetables or grains in the broth will give them enough flavor that you may not miss having your arsenal of spices from home.

- Bulk bins for nuts and grains to only get what you need for your trip. Quinoa cooks fast and doesn't need oil. Since quinoa needs to be rinsed before cooking to get rid of the bitter-tasting saponin, look for pre-rinsed versions.

- Pre-cut veggies. Buy an entire vegetable party tray and chow down throughout your stay. Look for pre-diced fajita vegetables and chopped mushrooms that don't need a cutting board, knife or container.

- Canned wild salmon.

- Rotisserie chicken. You may feel like it would be a waste to buy a whole chicken, but if you are going to be staying somewhere for a few days, the $7 you would spend on the chicken is still less than one restaurant meal even if you don't eat all of it.

- Tortillas. I find these more versatile than bread because I can make wraps or my favorite, little pizza-like tostadas. I recommend Ezekiel sprouted wheat or corn tortillas or Food For Life Rice Tortillas, which are found in the frozen section and are heartier and healthier than white flour.

- Eggs. You can find these already hard-boiled in some groceries, but buying a 6-pack of eggs and boiling them yourself is pretty easy in a hotel kitchenette. It also eliminates the need for oil to scramble or fry them.

- Fresh fruit or pre-cut fruit

- Bagged salads or make your own from the salad bar. Who says you need to actually make a salad at the bar? Just get the veggies and add-ons you want to use for the week or your next few meals and throw it in the bowl.

- Non-dairy beverages i.e. unsweetened almond, cashew or coconut milk. These come in smaller aseptic containers.

- Salsa and guacamole jazz up anything! Make sure your guacamole is guacamole. Some brands, like Deans, are chemical concoctions (forty-five ingredients!) with very little avocado.

- Hummus with minimal ingredients.
- Single-serving containers of plain Greek yogurt to use instead of sour cream or pair with fruit.
- Cottage cheese, minimally processed, to add to vegetables, fruit or eaten plain.
- Bags of frozen vegetables. Skip the ones in a sauce.

Do you see how there is not ONE frozen microwaveable entrée on this list?

For in-hotel recipes, check out the online bonus page.

Road Trip Nutrition

Packing for a car trip is easier than air travel because you don't have to worry about liquids. When I work in my home city, I pack a cooler or bag if I don't plan on eating out with a client. For Emergency Snack Attacks, I keep single serving bags of nuts in my car at all times. This helps when I'm starving to avoid making a bad decision and grabbing something unhealthy or going overboard when I do eat. It's also good to have Hangry snacks in your vehicle in case of emergency. I have two friends who have each sat on a highway for more than three hours due to an accident. In the South, when there has been snow or ice, people have been stranded in their cars or taken three to four times as long to get home. If you were already hungry, imagine how you would feel after three hours! For someone with diabetes, it's even more important to keep some snacks in the car in case your blood sugar gets low. Dried fruit works well too. The key is to make sure they are things that won't melt or freeze.

Some of my staples include:

- Nuts
- Homemade trail mix with nuts, seeds, and dried fruit
- Dried oats or muesli

- Individual packets of nut butter
- Protein powder
- Minsley pre-cooked quinoa or rice

Please don't store plastic bottles of water in the car in the summer. The heat makes chemicals leach into the water. Use your own stainless steel bottle or replenish your plastic water bottles daily.

There you have it. Strategies and ideas to cover all aspects of travel to make sure you eat for energy and not succumb to the typical jack and crash cycle.

For links and references to this chapter visit http://www.beyondtravelbook.com/signup.html and login with your email address. Use the password provided in the email for access to the bonus page.

6. Mobile Exercise

Exercising on the road takes planning, discipline, flexibility and creativity. If you are someone who has to have everything ideal to exercise, get over it and stop with the excuses! You are not always going to have the ideal gym or environment to get your workout in. You may not be able to do your favorite activities, but you can always find opportunities to exercise to maintain your health, weight, stress level and sanity!

If you are a regular exerciser, you're more likely to maintain your routine on the road and more likely to get stressed about it if you can't. A routine-breaker is one of the top stressors in the business traveler survey. Whether we are training for a triathlon or just trying to stay healthy, as business travelers we have to be very flexible. I competed in two Ironman Triathlons during my heaviest year of travel. I didn't always have perfect conditions, but I made it work.

Regular and non-regular exercisers can look for movement opportunities on the road to increase their energy, strength, improve their sleep and decrease their stress, all without taking up too much time or breaking a sweat. They can be thirty seconds, two minutes or ten minutes. Never underestimate what a quick two to three minute routine can do for your stress levels and energy. Will it get you a six-pack? No. But it will improve your mood and your health.

Sitting Disease

You've probably heard the phrase "sitting is the new smoking." The negative health effects of sitting are extraordinary and shouldn't be taken lightly. If you are a professional sitter, you risk a decrease in health, quality of life, and productivity, and may end up with a case of butt amnesia. Butt or Gluteal Amnesia is common among people who sit all day. The gluteal muscles forget how to fire from lack of use. This leads to low back, hip, knee, and ankle pain.

Prolonged sitting has been linked to:

- High blood pressure and cholesterol.
- Increase in the production of insulin after just one day of sitting, which could lead to diabetes.
- Greater risk for colon, breast, and endometrial cancers.
- Weak abdominals, tight hip flexors, and weak glutes.
- Poor leg circulation, varicose veins, and deep vein thrombosis.
- Weak bones.
- Slower brain function.
- Neck Strain.
- Sore shoulders and back.

One study took three groups of healthy adults; continual sitters, morning thirty-minute walkers who then sat all day, and sitters who took regular activity breaks equaling thirty minutes over the course of the day. The group with regular activity breaks significantly reduced blood sugar and insulin compared to the group sitting all day *and* had similar benefits to the thirty minutes all at once! The excuse that "I don't have enough time to make it meaningful" goes out the window. Five-minute opportunities work.

Standing and Sit-Stand Desks should be an option for everyone. Google, Facebook, and Twitter all cite resources for standing desks as alternatives. It pains me when my clients have to submit a medical request to get a standing desk, especially when a Varidesk costs as little as $275. I also have clients embarrassed to stand because no one else in their office does it. I'm guessing in about five years; the professional sitters will be the ones being stared at.

Back when I bought my desk about eight years ago, the options were minimal. I had to go for a medical desk on wheels, which works perfectly and has five shelves for me to house my computer, lamp, printer and peripherals. A video of my set-up can be found in the bonus chapter. Even when I work outside on my balcony, I get itchy to stand up. When I'm at a coffee shop or the airport, I look for a tall table where I can stand. I'm not on my feet all day because I like to sit sometimes when I'm talking on the phone, but I'm upright for most of it. I suggest a stool (I use a drum throne on hydraulics) for when you do need to sit. A stool or drum throne is great to rest one foot on the lower bar while standing to change positions throughout the day.

There is a plethora of options today, ranging from do-it-yourself by stacking your computer on books to $3000 plus desks on hydraulics. The *Varidesk* is nice because you can use it for sitting *and* standing. The versatility enables you to choose based on how you feel and the price point, $275-$650, is reasonable. For traveling try the *Ninja Standing Desk*, which weighs five pounds and can be hung on a doorframe.

My portable traveling desk of choice is the *StandStand*. The Stand-Stand, $69-$99, comes in Baltic Birch or Bamboo in three different sizes depending on the user's height. It weighs less than two pounds and fully collapses to the size of a laptop. I can fit my StandStand, laptop, peripherals and everything I need in my Cocoon Innovations Kips Bay bag. Half of this book was written in Umstead State Park on a picnic table using my StandStand.

When you get your standing desk, start using it in short intervals, fifteen to twenty-five minutes at a time. One of my clients had back pain after she went all out and stood most of the day as soon as she got her desk. Your body needs to get used to standing and maintaining good posture. Standing desks aren't a cure-all. Just like you can be a potato chip Vegan or a bologna-eating Paleo, you can also be a slumped over, hip-cocked stander.

Choosing a Hotel

The importance of a hotel fitness center depends on the time of year and what city I'm visiting. If it's winter and going to be dark and cold when I'm exercising, I'll try to find a hotel with a fitness center or make sure I am in a room big enough to do my workout. In the spring, summer and fall, I prefer to be outdoors, so it's not as important. If I'm going to be in an area that isn't very safe or nice to run outside, I may opt for a fitness center if I'm going to be somewhere for more than a couple of nights.

If you like to use fitness centers, treadmills, and stationary bikes and don't like the idea of walking or running outside in a strange city, make sure you check out the photos of the fitness center online. Hotels are great at making fitness centers look three times the size they are. You may also want to call the hotel and ask what equipment they have and if it works. The photos could be ten years old, and the treadmill could be broken. If a hotel doesn't have a fitness center or it's really bad, you can ask if they provide passes to nearby gyms. Sometimes this is an even better deal.

I used to travel frequently to Plano, Texas and chose a hotel because they **didn't** have a fitness center. Instead, they gave passes to 24-Hour Fitness two blocks away. That, coupled with a kitchenette and its location next to Whole Foods, made it my favorite place to travel for business!

Hotels always seem to have the fitness center right next to the pool, which means the rooms are very hot and humid. Even when they aren't next to pools, I find that they keep them too warm. Make sure you bring wicking clothes and have a bottle of water since you will sweat more. Since you packed your reusable water bottle, you can fill up at the fountain or cooler. Don't be the guest who uses fifteen paper triangle cups.

It helps to go at 'off times' which means super early in the morning, late in the evening or during the day, which usually isn't likely when you are traveling for business. Always check the times the fitness center is open before you book your room. Some hotels have them closed until 6 or 7am, which is a big fat **F** in my book. This says, "We don't care or know anything about business travelers!"

Having access to a fitness center in the evening is nice after a long day of meetings. Even if you don't want to get sweaty, walking slow, 2.0-3.0mph while reading The U.S.A. Today, a book or magazine, is relaxing and allows you to get a movement opportunity in. However, if the fitness center is busy, stretch and read instead. It wouldn't be fair to the people who are intentionally working out.

Explore

If you feel you are in a safe area, take advantage and run or walk outside. Hotels will often have routes at their desk you can pick up, or look up routes using different apps or websites. *WalkJogRunning* is $2.99 and has over six hundred thousand running routes that other users have submitted. *Runkeeper* enables you to track your run or walk via GPS, and you can share your information if you want to, via Twitter or Facebook. For safety reasons, I would be careful doing this if you don't want others to know that you aren't home and if you have a lot of friends or Twitter followers and your information is public.

Even if I work out in the morning, I will typically go for a walk outside to explore in the evening or just to get some movement after a long day sitting on a plane or in meetings. Ask the hotel front desk which direction is the best to walk or if there are any paths or green-ways nearby. Sometimes I'll tell the front desk that I'm going for a run and leave a note with my estimated time to be back and my phone number. If there were an emergency, at least someone would know to miss me. I always check back in when I get back and retrieve the note. Not once have I had anyone act like I was asking too much.

In Room or Parking Lot Exercise

Never underestimate how good of a workout you can get in your room. Remember, you may not be in your ideal situation, but it's an excuse, not a reason, to skip your workout. Suites-type hotels are ideal for in-room exercise, but even a small room can be used. You can take your equipment, borrow from the hotel or do bodyweight exercises.

139

Women are more likely than men to skip exercising on the road. They would rather have a tooth extracted sans Novocain than be caught at 6:00am on the treadmill, sweaty, parts bouncing, no makeup and their hair in a clippy. Why? Because the fit woman next to them could be the client they are meeting today, or the guy doing fingertip push-ups could be their new supervisor. While I've never been too embarrassed to be seen working out, I do empathize with not wanting to be bothered. At conferences or meetings, it always drives me a little bonkers when colleagues talk to me when I'm working out. That's my personal time; I'm not on the clock.

What can you do in your room? Underwear Workouts! If you don't like to pack a lot or you've forgotten your exercise clothes, you can work out in your room in your underwear and no one will know the difference. A bodyweight routine or a video online is perfect for a hotel because most videos are designed for small spaces. Yoga and Pilates are very easy to do in a hotel room and are great for the end of the day when you feel like you need to stretch out or just want to do something without getting too sweaty. Between meeting time and dinner, I go to my room, strip down, do a ten to twenty minute yoga series, put my clothes back on and go to dinner. I feel so much better, I'm stretched out from sitting all day, and I don't have to shower.

Portable equipment that I sometimes take includes:

- Resistance bands: Lightweight and take up very little space. I preferred *Rubberbanditz* brand and designed my kit for mobile professionals called the Jetsetter Gym Kit. Fifty-Five pounds of resistance in a 10-ounce bag. If you think you're too macho for bands, Ari Zandmen-Zemen, CEO of Rubberbanditz, is a 6'7 former college basketball player.
- Tennis ball: Self-myofascial release (SMR) is a stretching technique using a foam roller, ball or other assistive device and helps improve flexibility, muscle recovery, and movement efficiency, inhibit overactive muscles and reduce pain.

- Trigger Point Therapy Grid: Double up and use for SMR and core exercises.
- Collapsible Hoop.
- Travel yoga mat: Smaller than a regular mat and stickier than a hotel towel.

A lot of fitness companies are still behind the times and only offer DVDs instead of live streaming (I'm talking to you BeachBody), which makes it very inconvenient for travel. Most new laptops don't have DVD players and many people now use tablets and iPads. Thankfully, there are a ton of websites, subscription services, and YouTube videos available. Remember to look for something stating the instructor is certified to teach exercise or is a personal trainer. I've seen some videos that made me cringe with the potentially dangerous cues they were giving. Using an online service instead of a gym is great for the self-motivated people who like class formats. Paying $7-$20 per month for unlimited online classes you can do anywhere is a lot better value than $20-$100 a month for a gym you will only be able to get to one to two times a week if you're lucky.

Websites to try:

- www.doyogawithme.com. Yoga you can filter by the length of video, intensity and style.
- www.udaya.com. Unlimited access to a library of online yoga classes. Currently $12.00 per month.
- Marcey Rader YouTube Channel. Several fifteen to twenty minute bodyweight or Jetsetter Gym Kit workouts you can do in a small space, varying levels and intensity. I also have videos created exclusively for Extended Stay America Hotels for in-room exercise.
- ZuzkaLight.com. Workouts of varying intensity and length with a paid subscription option.

- Dailyburn.com. For $7 a month you get access to a wide variety of classes that can be streamed to any device, making it convenient to use at home and traveling. I have a client that subscribes to this site and loves the versatility.

Bodyweight workouts are also a great option. Don't fight with the ten people trying to use three machines in the fitness center. Stay in your room and do push-ups, mountain climbers, burpees, squats, lunges and triceps dips. Be considerate of the people below you if you aren't on the ground floor. Jump squats and donkey kicks at 5:30am can sound like the hotel is crumbling to the people below you.

Parking lots are great places to do plyometrics, sprinting drills, walking lunges and agility routines. Make sure you're in a well-lit area that has no traffic going through it. Stay alert and keep your eyes open. I've done entire workouts in parking lots that totally kicked my butt.

Exercise Routines

I've trained for ultra-endurance races through some of my heaviest business travel times. When I competed in Ironman triathlon, I was training fifteen to twenty hours a week. No one *needs* to exercise that much but if you think you don't have ten minutes to exercise or two five-minute opportunities, then I'll play the world's smallest violin for you.

The most important thing is to have a routine or trigger to compel you to move. I'm a morning exerciser, but I always find opportunities a few times throughout the day too. Morning exercisers tend to be more consistent than evening exercisers. First, they have fewer excuses, i.e., working late, plane delays, or too tired from traveling. Second, the cue is always the same *wake-up, then exercise.* It sets the pace for the day and is a keystone habit. I have a challenge with the website Coach.Me I called the 10 by 10® to exercise 10 minutes by 10:00am as a healthy, lifelong behavior.

Not a morning person? You can wake up ten minutes earlier and do something, anything, to get your heart rate up and get moving. The metabolism boosting effects can last up to an hour. My client S.S. does this twice each day. Her coffee brewing triggers the first opportunity. After she hits the start button, she does a four to five minute workout. Sometimes it's yoga, but other times it's an intense Tabata workout. Either way, when she normally would have just been staring, zombie-like into the bowels of the coffee pot until it was ready, she now uses that time to boost her metabolism and give her a keystone habit.

Opportunities

Opportunities can be found anywhere, anytime, in any clothing. Finding one- to five-minute opportunities throughout the day adds up. Bathroom break? Try some single-leg squats or sink push-ups for thirty seconds. Waiting for your plane? Throw down some triceps dips on the gate seats. Find something you do consistently to trigger you and create a movement opportunity.

Movement opportunity ideas from the arsenal of my clients and myself:

- Two minutes of single leg squats, wall squats or balance work while brushing teeth.
- Pull-ups after walking the dog.
- Squats while the dogs are taking a biology break.
- Plank pose after taking a birth control pill.
- Desk push-ups after each client call.
- Jumping jacks and high knees while the microwave is running.
- Five sun salutations each time they enter their hotel room (one client was in and out so many times in one day due to a conference in their hotel room that they did 45 sun salutations!).

Find a trigger. Create an opportunity. Be consistent.

"Taking opportunities to do quick workouts during the day has changed me. I find myself looking for times to get to do them, instead of dreading it! It gives me energy and makes me feel good about myself." Client, Michelle Scaraglino

When you're stuck in the airport, it's a perfect time for an opportunity to walk and move. I've done push-ups and triceps dips off the seats, single-leg squats, lunges and even burpees at an empty gate and whipped out my collapsible hoop and hooped while reading in a quiet corner of the airport. A few times, during long delays, I have pulled out my Jetsetter Gym Kit and got in a few exercises right there at the gate. No less than three people each time asked me if they could use it too. The kit got passed around between weary travelers and we shared a *business travel is glamorous* bonding moment waiting to board.

A friend of mine is a pilot and got stuck at O'Hare during a seven-hour layover. The flight attendants popped a squat at a Starbucks for five hours. He left his bag with them and walked *six miles* in the airport, using his pedometer to track it. He walked every terminal and gate. *Six Miles.* Candy crush doesn't burn that many calories.

Business Meeting Time Out

At some point during an all-day meeting, either during a break or at lunch, it's important that you excuse yourself and consider the opportunity to get in 5-10 minutes of movement. Doing this *before* you eat lunch will guarantee that you will do it and probably eat less because you'll have less time. You can do it after you eat, but you risk getting hijacked by your colleagues and not giving yourself the time out.

During the time out go to your hotel room, office, outside or even the bathroom and do a quick five-minute stretching routine and some exercises that won't make you sweat. It will make you feel better and more energized, get your heart rate up a little bit or slow it down if it

144

is a particularly heated meeting, and keep you from continuing to eat from the buffet. No one has to know you are doing this since many people pop back to their room or otherwise excuse themselves for some privacy. If you can, taking a walk outside is even better, and you may be able to find someone to go with you. Check out the bonus page for a Business Meeting Time Out Exercise Routine.

Oh, My Aching Feet

Traveling can result in aches and pains in places you never knew existed and is tiring to boot. I would treat myself once or twice a month and get my bodywork done regardless of the city. In some cities that I visited regularly, I scheduled routine appointments when I was in town. Massage, chiropractic, and foot reflexology will help your posture, muscles and your aching, tired feet. If you don't have the money or the time for bodywork, you can still do some things for yourself in your hotel room.

I've been doing ice baths for years. It feels like torture for the first couple of minutes, but if done in the evening, helps you sleep at night due to the rapid drop and then rise in body temperature. It also helps raise your pain tolerance and ability to withstand discomfort. Stop at a convenient store and get one to two bags of ice and put it in the tub with water up to your hips if you are sitting. I don't fill the whole tub, but just up over my legs and hips. I find that the ice baths help for aching legs and feet! The research proving positive effects for muscle soreness are mixed, but you may still find yourself addicted.

Self-Myofascial Release

I travel with a tennis ball and Trigger Point Therapy products. I've used them for over a decade and think it is the key to my long career of training and racing. Self-Myofascial Release (SMR) is performed with a foam roller or with TP Therapy products, which are far superior to regular foam rollers. For travel purposes, the TP Therapy Quadballer, Footballer and Massage Ball travel much better than a traditional foam roller because they are more compact. They also last longer and won't break down like a foam roller. I'm partial to the SMRT-Core Grid and stuff my clothes inside the core to save room. If you aren't ready to make the purchase of a TP Therapy kit, using a tennis ball can work on some areas too. Self-Myofascial Release can improve flexibility, muscle recovery, and movement efficiency, inhibit overactive muscles, correct muscle imbalances and reduce pain.

The most basic way to describe SMR is to roll slowly over the ball until you find a tender spot, then hold on that spot for thirty seconds. Gently roll it out an inch or two at a time. This is great to do while reading, watching a movie or listening to a podcast. At first it might be uncomfortable, some will even say painful. I may have even heard the term 'torture' used a few times. This is one area where *no pain no gain* is true. If you have pain, then your muscle and fascia is a jumbled up mess underneath that skin, and you need to perform SMR. I highly recommend enlisting the help of a Certified Personal Trainer first to teach you how to correctly foam roll. If I could only enlist one product or supplemental activity, I would use SMR and the TP Therapy system, hands down. If I could only buy one item, I would buy their SMRT-Core Grid Foam Roller and I encourage all of my clients to purchase one. An old tennis or lacrosse ball works well on small areas and takes up very little room in your bag. I keep one in my car too to work my chest and neck when I'm a passenger or when I'm waiting in a parking lot.

If you can't stand the thought of an arctic bath and don't want to spend money on products, you can always lie with your feet or legs elevated against the wall. Not only is this a restorative pose, it helps with swelling from flying on the plane.

Auto Exercise

If your job involves long road trips or driving around from client to client, you can still fit in opportunities to exercise. There is no badge or trophy for driving four to five hours without stopping. The only thing you're doing is putting yourself at risk for stale reflexes, butt amnesia, and zombie-like focus. Sitting just two hours reduces blood flow, raises blood sugar and drops good cholesterol levels by *twenty percent*. Excessive sitting is cited as a key factor in heart disease, stroke, diabetes and some cancer. Stopping every couple of hours may seem like a waste of time, but ten minutes to get your blood flowing, even if it's just walking into a rest stop will increase your alertness and maintain or improve your health.

Use the time at stoplights to do isometric exercises. Most people have a forward head posture from being on computers or smartphones all day. Simply pressing your head directly back into the headrest, while keeping your chin level, helps to strengthen your neck muscles. Hold for ten counts and relax. Press into the steering wheel at different angles with your hands; elbows slightly bent, to strengthen the biceps, triceps, and pectoral muscles. Perform these until the light turns green. For a rest stop workout and auto exercises, check out the bonus page.

Clothes and Accessories

Unless you're doing underwear workouts in your room, wicking clothes are imperative to pack so they dry quicker and are less apt to mildew. After your workout, drape your clothes over the air conditioning vent while showering and stuff newspapers (the USA Today sports section is appropriate) in your sneakers to help soak up some of the sweat. Sports clothing that wicks tends only to perform for about fifty washings. If you're still wearing the same shirt from REI after ten years, you probably aren't getting much wicking benefit.

If I'm working out in my room, I am sans shoes. Otherwise, I prefer low profile to minimal shoes. They are lighter and easier to pack. These are shoes like Altras, Nike Free, Inov8s, and New Balance Minimus. If you're used to a lot of cushion and support, start slowly with these types of shoes and wear them for short periods of time.

I keep a set of cheap spare headphones in my bag at all times, so I don't forget them. I can't stand running on a treadmill without watching TV or listening to music. I use my *Sprigs Phone Banjee* wrist wallet to hold my phone and my key card. It's made of wicking material, is washable and super lightweight.

Exercise and Jet Lag

Anyone who has experienced jet lag knows that exercise sometimes feels like the last thing we want to do. However, it is probably one of the three most important ways to counteract the effects. Exercise and light affects our circadian rhythms and tells the body to 'Wake up!'

Keeping the same exercise routine as much as you can when you travel will help you adjust to your time zone. If you exercise at 6:30am at home, try to exercise at 6:30am where you are. Your body has gone through a biological process when crossing time zones so you may not be running that eight-minute mile with the same ease or performing your bench press with the same amount of weight. This is especially true if you go from low altitude to high altitude. The first time I ran on a treadmill in Mexico City I thought I was ill because I was running so slow. I didn't realize I was at eight thousand feet! If I'm on a short domestic trip with a time difference of only one to two hours, I try to maintain my home schedule and get up and go to bed at the same time.

No matter where you are staying and what you have available, you can find time for movement opportunities.

For links and references to this chapter visit http://www.beyondtravelbook.com/signup.html and login with your email address. Use the password provided via email for access to the bonus page.

7. Mobile Health

Health is more than nutrition and exercise. It also encompasses sleep, stress management, illness prevention and more. This chapter is devoted to ensuring that travelers look at the big picture of wellness when mobile. Preparing for our trip so we aren't frazzled going out the door, eating for energy, finding movement opportunities, sleeping well, meditating and creating routine from non-routine, can help keep us from becoming the old, tired, pound-packing, burnout traveler.

Sleep

Sleep deprivation is considered an epidemic in the U.S. It affects over twenty-five percent of the population, with over ten percent of people reporting chronic insomnia. Besides the moodiness and acting-like-a-jerk syndrome that results from lack of sleep, Short Sleepers, who sleep less than six hours a night, are more at risk for infection, insulin resistance, obesity, diabetes, cardiovascular disease, cancer, arthritis, hormone imbalance and mood disorders. They have higher blood levels of inflammatory proteins and C-reactive protein, which is associated with heart attack risk.

Chronic Insomnia is associated with elevated heart rate and core body temperature, elevated nighttime cortisol (the belly fat hormone), and over-activation of the hypothalamus and pituitary axis. When we sleep our internal organs rest and recover, repair tissue, grow muscles and synthesize protein. Hormones are released to regulate appetite control, stress, growth and metabolism.

Sleep deprivation is responsible for a significant number of motor vehicle and machinery-related accidents every year. Being tired accounts for the highest number of fatal single-car run-off-the-road crashes. Combine this with being in an unfamiliar place when traveling and you have a double whammy. One night of insufficient sleep is the equivalent of drunk driving. When I used to compete in adventure

149

racing my teammates agreed the most dangerous part was the drive home after an eighteen to thirty hour race.

Besides the Busy Badge, people like to wear the Sleep Badge and brag about how they can get by on four or five hours of sleep a night. There are people who can do this, but it's not the majority, and it isn't something to brag or be righteous about. Sleep is when your body is repairing itself. I had very high energy when I was only sleeping 3-5 hours and was ultra-endurance racing year-round. However, it was affecting me in other ways, it just took a while to catch up.

Interesting Sleep Facts and Statistics

Did you know that children are insensitive to extreme noise levels? Keeping the house quiet during naps and bedtime makes it harder for them to sleep through noise later. As we age, our threshold for noise levels decreases (National Sleep Foundation).

People who struggle with insomnia or other sleep disruptions tend to have lower pain tolerances.

When you're awake, your brain builds up beta-amyloid proteins that are biomarkers for Alzheimer's Disease. When you sleep, your brain flushes some of these out.

Nature Communications reported that brain scans of healthy adults with a good night's sleep were able to regulate their desire for high-calorie foods better.

People with low Vitamin D levels are more likely to suffer from sleep apnea and complain of daytime sleepiness.

It can take two to three weeks for sleep to adjust to an altitude of 13,200 feet or more.

After drinking more water, sleep hygiene is one of the first things I work on with clients. I usually focus on this before nutrition and exercise because most people don't have good sleep habits. Healthy sleep increases energy, results in better decision-making, strengthens the immune system, heightens our alertness, focus, and creativity, improves our client interactions, improves our mood and increases our libido.

When we are tired, what kinds of foods do we reach for? Not energy foods like cruciferous vegetables, seeds or nuts, but refined, sugary foods and caffeine. Reduced percentage of sleep time and REM time are associated with higher intakes of fat and carbohydrates and more intense cravings for sweet and salty foods. We misinterpret our sleepiness as a need for fuel. Because we don't have the focus, impulse control or decision-making skills due to lack of sleep, we go for a poor choice to feed cravings instead of the right fuel our body.

Sugar and caffeine are counterfeit energy strategies.

Lack of sleep changes our hunger hormones, which can affect our weight and body mass index. Our satiety hormone leptin lowers, resulting in increased appetite and cravings. We have impaired glucose tolerance and insulin resistance, which explains the correlation with Type Two Diabetes. When lower levels of insulin are released throughout the night, a number of inflammatory proteins and blood sugar levels rise. When we don't sleep, we are up more hours in the day but have less activity because we are tired. The same parts of the brain control sleep and metabolism, resulting in a positive association between sleeping six hours or less and a lower resting metabolic rate (which you want to be high to burn more calories at rest) and more calories consumed.

When we sleep and dream, we are processing and assimilating the information we learned throughout the day. This occurs during deep rapid eye movement (REM) sleep. When we take sleep aids, anti-depressants and many over the counter drugs, we don't get to this REM state. Think of dreaming as what we need to do to digest information in the same way when we eat food, we need to digest it for it to give us energy and do its job. When we sleep, memory consolidation occurs allowing for formation and storage of new memories.

If you snore or have obstructive sleep apnea, it's important you take measures and see a doctor for your symptoms. Sleep apnea does not have to be a permanent condition. Losing weight, exercising, wearing a mouth guard and going on an anti-inflammatory diet can be very helpful.

People with gluten sensitivities or who have Celiac or other autoimmune diseases that are affected by gluten may find that eliminating gluten from the diet can affect sleep. I made several changes after I was diagnosed with Hashimoto's Disease, eliminating gluten being the biggest change. I can't trace it solely to this, but I now sleep extremely well eighty percent of the time for a good seven to nine hours a night and had already been practicing other sleep hygiene methods for a couple of years prior to this change. It may not be the answer, but test it out by going on a strict gluten-free diet for a month and see if it helps.

Hotel Sleeping

How many of you have laid in bed in a hotel listening to your neighbor's television, snoring or toilet flushing all night? As business travelers, we are in different beds, with different sounds, with different time schedules. Sleep is something we need to put first when thinking about having one more round at the bar or staying up late rehearsing our pitch one last time. Just like with nutrition, we can't pretend we're on vacation. We need sleep to be a priority.

The intensity, abruptness, regularity, intrusiveness, and familiarity of noises affect our sleep. If we are used to noises such as crickets chirping or traffic outside our door, the absence of noise may keep us awake. These types of noises can become the background for most people in about a week, however, noises that are important, like babies crying, alarms or our name being called can still wake us up.

I'm a fan of white noise ... from fans, air conditioners, or white noise apps. After I couldn't take one more middle-of-the-night serenade from the dog day care and boarding kennel behind our house, we bought an *Ecotone Sound and Sleep Machine* for home. It's a little pricey, but the sound adjusts to the volume of noise in the room.

I used to be an awful hotel sleeper until I started incorporating a few sleep hacks. First, I travel with an eye mask because I need darkness when I sleep. The light from the curtains that never seem to close all the way, coupled with the light coming in from the door to the hall-way is enough to keep me up. I use the *Dream Essentials Contoured Sleep Mask*. It looks like a bra for your eyes and doesn't lie flat against your face, so it's way more comfortable than typical masks. I keep a large binder clip in my bag to pull the curtains all the way shut, so that little bit of light doesn't peek through and I roll up a towel to put at the bottom of the door to block the hall light.

Some people can use foam or custom-made earplugs. I don't like the feeling in my ears, so I use a noise app instead. I use white noise all the time to drown out distractions, not just when I'm sleeping. I use my meditation app Calm.com to listen to white noise, rain, ocean waves or soothing music. It works in airplane mode (which your phone should always be in anyway if you are sleeping with it) and set the timer so it doesn't drain the battery if I can't plug it in. There is also a YouTube video called *12 hours of white noise*. Sometimes I'll put this on my laptop in the hotel room and then open the lid just enough that it stays on.

Blue Rays

Forty-three percent of polled adults say they rarely or never get a good night's sleep. Ninety-five percent of those people used a com-puter or phone within the hour before bed. To get to sleep easier, it's very important that you don't stay on your computer or smart phone until right before you turn out the light. Your brain needs time to wind down. This has much bigger implications than just sleeplessness.

Studies have shown that the bright light of a computer screen may suppress melatonin and affect body temperature and heart rate.

Melatonin is a hormone secreted by the pineal gland in the brain that synthesizes and secretes insulin. Melatonin suppression has been linked to increased risk of cancer, Type 2 Diabetes, metabolic syndrome, obesity and heart disease, as well as impaired immune function. As we age, our natural melatonin levels decrease. If you supplement, take the lowest possible dose first to see if it works for you. Melatonin occurs naturally in tart cherries and purslane (ancient therapeutic herb). Marijuana significantly increases endogenous melatonin, but the research is mixed on whether or not it helps with sleep and REM cycles.

Blue light is emitted by TVs, computer screens and phones and is the most melatonin-suppressive. Blocking blue light has been shown to be very effective in reducing melatonin-suppressing effects. I try to shut my computer down at least an hour before bed and limit looking at my iPhone too long, maybe just quick peeks at my calendar or the weather for the next day. I have a *Kindle Paperwhite* to read at night specifically because I don't want to use a computer screen.

To help with blue rays on your computer, download the program f.lux. It's free software that warms up your computer display at night and adapts to the time of day based on your time zone settings. Blue blocker glasses can also be helpful and can be very inexpensive if you go the Uvex route. Keep one set in your luggage and another set at home. Even regular light can suppress melatonin, so if you have issues with sleep, it's worth putting them on when the sun goes down. Embarrassed about wearing glasses at night? In a hotel room, no one will see you. At home, no one will see you except your spouse or your mates. Better sleep vs. feeling a little silly? There are a lot more people out there wearing blue-blocker glasses at night than you think. I vote for better sleep.

Besides the fact that the light 'plays' with your brain, do you want to get an email late that will upset you or tell you about a new task or project you are assigned to manage? You don't have time to do it, yet now it's on your mind and probably disruptive to your sleep. *People, we have to stop checking email and messing around on our phones in bed.* Put your phone in airplane mode, so you're not interrupted, or better yet, don't even have it in the bedroom or beside your bed. In a hotel, charge it in the bathroom or out of arms reach, so you aren't tempted to check anything at night. Plus, the research surrounding EMFs (electromagnetic fields) are enough for me to ban the Wi-Fi being turned on in my bedroom. I don't need EMFs near my head for 8-9 hours a night. Airplane Mode Please!

Prescription Sleep Aids

I admit it. I used to be a fan of a prescription sleep aids. I thought that half-drunk feeling the next morning meant that I slept hard. Being in clinical research, I decided to dig a little deeper into the safety and efficacy and since then, have never put one in my mouth. For two major sleep aids on the market, the effect with medication is falling asleep fifteen minutes faster. That's it, folks. It doesn't take much to be clinically significant. The downside to that precious fifteen minutes isn't worth the upside.

Prescription sleep aids have been linked to memory impairment, loss of balance, morning hangover, dizziness, sleep walking, sleep eating, sleep sex (as in, not remembering that you had it, which you would not want to admit to your partner), depression, headache, dry mouth, anterograde amnesia, and constipation. I could go on and on. I'm not anti-drug and I think for very short-term situations you may need sleep aids, but know that they interfere with the natural sleep/wake drive and can create a rebound effect leading to more insomnia later. Prescription sleep aids have also been linked to increased mortality. Is that extra 15 minutes worth it?

Healthy Sleep Hygiene Hacks

Creating a sleep routine at home and maintaining that routine as much as possible on the road will help you improve your sleep. Try one or all of these practices following and make sleep a priority. I used to sacrifice sleep to get in a long workout, when ultimately, I would have been better off sleeping an extra twenty to thirty minutes and making my workout shorter but more intense.

- Stick to a sleep schedule as much as possible, even on the weekends.

- Practice a relaxing bedtime ritual both at home and in the hotel. Gentle yoga, meditation, reading (but not a thriller), an Epsom Salt bath or an ice bath can be helpful.

- Eliminate as much light as possible. Use blackout curtains or blinds, an eye mask, and cover your alarm light. I even put black electrical tape on my smoke alarm light.

- Naps are great for energy boosters, but if you have trouble falling asleep at night, avoid naps late in the afternoon or for longer than fifteen minutes.

- Exercise daily. Some people need to avoid *intense* exercise three to four hours before bedtime. However, one study showed that insomniacs slept better if they exercised for thirty minutes as late as 7:00 pm.

- The room temperature for an 'ideal' sleep is between 60-67°F. Temps below 54° and above 75° can cause less restful sleep.

- Change your mattress every nine to ten years or per manufacturer recommendation. Update your pillow every one to two years.

- Expose yourself to sunlight as much as you can first thing in the morning.

- Wake up at your natural time whenever life allows. Use an app that wakes you at the right time in your sleep cycle, if you can keep it in airplane mode and have the discipline not to look at it before bed.

- Avoid alcohol in the evening. Alcohol is a double agent. Many people think it helps them sleep, but it disrupts the deep REM sleep cycle. When the sedative effect wears off, you're more likely to awaken during the night, and more so if you are female. This is one of the reasons why it's hard to wake up the next day after drinking. A rule of thumb from *Stanford's Sleep Center* is waiting one hour per drink before heading to bed.

- Avoid or limit caffeine after about 2:00pm. Even if you can drink soda at dinner or coffee afterward and fall asleep, it doesn't mean the caffeine isn't affecting sleep quality.

- Avoid heavy, spicy or sugary meals before bed. This can give you indigestion or stimulate your senses and make it harder to sleep. Personally, if I eat sugar before bed, I get nightmares. Food rich in tyrosine, such as cheese, soybeans, beef, lamb, pork, fish, chicken, nuts, seeds, eggs, dairy, beans and whole grains may keep you awake and increase energy. Test and find out.

- Lower carbohydrate diets can be beneficial for good gut bacteria, which can be helpful for sleep.

- Don't go to bed hungry. If you are already hungry (truly hungry, not just craving something) then how soundly do you think you will sleep for the next eight hours? Have a light snack with protein, fat, and carbs. To control blood sugar, I'll sometimes have a tablespoon of nut butter or coconut manna if I'm hungry.

- Try not to get into the midnight snack habit. It just trains your body to wake up and need a snack.

- Chamomile tea can be helpful for some people, but it's a diuretic and may cause you to wake up during the night to use the bathroom. Like you might with a child, I cut off my fluids a couple of hours before bed.

- Turkey isn't the best source of tryptophan. The reason you fall asleep at Thanksgiving is due to the massive amount of calories, mostly carbs, which you consumed. There is more tryptophan in chicken, shrimp and soy.

- There is nothing in milk that helps you sleep. If anything, it has a placebo effect.

- If you wake up during the night and can't go back to sleep after fifteen minutes, get out of bed and do something relaxing until you get tired again. DO NOT pick up an electronic device or start working. If I wake up, I read, fold laundry if I'm at home, or do a meditation to help me get back to sleep.

Meditation

"We live by the myth that stress is the enemy in our lives. The real enemy is our failure to balance stress with intermittent rest. Push the body too hard for too long — chronic stress — and the result will indeed be burnout and breakdown. But subject the body to insufficient stress, and it will weaken and atrophy. Few of us push ourselves nearly hard enough to realize our potential, nor do we rest, sleep, and renew nearly as deeply or for as long as we should." – Tony Schwartz, CEO, The Energy Project, Harvard Business Review.

For people who travel weekly, there isn't enough time for stress levels to drop prior to the next trip. According to the CWT stress index, this increases stress scores by four points. Even when your trip is easy, the underlying anxiety of traveling can take its toll. Stressful events include:

- Lost baggage
- Delays
- Strange rental car (where are the lights and windshield wipers?)

- No Wi-Fi
- Hungry, which can turn into Hangry
- Navigation in a strange car in a strange city

Our society has a pervasive, ill-conceived notion of what is 'impressive,' or worthy of awe, and tend to wear Busy like a badge. We have forgotten how to sit and be still and present. We can't stand in line or wait for a taxi without looking at our phone. We must always be doing. I am as guilty as anyone and feel like I should try to be productive everywhere, however, sometimes taking that mental break is what makes me *more* productive.

I recently conducted a workshop where participants spoke about how nice their office building was and that there was a path outside to walk. The funny thing was no one ever took advantage of it because they felt if they were seen walking outside, people would think they should be working. If they spoke about how busy or overloaded they were, people would remember that they were away from their desk! Since I was working with the entire group, I told them to reframe that and look at those people as renewing their productivity and energy muscles while they were out walking. The lazy brains and butts were the ones sitting all day.

Anyone that knows me personally would not describe me as woo-woo la-la. Much like yoga, it depends on the teacher, style, and environment. Several major companies including The Huffington Post, Goldman Sachs Group Inc. and Google have incorporated meditation training into their offerings to employees to help them focus, increase creativity and expand emotional intelligence.

Andrew Scheffer, an MBA who spent years in the professional world of private banking and Wall Street, has studied and practiced meditation for over twenty years. He left the corporate world to teach professionals how mindfulness not only improves their lives, but their businesses. He's worked with companies such as Warner Brothers

Home Video, The Four Seasons Restaurants and Jib Jab Media to incorporate meditation into their life.

While we are traveling and away from our every day habits, responsibilities, and distractions, it is a perfect time to learn and practice meditation. By taking a few moments to guide our attention and build up our mental focus and resiliency, we cultivate a skill and a habit that we can use for our normal hectic lives. Just like stepping into an air-conditioned room on a hot day can help bring relief and cool us down, even a few minutes of mindfulness and meditation can have the same effect on our mind and wellbeing. – Andrew Scheffer

Meditation or deep-breathing is going to the gym for your mind. There are more than *18,000* published studies on the physical and mental benefits. An NIH study showed a 23% decrease in mortality, 30% decrease in death due to cardiovascular disease and a decrease in cancer mortality. Is there a drug that does that?

Benefits of meditation include:

- Lowered acute stress response.

- Increased concentration of gray matter in the hippocampus of the brain, which is subject to the stress release of cortisol. The brain function of meditators is very different than non-meditators. Meditators have an enhanced capacity to concentrate and manage emotions.

- Reduced concentration of C-reactive protein, which is associated with heart disease.

- Decrease in active inflammation and increase in immune system.

- Lower blood pressure.

- Increased impulse control.

- Improved attention.

After several years of trying to meditate and beating myself up over not being successful, I installed an app on my smartphone from Calm.com and have managed to make using it a daily habit for over two years. I realized what I needed was a guided meditation with a voice I liked. If you try one style and it doesn't work for you, try another one. A friend of mine loves the meditations from a very well known woman, but I can't stand her voice. An uber-popular app right now has a voice of someone who sounds like the guy from Zombies Run! Using that app makes me hyper-alert to run from zombies! However, one of my clients loves his voice because she was never trained in Zombie evading.

What's great about Calm.com is that some of the meditations are only two minutes long. That's what I started with, just two minutes a day. There are different meditations for focus, anxiety, creativity, and forgiveness to name a few, that range from two to twenty minutes. If you feel less than stellar but are unable to sit in the moment for more than a few minutes, put on a two-minute meditation. It's two minutes out of 1440, but can make a world of difference. I tracked my streak on Coach.Me to help keep me motivated. Now I meditate daily for ten to fifteen minutes first thing in the morning while I'm taking my heart rate variability measurement using the *SweetBeat* app, before sleeping when my husband or I am traveling and short breathing cycles or meditations during the day as transitions.

In addition to guided meditation, I also use a breath I call the '4-6-8 breath.' I inhale for four counts, hold for six counts and breath out for eight. I can do this anywhere and don't need my phone. This is what I use between client calls, before starting a new task or if I feel rushed and am getting ready to eat. I typically do this for four to six cycles. My clients love this and find it works well for them.

"The 4-6-8 breath works! It kept me calm during a bout with my crying baby!" – A.P., Power Plan Client

If using the term meditation still feels too woo-woo for you, just call it deep breathing. There are a couple of apps, *BreathBuddy*, and

161

Breathe2Relax, which you can download to focus solely on inhaling and exhaling using the belly. Learning to belly breathe is important to counteract the shallow chest breathing we tend to do under stress.

Ideal times for meditation or breathing sessions:

- First thing in the morning to set your intention for the day.
- In the evening to wind down.
- In the car. Please don't meditate! Focus on deep or 4-6-8 breathing.
- Between tasks or projects to get focused on the next one.
- Between client interactions.
- Transitions from home to work and work to home.

My client S.B. uses the stop sign entering into the parking garage as her visual cue to start deep breathing and practices the transition to home. Upon arriving home, she does a 2-minute meditation in her garage before going into the house.

- Before turning on your computer.
- After turning off your computer.
- Waiting for the plane to board.
- Waiting in line for the train or taxi.

My client Y.H. has hypertension and knows that concentrating on breathing will help her blood pressure and stress levels. We found two triggers that work for her on the road: 1) Getting in the rental car and 2) Sitting in the seat waiting for the plane to board.

Meditation takes practice. For most high achievers, it starts out feeling like a waste of time. You sit for two minutes thinking of all the things you could be doing like reacting to email, clicking accept to the meeting invite, checking Facebook or watching TV. Start your session with the intention to accept what happens. So you think about what you're having for dinner or if your plane will be on time ... who cares? You're not being graded. Acknowledge the thought and move on. Eventually, you'll be able to focus on the guide or even just your breath. I'll often have an intention for the day or devote my meditation to someone, often a family, friend or client, who is having a particularly hard time, and send kindness his or her way.

Find something you do every day when traveling or at home and make that your trigger to meditate. It's more about the quantity and doing it consistently than if you had a long session.

Heart Rate Variability

The only way I've been able to practice self-quantification in more than a year is with the SweetBeat App by Sweetwater Health. I believe it's one of the keys to my recovering fully from my blasted immune system before my diagnosis, and I'm now healthy and racing again. Every single morning, whether I'm at home or traveling, I take my heart rate variability (HRV) measurement using a blue tooth monitor and my phone.

Heart Rate Variability is different than just taking your heart rate, which doesn't give you a full picture. It determines stress via the flight or fight response by measuring sympathetic and parasympathetic branches of the autonomic nervous system, using a technique in which the spaces between beats are measured. The higher the HRV, the less stressed you are.

First thing in the morning after I go to the bathroom, I go back to bed and put on my heart rate monitor and perform a 3-minute session, lying down, to determine my HRV for the day. When I'm stressed, I'll have a low score and know to take it easy that day with training, or skip a day altogether, cut out coffee and get more sleep. If I have a high score, I can do a harder workout. We don't always realize when we're stressed or detect how good stress (eustress) is affecting our nervous system. You can also wear it throughout the day to see how different events, like meetings, client calls, or traffic, affect your HRV. It works with *Fitbit, Withings,* and *MapMyFitness* apps.

Gratitude Journaling

I started gratitude journaling a couple of years ago. I simply list three things for which I'm grateful each evening before I go to bed. When I'm on the road, I write them down on any sheet of paper or say them out loud. There are gratitude journaling apps; I just choose not to use them. Your gratitude statements don't have to be profound or broad, like "my health" or "my family," they can be very simple like "they gave me extra guasaca sauce at lunch today," "my spouse made the bed" or "my plane was on time."

Gratitude journaling has been found to increase positive emotions, improve sleep, increase feelings of compassion and kindness and even strengthen the immune system. It's important that you don't let your gratitude get stale by stating the same thing every day. After a few days, your gratefulness for your cat kind of loses its meaning. Try to make it something new. Find a time of day where you can be consistent. It's easy for me to think about it at night because my journal is in my nightstand at home with my sleep mask. When I'm on the road, I think about it because I do a mental recap of my day and put on my meditation app. Thinking about what you are grateful for before you sleep can help ease any feelings of anxiety or overwhelm leftover from the day. This seeps into our subconscious mind while we sleep and gets replayed throughout the night. *See why you don't want to get that late night email from a disgruntled client or boss?*

A good friend of mine has a Gratitude Jar in her living room with paper and colored pens beside it. She invites anyone that is visiting her to write something they are grateful for, anonymous or not. Occasionally she takes the paper out of the jar and reads them. I LOVE this and routinely write something for her jar when I visit.

Bodywork

Some people find bodywork such as massage, acupuncture, pedicures, reflexology, chiropractic and Reiki to be effective stress and pain relievers. When I frequently traveled to Plano, Texas, I scheduled a massage every other visit. Bodywork or spa services aren't just for women and go a long way toward stress and pain management. Depending on the modality, it may help prevent or treat existing injuries. Don't discount bodywork as part of your self-care management.

Routine

When you are at home do you exercise, wind down at 8:00pm, make sure you eat at least a couple of servings of vegetables, stick to one to two cups of coffee, limit yourself to one cookie, and stop checking email after 9:00 pm?

When you travel do you hit the snooze button, check email until 11:00pm, eat fast food, drink coffee all day, take advantage of the corporate per diem at the bar, eat cookies out of boredom, and forget what a vegetable is?

What happens to us when we travel for business? It took me years to figure out how to get a handle on it. That per diem called my name to spend every penny. That tray of cookies at the all-day meeting whispered in my ear. The stress of my email made me stare at a screen until I tried to go to sleep. I watched TV in bed even though I forbid a TV in my room at home. How can you develop habits when you don't have a routine?

I have a client who feels like when he travels, he is on an all-expense-paid party that he has to host. He's wining and dining clients, afraid if he doesn't drink it will make *them* feel awkward. He's the first to show up and the last to go back to his room. He opens his computer, and before he knows it, it's 2:00am. Tired, he starts his day with an espresso drip and keeps it coming all day until his veins are shot.

You have to create boundaries. You're not on vacation. Your body doesn't care that you have $75 to spend or that you're celebrating a sale. Your brain doesn't give you any leeway to grow new pathways just because you have a deadline, and you need to stay up all night.

When you're on vacation, or you only travel once or twice a year — go for it. It's normal and healthy to let your guard down. But travel weekly or even monthly for your job? The only way you aren't going to burnout, get sick or end up with the Travel 20, is to set boundaries and stick to them.

Routine helps prevent stress. If you're traveling to a new city and can swing it, taking the time to explore and sight-see is great for energy renewal and sparking creativity. However, the stress of also being a tourist may seem like yet another thing you have to do. *I'm in Chicago staying on the Magnificent Mile, and I'm not going to leave my hotel? I'm a block from South Beach, and I'm not going out to the ocean?* Don't feel pressured to see the sights when you're traveling for business if it's going to make you feel more behind and stressed by doing it. Sometimes the best thing you can do is to continue your normal routine. If you work out in the morning at home, then continue to do that on the road. If you eat oatmeal for breakfast, then eat oatmeal for breakfast. Go to bed around the same time. Remember, you aren't on vacation. Business travel isn't part of your job. It's a lifestyle.™ Do what you feel comfortable doing. Don't pressure yourself to do any more or any less.

With travel, you always have to be prepared for Plan B, because so many things, air travel delays, the speed of your hotel Internet, the menu that the assistant decided on, is out of your control. Plan what you can and prepare for the rest.

Habits to keep as routine:

- Alcohol. Some people know they don't hold alcohol well. If you are one, be smart and don't let your career get derailed by slurred words, shuffling feet and flirtatiousness you wouldn't give out if you were sober. If you are always having after-work drinks or dinners out, set a limit. Maybe it's one drink per meeting or no more than three times in a week. Get a drink that looks like a drink if you don't want people asking you about it. Whatever you do, don't go on and on about why you aren't drinking. Just say you have to pace yourself through the week, it affects your sleep, or you need to be at one hundred percent tomorrow morning. Whatever you do, don't make them feel bad about it. Still feeling pressured?

Ask yourself:

- Do I want to do anything or say anything with this person that I might regret?
- Is this person my boss, peer or someone who needs to see me at my best?
- What do I need to do in the morning? Do I need to wake up feeling good since alcohol affects REM sleep?
- Do I want the empty calories?
- Am I only drinking out of social pressure?

Breakfast: Why is it that at home you eat fruit, eggs or a smoothie but on the road you eat sugary pancakes, waffles, bacon, and juice? Stop eating dessert for breakfast. Just because it's free doesn't mean you have to eat it, and have one of everything.

Exercise: Sometimes you have to do what you like and not necessarily what you love. Make do with what you have available. Deciding that the hotel gym is too stuffy, or it's too cold/hot/wet/sunny outside to exercise is just an excuse. It's not a reason. If you pick activities that don't require teams, equipment or special clothing you can still get in a good workout. Yoga, bodyweight exercises in your room or walking and running can all be done when traveling. If you exercise in the morning for forty-five minutes at home, stick to the morning when traveling and be realistic about how much time you have. I have a friend who is a serious traveler and avid CrossFitter. She finds CrossFit boxes wherever she travels.

Movement Opportunities: Find bursts or triggers throughout the day to get in thirty seconds to ten minutes of opportunities. Besides being a mega stress reliever, opportunities can give you energy. If you do nothing else, do ten minutes of movement every day that you travel. Join my challenge on Coach.Me to exercise ten minutes by 10:00am every day. The link can be found in the bonus page.

My client N.D. had a mantra, "Open the door and hit the floor." As soon as she got to a hotel, before she touched her phone, laptop or ate her dinner she brought with her, she put a towel down on the floor to do ten minutes of Pilates or yoga.

Email Processing: When I travel, my email schedule can fall to pieces because it's easy to check my phone out of boredom. Now that I use *Inbox Pause* I still stick to my two times a day schedule. If you use *AwayFind*, you can receive only the important emails, senders or communications from upcoming meeting attendees on your phone. Create office hours for your email just like you would at home.

Sleep and Wake Times: If you can, go to bed and wake up at the same time as at home, even when traveling for business. If you don't have a TV in your bedroom at home (please say you don't) then why do you have it on to lull you to sleep in the hotel? Unless I'm going to be somewhere for more than a few days, I don't adjust my sleep schedule at all.

- Phone. Are you available 24 hours a day when you're at home? Create office hours. Just because you're on a business trip doesn't mean you're working twenty-four hours the entire time you are gone. Use the Do Not Disturb setting to set a range of reasonable call times, yet provide access to your family. And please, put your phone in airplane mode when you sleep.

- Sugar. When we are tired, anxious, and lonely, we tend to reach for the sweets and treats. When that giant cookie tray is calling your name during the afternoon meeting, consider these options:

Have the cookie because otherwise you would be obsessed with it. It's right there in front of me. I can smell the cookie. The cookie wants me to eat it. Everyone else is having a cookie. Damn the person who ordered these delicious cookies. If this is you, try having half the amount you normally would have. If you have two, have one. If you have one, have half. The very act of trying not to think about the cookie is depleting your decision-making and ability to have more willpower later.

If you're eating out of boredom or keeping yourself awake, make a habit of saving some of your lunch for later in the afternoon.

Don't vilify the people eating the sugar. Focus on how it affects you and if you want to be at your sharpest.

If you are the person ordering the cookies, stop ordering cookies!

As a traveler, sometimes being boring when you travel is important to your health. If you feel pressure to see sites or close down the bar with your clients or companions, get rid of the guilt. You aren't on vacation. You're working. It's okay to keep the routine of putting yourself, your health, and your productivity first because your non-routine *is* your routine. Stick to what you can as much as you can. Socialize as much as you need to but don't go overboard. Self-care reigns supreme.

Help! I'm sick.

Scenario 1

It's 11:30pm and I'm staggering around London asking people "where's the nearest hospital?" People thought I was on drugs or drunk and kept crossing the street to avoid me. Finally, a policeman asked me how I was doing. I told him I was very ill and needed a doctor. It ended up being a very severe case of strep throat, dehydration, and flu.

Scenario 2

It's 11:30pm again and I'm driving around Ft. Lauderdale trying to find a pharmacy that's still open to buy a Thermacare for my neck, which is so stiff I'm unable to turn my head and it's not even safe for me to drive.

Scenario 3

It's 6:00am and I've slept about two hours. I was up all night calling the hotel staff every two hours to bring me Gatorade and whatever they had as far as over-the-counter pharmaceuticals. At 7:00am I called my manager to tell her there was no way I was going to be able to go onsite (to a hospital no less) because I wasn't keeping anything down. Her words were "We have to get this visit done. Take an Immodium, drink some Gatorade and get down to that site."

Being sick while alone and traveling isn't as bad as having your vacation ruined (done that too) but it still isn't rainbows and kittens. Preparing for being ill, or at least having a few things packed with you, can alleviate staggering around at night, trying to find a pharmacy or begging the hotel staff to bring you Tylenol.

Always carry your health insurance card and have it scanned into the cloud in a system like Evernote in case it gets lost. Some doctors and hospitals won't even look at you without proof of insurance. There is typically a number on the back of your card or on the insurance company website that you can call to find out if there are urgent care centers, minute clinics or hospitals nearby that accepts your insurance. Check that first, so you don't get a surprise bill later for going out of network. Most companies won't pick up your tab unless you got sick due to something from work.

Your company may participate in something like *eDocHome*, which provides 24/7 access to a doctor. You simply log in online or to your account, describe your problem and upload a photo (if necessary), then request to speak via phone or video to a doctor licensed in your State. Average call back time is sixteen minutes. One of my clients used a virtual physician solution for allergies and a possible infection and had a great experience. If your company doesn't have a virtual solution, they are very low cost, starting at $15 per month, and may be worth it for you and your family.

If you're hacking up your right lung and on a plane, do everyone a favor and wear a mask. Embarrassed that you might look silly? You'll be looked at with disdain without the mask so at least people may feel some sympathy since you aren't trying to spread whatever is growing inside you.

After a run-in with a cyclist who was also juggling in Brazil, I had to find my inner MacGyver and get creative with a pillowcase, ice, and an exercise band. When I started adventure racing and was required to carry a first-aid kit at all times, I realized that I could pack almost everything I needed for mere ounces. Prepackaged first aid kits are great, but remember to check them at least twice a year for expired products and replenish as needed. Also, consider that if a pain reliever has been in your below freezing or hot-as-an-oven car, it may have lost some of its effectiveness.

Items to have in your first aid kit:

- Antacids: Have these if you frequently suffer from heartburn. These shouldn't be eaten like candy or a supplement. Antacids can cause constipation, which is already an issue for travelers.

- Sunscreen: Not just for your beach weekend. Car windows can filter out UVB rays but not UVA rays. Unless your car has tinted windows, make sure you apply sun block. This isn't something you can keep in your kit all the time because the heat of your car will degrade it. However, it's a good idea to pack it for your trips. I use a refillable 2oz *GoToob* or take individual sunscreen packets.

- Anti-diarrheal medication: No need to pack the whole bottle, just a couple of tabs and repack as you need them. Nothing is worse when traveling than getting diarrhea, especially on a plane. Imodium will work and is sold in most hotels and airports. Do *not* take this prophylactically. It will delay the process of your body trying to get rid of whatever cootie is inside you. For a natural remedy, compliments of *The People's Pharmacy*, eat or drink anything with coconut, i.e. coconut milk, shredded coconut, even coconut macaroons.

- Motion sickness medication or wristbands: I hurled my guts up all night after taking the Vomit Comet from Dublin and missed the last dinner with my family before they left to go home. If you are prone to motions sickness, try an over-the-counter (OTC) product or wristband, or use a natural remedy like ginger.

- Bellyache: Travel with a couple of packets of ginger or peppermint tea to aid your digestive system.

- Moleskin: Cut these to whatever size you need. Great for blisters or friction spots.

- Body Glide: Great to prevent blisters or chafing. They come in mini containers to pop in your pocket if you are out for a long day and might need it.

- OTC pain medicine: Tylenol, aspirin, NSAID — whatever works for you. You can keep a couple in your kit, or you can pay $3.00 for a single at the hotel desk.

- Antihistamine: People who suffer from allergies are usually prepared with medication, but often we don't know if we are allergic to something until we are exposed.

- Bandages: A few different sizes.

- Hydrocortisone cream.

- Epi Pen if you're allergic to bees and have a prescription. These expire, so replace when needed.
- Antiseptic towelettes.
- Latex gloves.
- Tweezers.
- Duct tape: Wrap a piece of duct tape around a bottle to tear off and use if you need it.
- Tampon, pads and liners: For women, this is a necessity. For people who accidentally shoot themselves, this can stop the blood until you get to the hospital (true story). Sanitary products are like duct tape. They have all sorts of creative uses!

Most hotels stock sports drinks like Gatorade or PowerAde. This should only be considered emergency drinks because they are full of artificial colors, flavors, and sugar or artificial sweeteners. A better bet would be unsweetened coconut water. I've seen a few hotels start stocking them.

I highly recommend wearing a *RoadId* bracelet. Please have some type of ID if you take walks. You can put health information as well as your doctor and emergency contact information on it, in the event that something happens to you, and you are unable to speak. A colleague wrecked his bike and had a severe concussion. The only way he got home was that someone saw his bracelet and called his wife.

Incorporating even a few of these suggestions will help you stay healthy when you're traveling so you don't spend your time at home crashed on the couch trying to recuperate.

For links and references to this chapter visit http://www.beyondtravelbook.com/signup.html and login with your email address. Use the password provided via email for access to the bonus page.

8. Preparing to Travel

Are you the type to frantically rush out the door, forget your unders and deodorant, vow every time to start making a list and have constant anxiety that you've forgotten even more? This is an unnecessary behavior that needs to be changed. There's so much we can't control when we travel that we need to start off the trip controlling everything we can. The trip doesn't start when you walk out the door. It starts from the time you book your itinerary and includes packing your luggage.

Most business travelers travel solo, so everything needs to be taken care of alone. The Five Ps – Proper Planning Prevents Poor Performance can play a big part in helping you get through it. What can you *plan* to reduce stress?

- Schedule your flight at a time that is good for you (fly in the night before if you aren't a morning person).
- Get to the airport with plenty of time to get through security and to your gate.
- Pack snacks. Low blood sugar can lead to feelings of stress and anxiety.
- Wear clothes, shoes and accessories that are easy to remove for security.
- Pack noise-cancelling headphones.
- Schedule time for exercise and planning your opportunities.
- Maintain as much of your home routine as you can while on the road.

Global Entry and TSA PreCheck

Want to know the best way to invest $100? If you are a low-risk traveler, get a Global Entry pass. Global Entry helps you clear U.S.

Customs and Border Patrol fast by expediting clearance and using the touch-screen kiosks when you arrive into the country. To qualify, you have to submit an application, which takes about 15-30 minutes to complete, an in-person interview, background check and fingerprinting. Before you apply, see which airports do the interviews. The closest airport for me to interview is three hours away and took at least six weeks before they had an opening.

Getting Global Entry also automatically qualifies you for TSA's PreCheck program. Qualified travelers get to go through an expedited security line where they don't have to remove shoes, belts, coats, liquids and laptops. Global Entry is $100, and TSA PreCheck is $85. Why not spend the extra $15 and get the Global Entry in case you will be traveling internationally? Both are good for five years. If you hold an eligible American Express card, you get one Global Entry statement credit or one TSA PreCheck statement credit every five years.

Note that if your companion isn't qualified, they can't go through the speedy line with you at customs, and not all airports will allow you to take someone through with you for expedited screening. If you frequently travel with someone, it's helpful if they also have it.

Burner Laptops and Phones

Some regions, including China, the Baltic States, parts of South America and Russia, are notorious for installing spyware or breaking into your electronics while you're logging in at the hotel or airport. Some companies provide employees with "clean" business laptops that only have the bare minimum of what they need to be installed. Since most companies store their information in the Cloud, it can still be accessed but won't be stolen directly off of your computer. Use a burner phone with a pre-paid SIM card. Basic phones can be purchased for $30-$50.

Safety tips for electronics:

- Sanitize your phone, laptop, and any other portable devices by clearing your browser history, cache and saved usernames and passwords.

- Delete any saved or favorite sites that can expose personal information.

- Remove personal data or photos that you would not want to be seen on the Internet.

- Remove phone lists that could be stolen or made targets of fraud or phishing scams.

- Back up your device before you leave.

- Never leave a device unattended or assume it has been tampered with if you have. One website even suggested you sleep with them in bed with you. If you have to leave it unattended, use the hotel safe.

- Make sure all your antivirus software is up to date.

- Disable your Bluetooth and Wi-Fi when you aren't using it. Bluetooth makes your device more vulnerable.

- Don't install security or software updates while traveling. It could be malware or spyware.

- Phone conversations and email or Internet browsing may be intercepted. Privacy protections vary from country to country.

- Turn off your location-based services.

- Use a VPN connection if possible or consider all your Wi-Fi activities are being monitored. If possible, work only in your business facility or in a business that you trust.

- Report all stolen devices to the American Embassy or Consulate.

- Change your passwords and pins when you return.

Destination Research

I used to travel to Buenos Aires for work to perform corporate training. I loved the people and the city. On my first trip, I was walking out of the elevator with a colleague and was met by a man who proceeded to kiss both of our cheeks. I knew this was common and thought nothing of it. When he started speaking in Spanish, my colleague told him who I was, and he immediately got very embarrassed since it's not our business culture in the U.S. to kiss cheeks. The next day I learned he was so embarrassed he had told his colleagues about it. I asked the group I was training if they always kissed both cheeks and they said that both cheeks are when you are really happy or like someone, otherwise, it's just one cheek. I asked what they did if they didn't like the person. "Just a cheek. No kiss."

The next morning I stopped to get coffee at the Starbucks (Yep, they are everywhere!) and I saw the Kissing Gentleman outside the shop with a woman. I ran up to him very dramatically and kissed him on both cheeks to make sure that he knew that I was a good sport. We laughed, and he turned to the woman and stated, "This is my wife."

Needless to say, I only got the cheek.

I've made a fool of myself enough times to know how important it is to understand the rules of the country I am visiting. I've insulted men by insisting I pick up my bag, given my card with one hand instead of two in Japan, and looked at a woman with disdain in China when she let out a belch that would rival my Dad. When I was a corporate trainer in Tokyo, I didn't have a translator due to a miscommunication within my company and proceeded to do the training since they all spoke English. I thought they understood the training because the entire time they were shaking their heads and said they had no questions. I only learned later that in that situation asking a question would

178

have been considered rude, and I needed to probe more and ask them detailed questions to check for understanding.

Before you travel internationally, read a book or check out a website devoted to international business culture and where you are headed. Anyone remember when Richard Gere dipped and kissed an Indian Starlet at an AIDS benefit? Arrest warrants were issued; protests broke out and both were hung in effigy. Guess he should have read *Kiss, Bow or Shake Hands.*

Knowing your country customs goes far beyond how you greet people. Humor and physical affection in Latin American countries are welcomed, whereas countries like Germany, Austria and Switzerland are more serious. When the Chancellor of Germany, Angela Merkel, shrugged off President George W. Bush's shoulder massage, she wasn't expressing her dislike for him (or maybe she was) but it was reflexive because it wasn't appropriate for her in a business situation (is that appropriate for *anyone* in a business situation? Weird).

Know how people are addressed and if you need to use the formal terminology. I can't remember the last time I said "Mr. or Mrs." However not using Sensei correctly in Japan could cause you to lose respect.

Before I take an international trip, I glance through the major head- lines in my destination country to ask questions about when I get there. I try to stay away from controversial topics and never assume what religion a person is. One thing I always ask people is "what do you and your friends think of America?" I preface it by saying that our country has its good and bad as every country does. I've had the most insightful and unforgettable conversations after asking this question. It's best done when you've been around someone for a couple of days, and they feel comfortable around you. Warning ... if you don't have thick skin or aren't very open-minded, don't ask this question.

Businessculture.org and Worldbusinessculture.com are just two websites to help you navigate the customs of your destination country.

App

TripLingo is an app for both the consumer and enterprise level. It includes useful phrases with audio lessons and quizzes, a voice translator or connection to a live translator, a Wi-Fi dialer, tip and currency calculator, Slang in four levels and dictionary.

ICE, or In Case of Emergency, lets you list your medical conditions, primary doctor, and insurance information and can be accessed even when your phone is locked. It translates your information into ten different languages.

Luggage and Bags

There are so many different luggage types, and pros and cons to each; it really comes down to personal choice. High-quality luggage is a necessity if you are a business traveler. This isn't the time to go to Wal-Mart and get a $25.00 bag. This is not where 'good enough' works. You'll regret it when you are running down the terminal with your luggage case flopping along and your handle breaks.

Tumi is my carry-on of choice for the last seven years. The company is very high quality and has a stellar reputation. Unfortunately, I bought a coral-colored case thinking it would be easy to spot and wouldn't be accidentally picked up by one of the other five thousand black-bag-carrying people in the airport. The first time I checked that beautiful piece of luggage it came back streaked with black and incredibly dirty. I have never been able to get the stains out so for years I have strolled around with my dirty looking Tumi bag. It is almost unfortunate they are made so well because I am too frugal to switch it out when the only thing wrong with it is cosmetic. No matter what cleaning solution I've tried, it hasn't come out. Lesson learned — consider the color and if it's easy to clean.

Even though I wish I hadn't bought that particular color, I do not regret purchasing something other than black. It's too easy to accidentally pick up someone else's bag. I recommend using a colorful luggage tag. I've seen people tie ribbons or string onto their bag and then seen these torn to shreds in the conveyor belt. Once I had to wait thirty extra minutes for my baggage because someone's ribbon clogged up the machine. Get a tag instead.

If you were part of the inline skating generation, you probably know the difference between a cheap set of wheels and a quality set. You want your wheels to roll smoothly and evenly. Try to get a bag with four 360-degree wheels instead of a two-wheeled case. They are much easier to get down the aisle and can be pulled beside instead of behind you. This makes it much easier and safer to walk through the airport. With four wheels, it's less likely to fall over due to weight. When bags fall over its typically the sign of a cheaply made bag.

Look for an add-a-bag system if you frequently use a laptop or smaller carry-on. This typically consists of a hook or sleeve to attach the smaller piece to the larger piece and pull with one hand. Some luggage even has a strap to attach your coat.

Hard cases help protect your belongings, get less beat up in checked baggage, can be lightweight, and are less attractive to bed bugs. If you buy polycarbonate, make sure it doesn't scratch. My preference is softer, expandable cases with just a few pockets so I don't forget where I put things. Try to find fabric that is washable and water-repellant.

The largest suitcase I own fits in an overhead bin on most jets. Be careful you don't buy one too big unless you plan to check it. Whatever size bag you buy, you will fill it. On one trip that lasted a full month, I only used my Tumi carry-on and a backpack. Your case of choice should be light enough that you can lift it. Do some shoulder presses with it in the store to see if you can lift it over your head. If you are one of those women who are constantly asking the nice gentleman behind you to put your bag in the overhead bin, get a new bag or stop packing bricks.

Bags from Eagle Creek have interior compression wings to help you get more inside. Some of their cases integrate with their Pack-It system. If I were looking at luggage to replace my Tumi, I would seriously consider one of their bags.

A quality telescoping extended handle is a sign of a good bag. If you have ever struggled with your luggage handle, you know what it's like to have one that doesn't push down or pull up easily. It should be effortless. Make sure you walk around the store with the bag just like you would in an airport, to ensure that the handle is long enough you don't hit your heel. If you're short, like me, you want to make sure that the handle isn't so long you are dragging it four feet behind you and annoying your fellow travelers. If the handle is built inside the bag, it will take up more space and make it more likely to fall over.

Laptop Bags and Sleeves

Cocoon Innovations is my hands-down, absolute number one favorite vendor for laptop bags. Their Grid-It system stashes away your accessories and peripherals in an organized fashion that you can see, as opposed to being in several pockets. My bag of choice is the *Kips Bay*. I can fit my MacBook Air, peripherals, hangry snacks and my StandStand. It's airport friendly too so I don't have to take my laptop out of the bag and risk it getting bumped, scratched or stolen, and it fits easily under the seat.

If you have a sizeable laptop bag and can't get to your computer easily during your flight, consider getting a sleeve for protection and to use as a bag within a bag. I use the *Inateck Netbook Bag Envelope Cover Sleeve*. It has two pockets for a phone and peripheral, two inside pockets (which I use for my laptop and my Kindle) and comes with a small bag for a power adapter or mouse (which I use for my phone and cash). It's made out of sustainable and renewable materials that are biodegradable, and it looks cool too. The lining is mold-proof, and the felt material on the outside absorbs shock and protects your devices.

To keep my laptop from resting on my legs, which is particularly bad for the gents, I use a *Targus Slim LapDesk*. It folds flat and weighs less than a pound. Who says you can't have a mobile office?

Wardrobe

Having too many clothes makes for too many decisions on what to wear. I try to have only what I love; that goes with things I own, and can be mixed and matched. Save yourself the space in your closet, time and energy deciding what to wear, and money buying items that won't go with anything else, and donate, consign or sell.

Packing

Most people pack more than they need. Be realistic with how much time you will have, where you are going and what you will do. If you're in meetings from 8:00am-8:00pm, you probably don't need a casual outfit beyond what you wear on the plane. I used to travel with a guy who always wanted to go back to the room to change into jeans before he went out to eat. I felt it was such a waste of time and laundry energy to change clothes for one hour of dinner and then go back to your hotel room.

I've been asked so many times to show everything I put in my luggage I've even made a couple of videos about it. I can get by with very few things even for an extended trip. For a three-week trip with only a carry-on and backpack, I packed exercise and dress clothes, casual clothes, a pair of boots, dress shoes, sneakers, a Trigger Point Grid Roller and a collapsible hoop! I still could have probably packed less and find that I can almost always get away with removing one to two items in my suitcase. When my husband and I went to NYC for three days we each took a small backpack and that was it. It was so nice not to have to lug roller bags through the subway or along the sidewalks.

One thing I believe as far as packing is using an *Eagle Creek Pack-It Folder*. I have bought these as gifts for family members and recommend them to anyone that travels. They vary in size and help keep your clothes from wrinkling and provide compression so you can fit more into your suitcase. When packing, use any available space or holes. I stuff socks inside sneakers, exercise clothes inside my foam roller, belts inside shoes, etc.

I have duplicate toiletries so I rarely forget to pack my toothbrush, face wash, etc. and opt to leave all of my toiletries in my bag. I buy two mascaras, two eyeliners, two razors etc. For liquids like lotions, foundations and hair products, I use tiny *HumanGear GoToob* containers and pour in enough for a couple of weeks of travel. It takes less space, and I don't need to buy duplicates. Some people also just have one makeup bag or toiletry kit that they swap out each time. The main thing I discourage is doing a hybrid approach where you keep some things in your luggage and other things in your bathroom at home. It's too easy to forget an item. If you do find yourself without an item, most hotels will give you razors, toothbrushes and toothpaste for free at the desk. If you're only going to be somewhere for one to two nights, just using the shampoo, conditioner and lotion that the hotel provides is worth not messing with your own.

I have sneakers that are always in my suitcase, so there is no excuse to dismiss my exercise routine when I'm on the road. If you don't want to pack sneakers, you can still get a good workout in your room barefoot. Not all routines require footwear, so the *excuse* of not wanting to pack extra shoes isn't a *reason*.

Since shoes take up a lot of real estate, I try to have my clothes one color theme per trip and pack only one pair of dress shoes and maybe one casual pair, in addition to my sneakers. I try to get shoes that can work dressed up or business casual. Regardless, if you are a woman and wear high heels, you should always have some slip-on shoe or low-heeled shoe in the airport. I'm not talking about wearing sneakers with your business suit, but running through an airport in heels can be dangerous! I saw (and heard) someone break an ankle doing this. Not only did she miss her flight (she wasn't in her home city), she had to figure out a way to get to and from the hospital. Any chiropractor or podiatrist would tell you that you are seriously messing with your biomechanics running in heels. Be smart.

I try to buy wrinkle-free clothes along with the similar color schemes. If you are male, you could wear the same suit two days in a row and most people wouldn't notice as long as you changed your tie, however a suit definitely takes up more space in your luggage. Female clothing tends to be a little more distinctive so we might have to mix it up, but can still wear the same color scheme and bring along a scarf or some other accessory. If I'm visiting more than one client in a week, I re-wear my clothes all the time. Unless I sweat in them, which is doubtful if it's a business meeting, I take one pair of pants or a skirt and wear those twice and take two tops and one jacket. Clothes that are a little dirty (one wearing sweat and stain-free) but clean enough to wear again are *clirty* clothes (clean/dirty). My friend who is a traveler used to pack a pair of black pants for every day of the week she traveled. She now has downsized her packing *and* her dry cleaning bill.

There have been some great experiments on clothing and what other people notice. Most people notice little if you re-wear items that are neutrals or classics. This especially works with pants and skirts. Again, for guys, the tie is the thing people will notice, but only if it is a bright color or print. Unless your job is in fashion, you don't have to stand out. I have always been complimented on my clothes, so I feel like the neutral, wrinkle-free wardrobe with some fun or colorful accessory or shirt works great!

One thing I am thankful for in being female is that I do not have to pack a suit. One way to keep a suit jacket from getting wrinkled is to wear it on the plane, but not all men want to travel wearing their suit jacket. Some flight attendants will allow you to hang them in the closet. There are many great videos on how to pack a suit online.

www.businessinsider.com has a great one that I recommend in the bonus chapter.

The trick for looking for travel clothes that don't look like travel clothes are finding the ones with good fabric. There's a difference between travel-friendly clothes for business and vacation. Vacation-friendly travel clothes may result in too sporty of a look. If you search 'travel clothes' it often comes up with dowdy, unfashionable clothes that scream "In retirement and live to be comfortable!"

Brands to be on the lookout for include:

- Athleta, Royal Robbins, and Sahalie: Women's sports clothing that offer great business casual and travel dresses and skirts.

- Mizzen+Main: The pricey, but wicking and wrinkle-free shirts from Mizzen+Main are Tim Ferriss' go-to items for travel. You also won't look like you shop at sporting goods store.

- Ex Officio: Another Tim Ferriss and Rader Household favorite. If you go to the site itself, you'll find many more options besides unders and what is typically carried at a chain sporting goods store, some of which are fancy enough for business casual and travel wear. Wash, wear, and repeat.

Packing Lists

Any list making app will work to make a packing list. Whatever list making app you use, it needs to be something you can check off and then remove the checks *each* time you pack for a trip. It's so easy to forget one little item and even after all this time, I still use a checklist. I have a packing list for vacation, camping, racing, and business. I consider everything I will be doing: Travel, Business Dinner, Business Meeting, sight-seeing (sometimes it does happen), Exercise and Travel Home. I also think about the activities I will be doing while on that particular trip. Will I be standing a lot? Walking around a hospital for an hour? Presenting in an all-day workshop? Is the client a ten-block walk from my hotel? All of these things come into play making every trip a little bit different. This is what my latest checklist had, but it certainly varies depending on the trip and the climate. A * denotes having a spare packed at all times.

Business Trip Sample Check-List

CLOTHES

☐ *Casual or travel outfit:* Needs to be comfortable but *cannot* be pajamas. If you are over the age of six, you should never *ever* be wearing your pajamas, too-tight yoga pants or flannel lounge pants in the airport. You can be comfy without wearing PJs. If I'm not seeing a client right away upon arrival, I usually wear jeans, leggings or cargos (convenient at the airport). If I have a bulky jacket or sweater, I'll wear it to save room in my suitcase. You are your brand. If you meet someone while traveling, do you want to look like you crawled out of bed at 1:00pm in the afternoon?

☐ *Business clothes for each day.* Streamline by wearing the same color scheme and not packing bulky items. I stopped buying shirts that require ironing because I like ironing about as much as I like picking lint out of someone else's toenails. I also liken the sound of a hotel ironing board unfolding to a woman screaming in terror. I know there is some poor woman's spirit hiding in there that spent hours ironing other people's clothing.

☐ *Sweater, jacket or giant scarf:* Versatile and wrinkle-free for cold planes and meeting rooms.

☐ Underwear*

☐ *Bra* (if applicable): Consider the cuts of your tops to determine what type you need.

☐ Dress Socks and/or tights*

☐ Tie (if applicable)*

☐ Dress shoes

☐ *Belt:* Reversible belts are great to save space. Banana Republic has nice ones.

☐ Coat

☐ *Hat/gloves/scarf:* If you live somewhere warm and frequently travel to colder climates, keep a spare pair of cheap gloves in your bag. A big scarf or hat is great to have in your carry-on because you can use it as a pillow or to wrap around your head on the plane.

☐ *Pajamas:* I sometimes sleep in my exercise clothes to save space in my luggage. In the winter, I make sure I at least have pajama pants because I never know about the temperature control in the room.

☐ *Shoe Bag:* This keeps the dirt from your shoes from getting on your clothes. Shower caps work great for this too.

☐ *Jewelry case:* I use a day of the week vitamin box for my smaller jewelry, so it keeps it from getting lost, bent or broken. My necklaces I put through a straw and then in a cloth bag.

EXERCISE

☐ *Sports Bra* (if applicable)*

☐ *Workout Clothes:* Wicking clothes are important, so they dry a little before you repack them. If you are working out in your room just wear your unders and a sports bra (if applicable) and save the luggage space! Use the hotel dry cleaning bag for your used workout or dirty clothes to separate them from any other clothes.

☐ Athletic socks*

☐ *Sneakers:** Lower profile shoes save room in your bag. I'm partial to the Nike Free, New Balance Minimus or Inov8 Trailrocs.

☐ *Sprigs Wrist Banjee:* This holds my iPhone and hotel key while I'm working out and my ID and credit card when I'm in the airport. I also use mine when I'm out at the club so I can dance purse-free!

☐ *Exercise Equipment:* This depends on where I am staying and for how long and can include: Travel Yoga Mat, Trigger Point Therapy Grid foam roller, Jetsetter Gym Kit or a collapsible hoop.

☐ *Road ID:* Please get some ID if you take walks or run without your license. I pretty much have my Road ID on at all times when I travel. If something were to happen to me, no one would know whom I was and posting "who is this woman?" on the local news wouldn't save me.

☐ *Tennis Ball:* If I don't have a foam roller, I have a tennis ball. I use this for Self-Myofascial Release of my muscles. Not quite a massage, but better than nothing!

☐ Bandanna or clip*

TOILETRIES

Most of these should be duplicates that never leave your suitcase. Check Environmental Working Group ewg.org to find products rated zero to two. These products have less toxic substances you are putting on your body, your hair or in your mouth.

☐ Comb/brush*

☐ *Shampoo, conditioner, soap:* * I like small reusable containers from Humangear called GoToob. I use Dr. Bronner's lavender hemp soap for body wash and laundry detergent.

☐ hair product*

☐ *Face wash:* * Yes To Cucumbers Soothing Hypoallergenic Facial Towelettes (facial cleanser) is rated a one by ewg.org and isn't a liquid.

☐ *Face lotion:* * Badger Damascus Rose SPF 15 is rated 0 and smells delicious. Jason Fragrance-Free Facial Cream is also rated 0.

☐ *Sunblock:* * If applicable

☐ Deodorant*

☐ *Hand sanitizer:* * There's no need for the antibacterial kind. Check ewg.org to find one rated 0-2.

☐ Toothpaste, toothbrush, and floss* -

☐ *Makeup:* * Either buy duplicates or have one bag with all your makeup and move it back and forth between luggage and bathroom. Since you'll be putting on makeup before you leave, you won't leave it behind. My travel makeup tends to be powders or sticks, so I don't have to worry about melting, leaking or the liquids rule. I advise against having a hybrid system where you have some things duplicates and others not.

☐ *Hand lotion or balm:* * I love Aquaphor. It's cheap, rated one to two by EWG and can be used as lip balm as well.

☐ *Feminine essentials:* * *(if applicable)* Some things you never want to be without ☺

☐ *Razor:* * My husband and I belong to Dollar Shave Club to have our blades delivered right to our door.

☐ *Athletic tape or duct tape:* Wrap this around a pen or pencil. It comes in handy for all sorts of issues!

MEDICATION/FOOD

☐ *Vitamins/prescriptions:* * If you have regular prescriptions, keep some clearly-labeled, packed in your bag. The label isn't just for airport security. I've picked up a pill or capsule and asked my husband what it was. "I have no idea."

☐ *Snacks:* * Some foods I keep stocked in my bag and replenish after each trip include nuts, nut butter packets, tea, canned wild salmon, and protein powder. Minsley also makes pre-cooked single serving bowls of brown rice and quinoa that are perfect travel companions.

☐ *Protein powder:* * I love <u>Vega</u> and Deep30 products. For the most part, if you can get it from a convenience store, it isn't going to be a high-quality powder. You get what you pay for.

☐ *Sports nutrition:* * I use dates and coconut manna as my sports nutrition of choice when I travel. Both are easy to pack. Hotels often carry Gatorade or PowerAde, but both of these have artificial flavors, colors, and sweeteners. Rule of thumb, if you can buy it in a gas station, it probably isn't going to be high quality.

☐ *Travel mug and/or water bottle:* * Besides the environmental impact, they keep hot drinks hot, cold drinks cold and you're less likely to spill your coffee on the plane. I highly recommend the *Contigo Autoseal Vacuum Insulated West Loop Stainless Steel Travel Mug*. Spillproof and keeps your drinks hot or cold for hours.

LOGISTICS

☐ Purse, wallet or utility belt, Sprigs Wrist Banjee

☐ *Credit cards/cash:* Always have at least ten dollars in cash so you don't panic at unexpected tolls or get to the hotel and realize your only choice is to valet park, and you haven't any money to tip. A dollar in quarters is also handy for parking meters. I made the mistake of driving in Florida, the land of tolls, with no cash. It took me an extra 45 minutes to get off at an exit, find somewhere that I could take cash out and proceed with my trip.

☐ *Passport/ID:* I have scanned copies in my Evernote in case I ever lose them. It's much easier to complete a police report when you at least have some evidence that you exist, even if it's a scanned copy, so you have the number for both.

☐ *Tickets:* Downloaded onto phone or printed

☐ *GPS:* Directions loaded

ELECTRONICS

☐ Phone

☐ Laptop or tablet

☐ *Phone charger:** I keep a spare cord in my laptop bag. If you forget your charger, always ask at the hotel desk lost and found. They are the number one most forgotten item, so you may be able to snag one since most people don't have it shipped from the hotel if they leave it behind.

☐ *Laptop charger/spare cord:** It's worth buying a spare cord when you buy your laptop, so you don't have to crawl under your desk every time you leave to travel.

☐ eReader (Kindle, Nook)

☐ Power adaptor (International Travel)

☐ *Headphones:** Keep a spare pair of cheap ones in your luggage or laptop bag in case you forget your good ones. Also great for pretending you are listening to something on the plane when you don't want to be bothered. Half the time my headphone cord is just tucked into my pocket. Shhhh…….

MISCELLANEOUS

☐ *Umbrella:* Check the weather ahead of time. A compact umbrella may be worth the luggage space.

☐ *Mini First Aid Kit:** Keep stocked with bandages, antiseptic towelettes, anti-inflammatories. A small amount of real estate, but worth it not to pay $5.00 for one aspirin.

☐ *Sunglasses:* Have a cheap pair for travel since they'll probably get banged up.

☐ *Hand warmers/toe warmers:* * – I have Raynaud's Disease, so I always keep packets in my suitcase. I've even used them in frigid conference rooms.

☐ *Sleep sack/liner:* * I have a silk sleeping bag liner for when the bed looks suspicious, or I don't want my skin irritated by the bleach they use to clean the sheets.

☐ *Sleeping mask:* There isn't one better than Dream Essentials Contoured Face Mask. You'll look like Batman and sleep like Beauty.

☐ *Sandwich bags:* * A few for extra food or in case something leaks.

☐ *Extra-Large Ziploc bags:* I pack entire outfits in one giant bag. It keeps them separated and compact and makes it easy to get dressed in the morning.

I try not to check luggage unless I have a long layover, where I might want to be able to walk around the airport. Lugging a roller bag and a laptop bag will prevent me from doing that as easily. I use a wristlet or a Sprigs Banjee for my money, credit cards and phone.

Having a suitcase half-packed all the time is such a timesaver. I always have everything ready in advance. What I am *not* good at is unpacking. If there were an Unpacking Fairy, I'd be the first to sign up. I make myself unpack twenty-five things before I sit down to do anything, no matter what time of night I get home. The number is arbitrary, but it usually ends up being most of my bag, so I end up finishing anyway. Otherwise, it can sit there for a week, half un-packed. We live in a three-story house, and the first room I walk into when I arrive is my office. I put all my office stuff away, then carry my suitcase to the middle floor kitchen and unpack travel mugs or water bottles and any food I have with me, then up to the top floor where I throw my clothes in the laundry. Waiting any longer puts my workout clothes at risk for mildew. The next day, after I wash and dry, the clothes go right back into the suitcase if I'm going on another trip. I try to avoid clothes that are dry-clean only because it's another errand I have to run, is costly, and most dry cleaning is harmful to the environment. I do this routine because I am the World's Laziest Unpacker.

Sometimes I save clothes to get rid of when I'm going on vacation or somewhere that I know I will be shopping. Clothes that I plan to give away because I no longer want them, not because they are stained or torn, are my donate clothes. This way as I wear them I can neatly fold them and leave them for housekeeping or lost and found for someone to take. I had a few sweaters that were too big for me and instead of taking them to Goodwill, I neatly folded them and left them on the bed with a note that said 'I no longer want these. Please feel free to take them if they fit." Housekeepers don't make a lot of money. If they don't want them they can give them to someone else or if they don't want the hassle they can throw them away. I had a manager send me an email once and said even though they would never officially encourage it, the housekeeper was thrilled with the sneakers and sweater I left in the room. Old t-shirts or items that have seen their last days, I sleep or exercise in and toss them in the trash when I leave.

Apps

Papilia is a personalized travel app that provides packing guidance tailored just for you. First you enter your age, gender, size, style aesthetics and the average price of a pair of shoes in your closet. Then you enter your details for your destination and the type of activities for your trip. Papilia sends you curated shopping advice, a packing list and culture tips.

Stylebook is a closet app to create and store outfits. The setup takes awhile because you have to take photos of all your clothing items, but the results can be worth it. I created different outfits using my clothes and realized pretty quickly I had some items with nothing to match.

After you have your outfits created you can assign calendar days and get a cost per wear if you have the price of the item. It's probably best on iPad because the outfits are a little hard to see on a phone screen, but I still like it.

TripIt keeps track of your itineraries for the car, plane, and hotel. If you pay the yearly fee, it will also keep track of all of your rewards points and miles. If you are a very frequent traveler, it is worth it not to have to check five different airlines and four different hotels to see what your rewards status is.

In addition to tracking your itineraries, *iFly* can tell you what cafes, restaurants and amenities are in the terminal of the airport you are in. It's helpful if you are trying to plan what to do or eat during a layover.

Find My Friends may feel a little 'big brother', but you can share your location with chosen people and turn it on and off when you want to. When I travel I turn it on so my husband can see where I am. Not because he is cyber stalking me, but because I travel alone most of the time and if I were to fail to show up for an event or meeting it may not be apparent or alert anyone that something is wrong. At the very least, if someone called my husband to say "Marcey didn't show up for the meeting," he could see via GPS where I was. We've also used this when we were meeting somewhere because it can alert you when the person left and when they arrived (great for concerts!). It's easy to turn off if you don't want someone knowing where you are all the time. When I travel, I have nothing to hide from my husband, and I feel better knowing that *someone* knows where the heck I am.

For links and references to this chapter visit http://www.marceyrader.com/signup and login with your email address. Use the password provided via email for access to the bonus page.

9. Air Travel

In the Carlson Wagonlit Travel study, one of the highest stressors for females were 'routine breakers' and included not being able to eat healthy meals. A delay or canceled flight can put you on a path of anxiety and stress and can have the most effect on your routine.

Airplane Hygiene

Airplanes are a breeding ground for what ails you because they are hardly ever disinfected. I have no shame in my game and am not embarrassed to pull out a disinfectant wipe on the plane to wipe down the seatbelt, headrest, armrests and lap tray. I'm not a total germaphobe and don't slather my body or hands in antibacterial anything, but airplanes and some parts of a hotel are exceptions to the rule.

Bacteria that have been found on tray tables include e-Coli, streptococcus, and staphylococcus. Once I saw a woman put her shoes on the tray table. I also don't put any food in the magazine pouch. I have discovered a poopy diaper and leftover food from previous travelers hiding between the magazines. Because planes need to be boarded quickly, the cleaning crew are only picking up visible trash. If you're sitting near a window, wipe down the window with your wipe. Who knows how many heads have been leaning against that window? Speaking of which, did you know that the windows are not UV-proof and that UV levels increase up to four percent for every one thousand feet? Rays could be one hundred fifty percent stronger than on the ground. Pull down the shade and make sure you wear sunscreen.

If you go to the bathroom, don't touch anything with your bare hands. Pick up a tissue and use it to touch everything inside. When you get back to your seat, use alcohol, not anti-bacterial, sanitizer. Plain alcohol sanitizer is much better and is enough to kill most germs and viruses. Bring your magazines, especially if it is at the end of the month and hundreds of hands have touched that magazine. Seriously, do you need to buy a $300 watering bowl with a fountain for your pooch anyway?

Jet Lag

Jet lag is not in your head. It's a real physiological phenomenon and is even worse when traveling on international or long-haul flights. The condition occurs when time zone changes affect our body's natural biological clock or circadian rhythm. Circadian rhythms are measured by the rise and fall of body temperature and plasma levels of specific hormones. These are affected by our exposure to sunlight and help determine sleep and wake times. Circadian rhythms cycle every day and can affect things like body temperature, immune system, your power and aerobic capacity and even your handgrip strength.

According to CWT, lost time and productivity for international flights is approximately fifteen and one half hours. Unfortunately, most companies don't consider cost-benefit in lost productivity when choosing to fly their staff economy, business or first-class. If the traveler is stressed, tired, non-productive or exhausted, how well will they perform? If they haven't been able to work any during their flight, now they are also behind in their work and have to make up for it when they get to their destination.

Symptoms of jet lag include:

- Fatigue
- Insomnia
- Loss of appetite
- Reduced concentration
- Reduced fitness capacity
- Nausea
- GI distress (also caused by altitude)

- Joint swelling and stiffness (also caused by altitude)
- Muscle pain and stiffness

The hypothalamus regulates our sleep cycles, temperature, and appetite. It responds slowly to changes in external time and light levels. It is estimated that it takes one full day of recovery for every one hour of time difference. Traveling east is harder than traveling west because it's much easier to stay awake in the evening then wake up three or five hours earlier. If you live in San Diego but are doing business in Raleigh-Durham and normally get up at 6:00am, you are now getting up at 3:00am and are expected to perform your best even though you just flew in the night before.

No matter how experienced you are as a road warrior, jet lag affects you. It still affects pilots and flight attendants even after years of travel; they just get more used to managing the symptoms. If you are traveling across several time zones, you may need to give yourself an extra day or two to mentally and physically prepare for your meeting or event. You could still work, but maybe not meet with a client or save your easier, less brain-intensive tasks for the first day. Better yet, take a day or two as vacation and *leisurely* see some sights and then start your meeting.

The *Argonne Diet Protocol* was developed by Charles Ehret of the US Department of Energy Argonne National Laboratory and has been shown to help reduce the effects of jet lag. It was designed to help travelers and shift workers who have to rotate work hours. It was tested and found that those who managed to complete it were seven to sixteen times less likely to experience jet lag. Unfortunately, it's hard to follow and isn't much fun because it involves alternate feasting and fasting for up to four days before travel and no eating on the plane. If I am on a super-long flight, eating on the plane helps to break up the monotony and I look forward to it. The full protocol can be found in the online bonus page.

The modified Argonne Anti-Jet-Lag Diet Protocol is to eat a normal breakfast and lunch the day you travel then fast right before and during our flight, only drinking water. As soon as you land you have a meal at the normal time for that time zone then continue to eat at local times. The fasting should occur for fourteen to twenty-four hours. Breakfast should be high protein, and dinners should be higher carbohydrate and very low protein. Caffeinated beverages should only be consumed between 3:00 and 5:00pm local time. Personally, I have not tried this because again, I like to eat, but for those of you that wish to try it, let me know how it goes!

More hacks for Jet Lag include:

- Select a flight that arrives in the early evening and stay up until about 10:00pm local time.

- Try not to take any naps during the day for longer than two hours so you can go to sleep at night. The shorter the nap the better so you're tired when you should be tired.

- Change your watch to the destination time zone as soon as you board the plane and start your routine as if it were that time.

- Avoid caffeine or any other stimulant on the flight.

- Avoid alcohol or caffeine at least four hours before going to bed. Alcohol may make you feel drowsy, but it doesn't let you get into deep sleep.

- Avoid heavy meals or intense exercise before bed. Light exercise is best after a long flight due to the sedentary nature of flying and altitude effects.

- Get outside as soon as possible to help regulate the biological clock. The more you are indoors, the worse your jet lag can be.

The *Entrain App*, developed by the University of Michigan, works for jet-lagged travelers by exposing different types of light on a schedule to work with your circadian rhythm and adjust to your new time zone.

Supplementation for Jet Lag

Melatonin is a hormone that controls circadian rhythm, is secreted by the pineal gland in the brain, synthesized from the amino acid tryptophan and is released at night in the dark. Watching the blue rays from a laptop, phone and TV screens can affect your sleep because it prevents melatonin from being released. Studies are inconsistent on whether supplemental melatonin helps with jet lag, but if you do choose to try it, dose timing is important. You should wait until you land in your new time zone to supplement. Studies suggest .5mg to 5mg of melatonin for three nights, one hour before normal bedtime after you've reached your destination. If the trip is short, just a couple of days, melatonin won't do much for you. It does seem to have a powerful placebo effect on some people no matter when or how they take it.

Because melatonin can be purchased over the counter, it is seen as ultra-safe. It has cancer-fighting properties and is a powerful antioxidant. Melatonin is a hormone and over time, you could become dependent on it. It's much better to generate your melatonin by practicing good sleep hygiene. If you do take the supplement, you should take the absolute smallest dose due to a Goldilocks affect...too much, and it will *prevent you* from sleeping.

Security

I try to be fast through security by preparing before I leave home or when I turn in my rental car. If I'm leaving from home, I'll just pack my belt and jacket until I get through security and then put it on. I try to wear shoes that are easy to get on and off (but still comfy). Since I usually wear a Sprigs Banjee when I travel, my phone, ID and credit card are on my wrist, and I can pull it off easily. My liquids and laptop are removed from the bag. I put my items in the bin in reverse order of what I will be retrieving them in and I always put my shoes last because I will not leave security without my shoes, ensuring nothing gets left behind. A great tip from smartwomantravelers.com is to remember PLLS - Purse Laptop Liquids Shoes. Most of these steps are irrelevant if you have Global Entry and can go through the expedited line.

If I'm wearing shoes without socks, I'll try to remember to have some handy in my carry-on, so I don't have to step barefoot through security. When I forget socks, I try to think happy, fungus-free thoughts.

Always watch the bins go through the scanner prior to going through security. If you send it through too early, someone could accidentally (or intentionally) take your things. In the rush of getting everything together, it's easy to forget something. If you do, contact Transportation Security Administration Lost and Found. If you leave something in the airport at the gate, terminal or parking garage, contact the Airport Lost and Found. If you leave an item on the plane, contact the airlines directly. I keep a business card in all my coat pockets and bags to make it easier for people to contact me if I've left something.

Have a photo of your luggage in case it gets lost. You can send it to the airlines to help them locate it. If I were packing something valuable, I would take a photo of the inside as well. I make a habit of taking photo or video of everything in my home once per year and store it in the cloud. If there were ever a fire or theft, I would have proof of what I had for my insurance company.

Safety

Most business travel is done alone and often to unfamiliar areas. It's very important that someone know where you are when you are traveling. You can use an app like *Find My Friend* or with TripIt, you can have someone you trust on all your travel itineraries.

Your cell phone should have an ICE number – In Case of Emergency. I have ICE in the name of my husband and two girlfriends so that if something were to happen, the police or fire department could just search ICE instead of guessing to whom I belong. If you are traveling outside of the country, always have your passport with you, so they can call an embassy if necessary.

For links and references to this chapter visit http://www.marceyrader.com/signup and login with your email address. Use the password provided via email for access to the bonus page.

10. Hotels

An entire trip can be won or lost by the quality of the hotel. When traveling for business it is your respite. You may have to be 'on' all day for meetings, have meals with colleagues and clients and be expected to sit next to your boss on the plane. The only time you have to yourself is in the hotel room. I'm a big fan of hotels with kitchens, with space for me to exercise and fast Internet. When I was approached by Extended Stay America about partnering with them, it was an easy decision based on one thing ... their full kitchen! We've already covered hotel nutrition and exercise. Now for a few other things.

Avoiding Illness

Unless you live in a bubble, it's impossible to avoid *ever* being sick, but paying special attention to some of the things listed in this book will certainly help in prevention. Hotel cleaning crews have tough jobs of getting rooms turned around quickly. This sometimes results in rooms not getting as clean as they should.

I carry cleaning wipes in a sealed storage bag and wipe down the bathroom faucet handles, all of the door handles and light switches, toilet seat and handle as well as the desk, nightstand, remote control and surfaces that may come into contact with food. It takes me about two minutes. Bedspreads may only get cleaned once every couple of weeks. I usually take it off of my bed and put it in the corner of the room, or if the room is cold, I'll just pull it up hip high when I'm sleeping. If you're a member of a hotel honors program, you can even request in the settings to have your comforter removed before you get to the room.

Carpets don't always get swept between each guest. I recommend wearing socks or slippers on the carpet and using a bath towel as an exercise mat.

The coffee maker may get rinsed out, but rarely is washed. I would wash it out *with soap* if I were going to use it. One hotel insider website states they have found vomit, urine and cigarette butts in the coffee makers. I never drink out of the glassware or coffee mugs. Sometimes these just get wiped down with whatever rag is being used to clean the rest of the room. Only drink out of the disposable cups or use your own. Also, never use the stir sticks unless they are in packaging. Who knows where that thing has been or who has touched it! I once saw a barista at a very famous coffee chain drop an entire box of stir sticks on the floor, scoop them up and put them in the container for customers. He thought no one was looking, but my eagle eye saw it all. I like that Extended Stay America Hotels requires that dishes, utensils, and cookware are cleaned and sanitized, wrapped in plastic and stored outside the rooms in a central location. Guests can request different types of kitchen packages be brought to their room upon check-in.

In the bathroom, the towels aren't always changed if it looks like they haven't been used. A former colleague of mine stated that she throws all of the towels on the floor before she leaves so they will wash them for the next guest. I reuse my towels just like I would at home if I'm going to be staying there for a few days. I typically end up using all the towels because I use one as an exercise mat and put another on the desk chair since I sometimes get sweaty working out in the room. Since I don't have the cleaning staff come to my room every day, by the end of my stay, most of my towels are used anyway.

Use the ice bucket with the plastic liner inside it. They don't often get cleaned, and people use it for more than storing ice. I know someone who routinely uses it to soak her feet (and I've seen her feet!).

The remote control is the absolute dirtiest thing in the hotel. You can clean it with a wet wipe or simply stick it inside of a bag or shower cap, so you are only touching it through the plastic.

I rarely swim in hotel pools. The CDC found that 16,500 hotel and motel pools had the highest rate of closure due to serious code violations such as fecal matter, urine, shigella, and norovirus. This is about one in every six hotels. The bacteria and viruses thrive because most hotel pools are heated. The hot tubs are worse and are akin to giant petri dishes. Neither pools nor hot tubs get regularly cleaned in hotels.

If a fitness center has wipes, use them. When I have the time to fill out the hotel questionnaires, I always request this if they don't have them already. Otherwise, always use a towel and try to avoid touching your face while you are working out. Fitness centers get a cursory wipe by hotel staff and are rarely disinfected.

Again, I'm not a total germaphobe, but if something is going to come into contact with food or there is a chance that I could get e-coli from someone else's refusal to wash their hands after they go to the bathroom, I'm good with taking one to two minutes to prevent it.

Don't Let the Bed Bugs Bite!

Bed Bugs have been a hot topic in the last few years for good reason. Hotels can get infested with them, and if you bring them home, it is extremely expensive and inconvenient to get rid of them. It doesn't matter how luxurious the hotel is since they have even showed up at the Ritz-Carlton. You can check out bedbugs.com for hotels that have had issues, but by the time it's listed, the hotel has probably taken care of it. Those hotels may be the cleanest of all because they are hyper-aware and probably fumigating more often. Bed Bugs can hop from luggage to luggage in overhead bins or be hanging out in the trunk of your rental car waiting to hitch a ride. They are not always guaranteed to come from a hotel. There are some things you can do to help prevent them, but there is nothing foolproof to one hundred percent guarantee you won't take them home. I do a few of the prevention methods below:

- Use a business card to run along the cracks and crevices around the mattress, bed frame or headboard to see if there are any bug remnants.

- Travel with a small flashlight to inspect for fecal or blood matter.
- If you see signs, alert the hotel immediately and move to another floor. Bed bugs travel up to fifteen feet so moving to the next room is not an option.
- Leave your clothes in your luggage away from the bed. Don't put them in the drawers. I keep my luggage in the bathroom or on the valet.
- Fabric luggage is more attractive to bugs than hard-shelled luggage.
- Travel with a large plastic bag. If you think you may have been exposed, encase your luggage.
- When you get to your car at the airport, put your suitcase in a plastic bag prior to getting in your car.
- Leave your luggage in a hot car or hot area, like a garage, for a couple of days. Just remember to pull out any toiletries or meltables.
- Laundering your clothes in hot water or dry cleaning is recommended, however, unless I thought I had them, I wouldn't do this. I don't wash anything in hot water because most clothing doesn't react well to high heat, and it takes a lot of energy.
- Inspect suitcases before putting them away.

Not everyone reacts to bedbugs the same way. I had a client who had bed bugs and didn't react to their bites. Her sister came to stay with her, and they slept in the same bed and she woke up with bites all over her. That was the only way she knew her home was infested. It cost her a few thousand dollars and a couple of weeks of inconvenience to get rid of them.

A colleague woke up with bites all over her after staying in a very nice hotel in NYC. The hotel offered to move her to another room. She was encouraged by her colleagues to ask the hotel to pay for dry cleaning and a couple of new outfits since the chance that her clothes were infested were high and moving to another room would just take them with her. The hotel refused to buy new clothes, but did pay for the dry cleaning.

If you don't want to sleep on the sheets, I recommend a silk sleep sack. It's lightweight and folds up next to nothing in your carry-on. I just crawl in and put the hotel sheets on top. If I'm in the sleep sack because I'm worried about creepy-crawlies, I stick it in a sealed, plastic bag before I put it in my luggage and throw it in the laundry when I get home. Even if the sheets are clean, the detergents and bleach they use are so strong that I've known people to get rashes from irritation.

Hotel Safety

Hotels have the potential to be dangerous places, especially for women, but there are ways you can protect yourself and be smart. When checking in, ask the hotel staff not to state your room number out loud. Ask for two key cards at the hotel. First, it doesn't alert anyone around you that you are traveling by yourself. Second, you keep one card on your person in a pocket and another in your purse or bag. That way, if your purse or bag were to get stolen, you would still be able to get into your room. I take a photo of my hotel door to remember the room number.

Be careful when going *into* your hotel room. If someone is in the hall with you, wait until they have passed by before opening your door. It's easy for someone to push their way in and trap you inside. Once inside, *shut* the door but don't lock it with the deadbolt yet. Before you use the deadbolt and bar, check the shower, behind the drapes, the closet, and the sliding glass doors, to make sure that there isn't anyone waiting for you. Check to make sure the door is all the way latched when entering and exiting and use both the deadbolt and chain or bar. Once I got out of the shower to find housekeeping in my room when I didn't use the bar.

Label your things, just like summer camp. I have a label on the outside of my suitcase as well as a business card on the inside in case the outer label gets ripped off. As much as I don't want to mar my beautiful MacAir, I have a label with my phone number on the bottom. When I had a less beautiful laptop, I just taped my business card directly on the bottom. I highly recommend this, as well as putting your IT number on the bottom. If you can't get your computer to work, having your IT number saved in your *Contacts* isn't going to help you.

Fire department ladders typically don't go above seven floors. Consider staying on a lower floor, even though you may not get the best view. On the other hand, staying on a ground floor can open you up to theft easier. If you are staying at a hotel with rooms that open from the outside, try to stay near the office or some other semi-busy area. Try to avoid staying in a room that adjoins with another one unless you know the person in it. If you can't avoid it, put your luggage rack or the office chair in front of the door so you will hear if someone tries to open it.

Do not prop your door open while you are getting ice or while you are waiting for room service. Never open your door to anyone without making sure that they are indeed hotel staff. If I'm not expecting a visitor and receive a knock at the door, I ask their name and call down to the desk to see why they are there.

I use my *Do Not Disturb* sign the entire time I am in a hotel. I typically decline housekeeping unless I am in a room for more than three days. I don't clean my house every day at home and don't need service daily on the road. Plus, it keeps people from being in my stuff. If you hang out the sign that the room needs attending, it's a sign to thieves that you are not in the room. Many people also leave the radio or TV on. I have a hard time with this because I try to be energy efficient, so sometimes I do and sometimes I don't. This is your call.

Always use the in-room hotel safe for your jewelry, valuables, phone, extra cash, passport, and laptop, even if only for a short time like a trip to breakfast or the fitness center. I test out the code and make sure it's working before I put my things in it to ensure something doesn't get locked in that I can't get out. Use a code you will remember like your house number, part of your zip code or your PIN. Don't use easy-to-remember codes like 1234 or 0000.

Tipping

Tipping gives you good karma. If you are a business traveler you are getting your trip paid for and reimbursed for tips so, don't be stingy. Don't be ridiculous either or your company may single you out. Service workers to include: Airport skycaps, shuttle drivers (especially if they handle your bags), taxi drivers, hotel housekeeping, room service (check to make sure it isn't already included), valets and the concierge. If you are paying for your trip yourself and you are watching your budget, avoid using valet parking if you can and opt out of housekeeping every day by putting out the *Do Not Disturb* sign.

How Much?

The most common tipping amounts:

- Airport Shuttle Driver: $1-2 or $1 per bag
- Skycap: $1 per bag
- Bellhop: $1-2 per bag or $2 minimum if they are taking it to your room
- Hotel Housekeeper: $2-$5 per night (the messier you are, the higher you should tip). Tip daily if you use housekeeping every day because you may not have the same housekeeper. If you don't use housekeeping tip at the end of the stay.
- Parking Valet: $2-5 to bring the car to you. If the weather is bad, tip on the high end.
- Hotel Concierge: $5-20 depending on the level of service. No tip is necessary for asking simple directions or recommendations.

- Room Service: 15% of the bill or at least $2 (not required if gratuity is included)

- Wait staff: According to Lizzie Post of the Emily Post Institute, you don't need to tip on the tax at a restaurant because that's the part the government gets. For excellent service tip 20% and tell the service person and their manager that the service was outstanding. For good service tip 15%. If the service is poor, you should still tip 10% and inform the manager about the issue.

- Wine Steward: 15% of the cost of the bottle

- Bartender: 15-20% of drink tab, $.50 soft drink or $1 per alcoholic drink. Make sure you always tip your bartender if you get something before you head to your table.

- Food Delivery: 10% of the bill (excl. tax), 15-20% if delivery is difficult due to weather or traffic or $2.00 minimum. The delivery charge doesn't always go to the driver so be sure to tip!

- Coatroom Attendant: $1 per coat

- Washroom Attendant: $.50-$1

- Taxi Driver: 15% + $1 per bag

For links and references to this chapter visit http://www.marceyrader.com/signup and login with your email address. Use the password provided via email for access to the online bonus page.

11. Auto

Unless you're in a city where trains or subways are the norm, it's hard to take a trip without renting a car or taking a taxi, even if you are walking from your hotel. Sometimes being a traveler always means traveling by car, like my client who covers the entire state of North Carolina and is in a different city every day.

Rental Cars

A lot of travelers forget where they parked their rental car or even what kind of car they are driving. I don't know how many times I've picked up a car in the evening, not paid attention to the color, make or model and driven to my hotel. The next morning, I wasted precious time wandering through the parking lot trying to figure out which car was mine. I have opened trunks or started the alarm to find it, and when the car keys didn't have either option, I even tried unlocking doors. Now I take a photo of the car and where it's parked before I walk into the hotel.

When I park my car at the airport, I write the location on my ticket stub since I have to pay in the airport before I walk into the parking garage. I sometimes take a photo of the location that I have parked at the airport, too. There are apps that will locate your car via GPS, but so far I have been ok just taking the photo and then deleting it when I'm finished. It only takes one very late night of walking three floors of the RDU parking garage to make me diligent about knowing where I park.

Have your itinerary and directions stored in your phone, entered into your GPS or printed out and with you at all times. You don't want to be fiddling around with it in a parking lot or driving around in circles late at night. Ideally, use voice GPS so you can look at the road while being directed where to go. You also want to find out where your lights, wipers and door locks are as soon as you get into the vehicle.

Most airports will escort you to your car if you are uneasy about where you parked, especially at night. Hotels will too, which is another reason it's good to have the number of the hotel handy on your phone before you get there.

If you're walking alone in a parking lot, do not be distracted by your cell phone. On the other hand, if you think you *are* being followed, some security experts recommend *pretending* to have a phone conversation. Your assailant may be worried that whoever you are talking to could call the police and there would be a witness, even if over the phone. Pretending to be on the phone is different than being distracted and talking to someone on the phone.

If a van is parked next to the driver's side door, it's easy to be pulled inside. Consider entering from the passenger side. Always glance into the back seat before you enter your vehicle to make sure you don't have a surprise passenger.

Put your laptop in the trunk *before* you leave for your destination so that when you park if you aren't taking the laptop inside with you, no one sees that you have one in your car. At a work dinner, three colleagues put their laptops in the trunk before entering the restaurant. Guess how many laptops were stolen over steak and salad?

Don't underestimate your ability to forget an item in the car. Something could fall under the seat or into the side of the door. Phone chargers are notorious for staying behind from rushing travelers trying to get to their flight.

Key tips for car rentals:

- Don't prepay for gas. It's almost always going to be in the rental agency's favor. You are paying a hefty amount for the convenience of not refilling.

- Scope out a gas station on the way *out* of the airport. One of my travel pet peeves is getting back to the airport before I find a gas station and having to circle back out and waste time trying to find one.

- There's rarely a need for insurance because your company, your personal insurance and / or your credit card will cover you.

- If upgrades aren't the highest priority, wait until you get to the counter to ask for one. Better yet, wait until the agent asks you and find out what their best deal is. Sometimes they need more lower-priced cars on the lot, and they are happy to get rid of their upgrades.

- Take photos of any dings or scratches before you leave. Many of us take a cursory walk around the car before and after (if at all). If there is anything on that car you hadn't pointed out before you left with it, you are 100% responsible.

I've often wondered why rental companies give you two keys until someone at a conference accidentally took my key. Thankfully, he turned the key into the rental center when he realized his mistake, although the right thing to do would have been to drive it back to me. I was two hours from the airport and my options were to have a tow truck come and tow the vehicle and take me to the airport or have someone at the conference center drive four hours round trip to take me to get the key. The charge for the key alone would have been $140, and the tow trip would have been $300. What a great money-maker for them!

Taxis/Uber

I don't particularly feel safe in taxis in all cities, but I often can't avoid them. Some cities the cars are unmarked, and it feels risky before even getting in. Always ride with licensed taxi drivers only. Take a photo of their license, which is usually on the back of the seat and clearly visible to you. This is a good idea in case you leave something behind. Calling a taxi service and saying you left your book in a taxi in NYC is like telling Wrigley you dropped your red marble in a giant vat of Skittles.

It's helpful for the driver if you have the exact address of your destination. I didn't know there was more than one Hotel Millennium in Manhattan, the driver didn't ask me which one and I was dropped off at the wrong place. It took me an hour to get to the correct hotel, and I had to pay for the error. Have a general idea of the direction you should be going and how long it takes. Map the route on your phone to make sure the cab driver isn't taking you the longer route.

I'm a fan of Uber at home and when I travel. I like that I can see via the app and GPS how close they are to my location in minutes, a photo of their face, so I know who I'm looking for, and what kind of car they are driving. I especially like that I know how much money it's going to cost me, and I don't need cash. Everything is done via the app.

Personal Cars

One woman I met in a workshop said that when her husband drives her car it's like someone has driven her desk around and moved all her important things. She has her car organized like most people do their desks, and anything out of place throws off her rhythm.

Items to keep in your personal car:

- First aid kit
- Napkins
- Tissues
- A couple of shopping bags for trash
- Hangry snacks
- Spare change for tolls or parking
- Umbrella
- Jumper cables and emergency equipment

- Emergency blanket
- Phone charger specifically for the car
- Extra business cards and marketing materials

Rage Prevention

The stress of commuting and driving can seriously take its toll on a regular trip. When you are traveling and driving in an unfamiliar place in an unfamiliar car, it can compound that stress ten-fold. The anxiety, frustration, fear or anger that can be triggered from driving can affect your alertness, focus, blood pressure, blood sugar and mood. How many people have shaken their fist, yelled at another driver or honked their horn angrily when someone pulled out in front of them, swerved into their lane or were driving too slow? It's natural to get irritated, but threatening someone's life or acting in a way you wouldn't act if you were face to face, rather than behind a large vehicle, is cause for stress management.

A daily car commute over 10 miles can raise your risk of high blood sugar, high cholesterol and depression *(American Journal of Preventive Medicine)*. After fifteen minutes of commute time happiness levels fall and anxiety levels rise. People who commute longer than forty-five minutes each way report lower sleep quality *(Regus Work-Life Balance Index 2012)*. If your commute lasts between sixty-one to ninety minutes, overall stress increases greatly. *(U.K. Office of National Statistics)* The longer time spent driving, the less productive you are and the more lost work days, late arrivals, higher turnover and decreased job satisfaction you enjoy.

I recommend a short meditation when first getting into a car, even if it is only four to six cycles of breathing. One of my clients performs deep breathing in the car as a meditative technique. Another client uses his commute home to think about what he was grateful for that day. When someone irritates me, I try to think of a reason why they did whatever it is that irked me. Did they pull out in front of me because they just received a call that their wife is in the hospital? Did they take the parking spot I was waiting for because they were distracted after receiving a pink slip at work? They could just be a jerk, but giving them the benefit of the doubt takes some of the stressor away.

One thing I don't have a lot of patience for are people who talk on their phones while driving. I don't say I *never* do it, but it's the exception rather than the norm and I'm usually lost and trying to find my destination. I refuse to talk to my family or clients when they're driving. It's dangerous and no matter how good you think you are at it ... you're not. Not only are you not paying attention, you're almost always driving slower than the cars around you.

I use the car ride to listen to podcasts, NPR or music. I don't fiddle with the stations and set my phone, the sound of choice and Shoeboxed receipt app before I start driving. My phone is on Do Not Disturb so I'm not tempted to look at it if I hear a buzz. I admit to sometimes switching up something on my phone or checking my directions when I'm at a stop light, but I really try not to because I don't want to be one of those people holding the line up when the light turns green because I'm scrolling and tapping.

Apps

How many times have you taken an exit only to find out that the gas station was four miles down the road? *Road Ninja* can help you map out your trip, tell you what gas stations, cafes, pharmacies and restaurants are at each exit and how far you will have to drive to get there.

If you've already downloaded Shoeboxed for receipt tracking, you can have it perform double duty and track your mileage as well. It calculates the reimbursement rate automatically and a receipt or report can be run to submit to your employer.

For links and references to this chapter visit http://www.marceyrader.com/signup and login with your email address. Use the password provided via email for access to the online bonus page.

12. Home

Being a traveler doesn't just require health and productivity on the road. To be at your most awesome, you also need to have a system at home as well. What's tough about being a business traveler is you sometimes have to have two triggers for a behavior. If you normally meditate after you take your dog out in the morning, you have to find a trigger to meditate when you're on the road. Every traveler knows that being gone for three to four days means catching up at home on the weekend. We want to eliminate as much of that catch-up feeling as possible and be able to relax or do what you need to do now.

Physical Clutter

I've had several people come to my home and remark how clean it is. I always tell them it isn't that my house is clean but more that I don't have a lot of clutter, which gives the illusion of cleanliness. However, the less stuff to dust, pick up, sweep around and put away, the faster any cleaning routine is!

Having less stuff, in general, is helpful as far as clutter and decision-making. When I drastically reduced my wardrobe it made it easier for me to pack and get dressed because I didn't have as many choices to make. I also made sure that every time I bought something, it already went with something I had or could serve more than one purpose.

One person's clutter is another person's treasure. If you are embarking on a quest to declutter, I recommend the book *Unclutter Your Life in One Week* by Erin Doland. While I don't think one week is reasonable or necessary, the steps she offers are easy to follow and make sense. Hiring a professional organizer is worth the money to help you separate your emotions from the book your ex-boyfriend from college gave you or the ugly sweater your Mom bought you for Christmas that you feel bad about giving away. If you're being swallowed up by the Paper Tiger, find a Productive Environment Specialist or a Professional Organizer in your area or work with one virtually (like me!) to

221

help you with your paper mess. One client I worked with got rid of three kitchen-size trash bags of paper just from her home office. She was able to remove an entire filing system and now has a cozy sofa to sit on during breaks.

Questions to ask when decluttering or bringing something new into the house (some questions adapted from Unclutter Your Life in One Week):

- Do I already own something like this?
- If yes, am I ready to get rid of the older item?
- Will it make my life easier, save me time, or save me money?
- Is it sentimental to me?
- Is it sentimental to other people so I think it should be sentimental to me? (Your memories are not your grandma's memories).
- Where will it live in my house?
- Is it the best price for the best quality?
- Will I use it before it expires?
- Would I buy this again? This is helpful when you are looking through your closet. I realized I was wearing things just because I owned them, not necessarily because they were my current style, or what I *wanted* my current style to be.
- Does it help me be the person I want it to be?
- Does it have a soul?

The last question is my favorite. We attach so much emotion to inanimate objects, even worse, other people's inanimate objects. I've never been a collector of things, didn't have a binky or a blankie and if something were to happen to my house, I would find it more of a nuisance to replace things than an emotional devastation that my belongings were gone.

One of my close friends is struggling with decluttering while at the same time her parents are downsizing and getting rid of their clutter while trying to pass it down to her. Now she has to make the decision to bring their clutter in or feel guilty about not accepting it, even though they aren't her memories. On the flipside, many adult children still expect their parents to have real estate in their home devoted to their trophies, medals, yearbooks and their Senior Prom Dress. It's your stuff. Don't force it on people and don't take it from people unless it's something you or they want. It's not fair to either party and especially not worth it when it's something useful that someone else could be using. One family member couldn't bear to get rid of her deceased father's tools. They just sat in the garage, unused for at least a decade. By the time she was ready to donate to the shop class at a local high school, the tools were outdated, and they wouldn't even accept them.

How to start? Begin with one drawer, one zone, or one room. Make a numbers game and find twenty-five things to trash or donate or set a timer and declutter for a set amount of minutes. One of my clients wanted her daughter to declutter but wasn't sure if she would be able to handle it due to the emotional attachment. My suggestion was to make it a game, and since she was twelve years of age, she had to find twelve things every weekend. It worked!

Making Your Home Easier for Travel

When I used to travel weekly, I felt like all I did on the weekend was catch up on my life tasks before it started all again. Traveling for business requires organization and planning if you don't want your house to fall apart. Common issues include mail not getting picked up, bills are not getting paid, the house not getting cleaned, clothes not washed, groceries not bought, and appointments not scheduled.

Mail

We've already talked about switching to automatic bill pay and File This Fetch. The less paper mail you receive, the less you will have to contend with, and the less waste in your recycle bin. If I'm going to be gone more than a week, I put a hold on my mail. I know some people who travel so much they use a P.O. Box because they don't want their mail sitting in their mailbox at all. I have a lock on my mailbox, so it doesn't worry me to be gone for security purposes. For safety reasons, you should have your newspaper (if you still get them) stopped while you are gone. An easy target for thieves is a home with a few newspapers out front. It's too obvious you aren't home.

Paper Junk Mail

Need to get rid of paper clutter and junk mail? I've eliminated most of my unwanted mail and some days I even have an empty mailbox.

DMAChoice.org (Direct Marketing Association) is a free mail preference service where you can opt out of junk mail via email. If you don't want any catalogs, magazine or credit card offers, you can opt out of that category entirely. It saves you from having to recycle and from seeing something you have to buy to keep up with Mr. and Mrs. Jones. Unfortunately, there is no opt-out for political ads. You can also register on DMAChoice for the deceased or as a caretaker.

CatalogChoice.org is complementary to DMAChoice if you only want to opt out of specific magazines and catalogs. A great feature is the ability to opt-down instead of opt-out. If you want Victoria's Secret quarterly instead of weekly, the site has the capability to do that for companies that will allow it. I've saved three fully-grown trees, 935 pounds of greenhouse gas, 332 pounds of solid waste and 2250 gallons of water by opting out.

OptOutPreScreen.com will allow you to opt out of credit cards for five years or permanently. I only have one credit card that I've used for 15 years. I've frozen my personal and my business accounts. This helps protect me from identity theft because a credit card can't be opened in my name without me unfreezing or thawing the account. It only takes a few minutes to thaw if I needed a new credit card. If you're someone who opens up new cards all the time to save ten percent or have an issue with your credit, it may be worthwhile to perform this step to set yourself up for success and make it difficult for you to do.

Paper Karma is an app for your phone. Simply snap a photo of the envelope with the Sender and Recipient in focus and they will contact the mailer to have you removed from the distribution list. I snap my photos right over the recycle bin before the mail ever goes in my house.

House Cleaning

I've already spoken about housecleaning being the best outsourcing a traveler can buy. However, if you opt not to go that route, you may have to adjust your standards or learn to live with toothpaste in the sink. I have different cleanliness standards than my husband, but they have also relaxed over the years too. I realized that tasks like dusting the baseboards every week aren't a necessity and can be done once every couple of months. If you are dividing up your chores with someone else or with children, one option to try is to divide your house into zones and assign specific rooms or divide the chores up into vacuum, dust and glass, bathrooms, laundry, etc. Divvy up the chores each week depending on everyone's schedule and realize that some weeks, not everything is going to get done. If you have a heavy travel week, maybe you need the lightest chore. You shouldn't spend your whole weekend cleaning your house. Make a list of tasks for each zone so it's clear to everyone what is considered clean.

Timecap your house chores. Set a timer and do what you need to do as fast as you can until that timer goes off. What's done is done. Don't let your Saturdays and Sundays fly by with only a clean sink and sparkly floors to show for it.

Organization

There's a difference between hyper-organization and orga-nized *enough*. If I were to open your pantry and find everything labeled and facing the same way you might be hyper-organized. If you have an inbox full of folders with folder children, folder cousins, and folder friends, you are wasting your time. I'm very organized, but **for some people the act of organizing is a mask for procrastinating.** At some point, there are diminishing returns for spending your time organizing and making things 'just so'.

Back in the day, before there were smart phones, and before there were flip phones, we had actual cameras. Flip phones took crappy photos, but then smartphones changed the game. Current phones take great photos and for most people, unless you are a true photographer, the quality is 'good enough.' I think there is a level of organization that's also *good enough.* Good enough means that you feel comfortable, productive, don't waste time looking for things and it doesn't affect people in a negative way. If your organization efforts are one-offs that are easy to maintain with a routine check-in to see if it's working, go for it. If your efforts are a way to procrastinate against doing what you really should be doing, reevaluate.

Working Remotely

If you have the ability or luxury to have a home office, even if only part-time, it's important to make sure that the environment feels productive and puts you in your focus and creation zone. As a traveler, you need to adapt to be able to work from anywhere, but to work from home can sometimes be even more challenging than working from a plane, train or hotel room.

Benefits to working remotely:

- No distractions from colleagues stopping by your desk.
- No temptations from the never-ending birthday and promotion cakes.
- Guilt-free lunches.
- Less cost for commuting, clothes, and food.

- Working hours that make sense for your energy levels (many companies still make you work specific hours, but it's a little more flexible).
- You can throw in a load of laundry or empty the dishwasher during a break.

Challenges to working remotely:

- Your work is never gone. It calls you from the office, kitchen, and laundry room.
- People expect you to answer email and phone at all hours.
- You don't have as much of an excuse to prevent glute amnesia and get off your butt and move. The steps you take are fewer from office to kitchen or bathroom than from the parking lot to your desk.
- Staying in your pajamas all day or otherwise not looking presentable for the UPS driver can subconsciously put you in a funk.

Companies often make the assumption that remote workers feel isolated or don't have an attachment to the organization. A study done by Fonner and Roloff using social scientific, quantitative research surveyed eighty-nine remote workers and one hundred and four office workers. The remote workers worked from home at least three days a week and tended to be older (average age 42.5), married, have children and job tenure. What they found was interesting, against the current way of thinking and what every manager needs to know.

- For both remote and office workers, frequent communication did not increase feelings of closeness with others, no matter what the mode of communication.
- Remote workers reported similar levels of closeness to colleagues in their workplace interactions as office workers.

- The more communication using email and instant message, the more stress they had from being interrupted, causing frustration and feeling *less* attachment to the organization. Office workers over-communicate with remote workers to "keep them in the loop." *I had a manager that worked in the office, whom I felt was always checking up on me. It made me feel distrusted since she never had a reason to do this. I got so fed up with it I took a job with another company.*

- On the other hand, office workers had more stress from interruptions but it didn't decrease their attachment to the organization. Fonner and Roloff suspect that it's because office workers expect interruptions, whereas remote workers expect autonomy. Office workers can close their doors or put up a sign, but a remote worker doesn't have the same visible boundary.

I have a client now who works from home one day a week. She feels like she needs to have her Instant Message on and be available all day so that people don't think she is sitting around on the couch. Leaving her IM on is distracting and results in more 'conversations' than she would normally have in a day at work.

What should a company or team do? Have a process or guidance around communication with the entire team, not just the remote workers. Don't expect your team to be on IM all day (I have guidelines for each of my clients depending on their jobs) or to email immediately. Don't *reply all* unless it's important to reply all. Don't send group emails out of laziness if it doesn't apply. And most importantly, trust your remote worker to be doing their job. If you don't trust them, they shouldn't be working for you, whether it's from the office or their couch.

When I worked remotely for corporate, I had to prep my food for the week even though I was one flight of stairs away from my kitchen. I didn't have time to fix meals because I was on back-to-back calls and sometimes delivering training. I would have to eat while working or listening to yet another meeting. I still got up at 5:30 or 6:00am to make sure I was done working out in time for 8:00 or 8:30am calls and sometimes didn't have time to shower until the afternoon.

Try incorporating some of the following techniques to be healthy and productive while working remotely.

- Set a schedule and stick with it. It's easy to get sucked into 6:00am and 6:00pm meetings. Blocking out time on your calendar for when you start and stop your day is important. Yes, you *could* be available but it doesn't mean you have to be. Exceptions should be discussed with you prior to meetings being scheduled. Business traveler? Same deal. Just because you are in a hotel doesn't mean you are required to do evening meetings. You teach people how to treat you and your calendar. Keep it sacred. If you allow people to schedule at all times, then the abuse will continue.

- Set up a real workstation. Your couch, dining room table or a chair at the airport can work in the short-term or even as a break from your regular environment, but it shouldn't be your permanent office. It's not going to help you feel professional or inspired sitting in the same place you eat dinner or watch The Walking Dead. Get a standing or adjustable desk, proper lighting, a whiteboard ... whatever you need to make you feel like creating. I have a couple of pictures that make me smile and remind me that I'm a person.

- Distract yourself. Right now, if I were to turn off my background music, I would hear dogs barking at the day care behind my house. This would be incredibly distracting to me, but not in a good way. I need to be distracted from the distraction! At home and on the road I use *Focus At Will*, a neuroscience productivity tool. It's a low-cost program I can set a timer; choose what types of background music I need and the tempo and energy level. Music with words distracts me so I save the

Spotify for when I'm doing easy tasks. The din of a coffee shop has been shown to increase productivity for some people. The background noise has even been recorded and can be purchased in an app or selected on Focus At Will.

- Use a document-sharing program. I came from a company that had a document sharing system that people hated using. Instead, they would keep attachments on their computers; send them back and forth, with no one ever having the latest version. This is pretty common with almost any company I consult with. Use your sharing system.

- Have a real office number. I use a Vonage number for my office line that simulrings my cell phone. I don't want two mobile phones or people I don't know texting me.

- Check email at regular intervals. Have a defined start time that signifies you are in work mode and when you shut down for the day. Then, shut down.

- Get your work done when you say you're going to and eliminate micromanaging. This can help with getting a little more flexibility in your hours.

- To get yourself to stop working at a reasonable time, pretend you have a child waiting for you at the bus stop at a specific time of day. Don't lie to your boss and say you have a child; this is just pretend for you! People that have children don't get as much pushback when they have to leave at a certain time. Pretending you have a kid freezing at the bus stop or that you're being charged by the minute at daycare makes people end their workday with a sharp transition. I knew a woman that worked at a company for three years and left for home every day at 5:30 to let her dog out. They never knew she didn't have a dog.

- Create a transition ritual. Whether that's a two-minute meditation when you start and end work, doing twenty-five squats and pushups, or rewarding yourself by checking social media at the end of the day, choose something that becomes a clear indication you are starting and stopping.

- Prep and make meals for the week, so you aren't grabbing a Lean Cuisine or worse. Act as if you have to take your lunch with you every day, so you have plenty of options to grab. People who work remotely often skip lunch because they feel guilty, or anxiety about stepping away or they are in back-to-back meetings. If you have to, get a dorm fridge for your office and stock it with water, hangry snacks or maybe even your lunch for that day. Make a smoothie in the morning to have for lunch if you have to be at your desk.

- Take energy renewal breaks every hour or two. Take a walk outside or do a walking meeting while talking on your cell phone, do fifty squats every hour on the hour, practice balancing moves while on a call, run up and down your steps after every email processing time or take a five-minute hoop break (my renewal of choice). If you feel like you don't have thirty seconds to drop and do some push-ups or a few stretches, then that means you probably need to do it even more.

- Get a standing desk with an option to sit when you're tired. You can burn as many calories in a year as running a marathon. Plus, it keeps you more alert.

- Take a shower and get dressed. Something about actually 'getting ready for work' that will put you in that zone. I'm not talking dress up and fix your hair, but at least get out of the clothes you slept in. Sometimes I may end up in my workout gear for a couple of hours but I'm definitely in alert 'Let's Go' mode for my day.

Marcey Rader

Five Things I've Learned About Organizing a Home Office

1. You will take up as much room as you give yourself. I used to have a very large desk and two filing cabinets. When I decided to move to a standing desk, I downsized to one two-drawer filing cabinet and an Apprentice caddy. You may think you need more room, but you're probably keeping things you don't need or don't have your space appropriately organized.

2. Beware of the Container Store, Staples, and Ikea! It's easy to spend a ton of money in these stores on all sorts of gadgets you think you need. I love organization stores, but most of the little accessories are just contributing to the clutter. Know exactly what you need before you walk in the door.

3. Use an external monitor. I think this is one of the best ways to increase your productivity wherever you work. I have a lot of windows open when I'm working so having an external monitor to drag items from one screen to another, view two to three documents at once without having to squint or simply to avoid having to open and close windows saves me time. Do your eyes a favor and invest.

4. Have what you often use within arm's reach and put away the rest. Have you ever noticed that a flat surface tends to collect things? You put a set of keys down, then a pad of paper, your headset and then it just becomes a pile of *stuff?* Having a clean, clear surface is more aesthetically appealing as well as more practical. If you only use a stapler a couple of times a month, put it in a drawer. I was hanging on to a 3-hole punch because it was a nice one. I finally realized I don't even keep enough paper to have a binder, so I donated it to a teacher.

5. Don't buy in bulk. Your office is an area that can easily start to become cluttered with pens, paperclips, extra staples and files. If you are in an office environment, take only what you need and put the rest back in the supply closet. If you work remotely, see if there is someone you can split your order with. Who needs 250 paper clips? The guilt of throwing away perfectly good binders or file folders weighs heavy on people who believe in recycling and less waste. I'm one of them. After calling six schools and being told they don't need more file folders or binders, I started recycling my old file folders and taking my binders in good condition to Goodwill.

Relationships and Connection

If you are a very frequent traveler, it's important to prioritize activities to ensure that your relationships don't suffer. When I first started traveling, about five years into our marriage in 1998, it was fun and exciting for both of us. My husband could stay up late, play his drums, order pizza and hang out with friends. It felt like he was a bachelor again, and it was fun. I could walk around new cities, hang out in hotels and not have to consider housework or chores. On the weekends when I was home it made that time more special. Fast-forward a year and the remodeling of a house. My husband spent all week remodeling, and I spent all week traveling. On the weekends, all I wanted to do was work on the house and eat simple meals at home because I was sick of restaurant food. My husband just wanted to get *out* of the house and eat at a restaurant. He's now a touring musician and travels on the weekends so creating a routine where we can is important.

Being the partner or the traveler has its pros and cons. Sometimes it's just nice to be alone and have the space at home to do your own thing. It's also nice to be in a hotel, where you can't do household tasks even if you wanted to and can practice self-care or walk around the city you're in. On the flipside, who does the chores? Who's taking care of the children? Who's sitting in an airport after the fifth delay? It can easily lead to resentment and stress for both parties.

According to the Carlson Wagonlit Travel (CWG) report, the ability to connect via text, phone or email with friends and family has major affects on business travelers and even more so for women. I know some parents who miss the bedtime routine and stress themselves out because they aren't there. Guilt overrides everything else, and it makes the trip more difficult. If there is another routine you can perform when you're away it might be helpful to know you are still participating. One of my clients records a message via her memo app and emails it to her husband every day to play for the kids at bedtime. She doesn't get stressed about being available at 8:00pm and her kids love it.

When training a group of travelers I had a 50/50 split on how many people call their children each day. It seemed the younger the kids, the harder it was for both the parent and the child to talk to each other. It made the parent feel guilty and miss them more, and the child remembered Mommy or Daddy was gone and then acted out. For the other half, they said it worked great, and they were able to participate in bedtime by Google Hangout, Skype or speakerphone.

Determining how often and what type of contact to have with your family is important. What you may think is enough may not be for them. I used to call my husband every time I landed until I realized that it wasn't a concern for him, and he didn't expect or need that call. Emily Pines, Director and Founder of The Energy Project, has worked it out with her husband that each morning they record a video message to each other. They travel across time zones so nailing down times to talk can be stressful. They stay connected without being tied down to a clock. Find a communication channel that works for you.

If you use a Google Calendar, you can share your calendar with your spouse so they know where you are and can plan around your travel. Even if you use Outlook, there is almost always at least one more option to send your itinerary. Use that email address as your Google option to block out your personal calendar. I have access to my husband's work calendar, band calendar and even some of my clients' calendars. I just check the box to show the calendar when I want to plan a weekend with my husband or need to know what city he is going to be in. If the email is coming directly from your travel itinerary, like TripIt, it can show your travel specifics with airline and hotel.

Ideas to stay connected:

- Have a weekly date. My husband and I had a date, just the two of us, every week from October 1993 to 2014, except when I was gone for more than a week. When we were really busy and I was gone for part of the week and then had people staying with us on the weekend, we would at least sneak out for a coffee to make sure we had alone time. When I started my business, I didn't want to spend the money, so we started having breakfast and coffee together every morning. I have to start and end work later, but that's okay. Now that ritual is sacred when we're both home, even if we have to set an alarm.

- Do something before you leave that will make their life easier. I use Sundays as prep and cook time for the week. I cut vegetables and cook entrees and sides. If your family appreciates this and won't let it rot in the fridge, it's a nice gesture. If they're still going to eat pizza and fish sticks anyway, don't use your precious time on a task that only you would value. If you don't cook, think of some other household task that you could do or something that can be done remotely like pay bills, schedule appointments, interview contractors, etc.

- Share your riches. I used to bring home sweets and treats when I was a sugar addict. Then I started buying healthier snacks in airports like bags of nuts or fruit salad on my way out of the airport to take home to my husband for work the next day. When I was paid a set amount per day instead of reimbursed for my receipts, I loaded $10.00 on his Starbucks card every time he took me to the airport. I preferred it to parking in the garage, and he got free Starbucks.

- Watch a show together. One of the best decisions I have made in my adult life (and I'm not kidding) is getting rid of cable and television. Not only is it expensive, but it's a huge Timesuck. Instead, we have Netflix and Amazon Prime. If you

have a show you like to watch together, decide how many epi-
sodes you can watch independently, so you are always caught
up to continue the series when you are at home. I know one
person who watches the show with his wife at the same time
because they like to pause and talk about it at different points.

- Check out the website
  http://www.everydaybetterliving.com/love_danger_signs/100_
  questions.html to get ideas for questions to ask your significant other on the phone. Not everyone has an exciting day but
  asking a new and thought-provoking question every call can
  be fun! My husband and I spent a year going through the book
  If – Questions for the Game of Life when we were camping or
  on road trips and my girlfriend and I used it on our Rim to
  Rim to Rim hike across the Grand Canyon. I highly recommend it for couples and close friends.

- Connect in different ways besides the phone. Google Hangout,
  Skype, Facetime, texting, SnapChat and emailing all give variety. A handwritten or sent card in the mail is thoughtful. I
  only did this once because my husband rarely gets the mail
  when I'm gone so I ended up picking up my own letter!

- Take your significant other with you. I know a woman who
  owns her own business and can do most of the work remotely.
  She travels with her husband when he is traveling by car. They
  get to have a nice dinner, and she can sometimes take in the
  sites of the city she's in. My husband has only opted to join
  me a couple of times, but my brother has gone to Tokyo, Beijing, and Miami with me. It was fun to have him with me,
  made it safer to tour around and he got a free hotel!

- Schedule your time with friends. Having a regular coffee,
  lunch, walk, or dinner once a month is important. I had a
  docudinner night once a month with two girlfriends for almost
  two years. We would rotate homes, cook dinner and watch a
  documentary.

One thing to be conscious of for both parties is the routine when you get home after traveling. I used to walk in the door and immediately start emptying the litterbox, dishwasher, and taking out trash, basically showing my husband in a passive-aggressive way all the things that should have been done while I was gone. I know this isn't a female/male characteristic because my girlfriend says her husband does the same thing as soon as he walks in the door! When my husband is traveling, I try not to bombard him with tasks as soon as he gets home. While I would prefer it to be different, after fifteen years of traveling, I know that when I arrive home, the mail will not be picked up, and there will be no groceries in the kitchen. Ideally, you can work something out and compromise that the things that are most important or at least visible to you as soon as you walk in the door will be done so you won't be in tyrant mode after you cross the threshold.

Use the time on the road wisely so you don't have to do it at home. If I have things I need to read or research, I try to do as much while traveling as I can so I have more time when I'm at home. Having a partner or spouse as a traveler means a more conscious effort to maintain the relationship. Trust and empathy are key. The partner at home needs to understand how tiring the travel may be and that it isn't always nice restaurants and cush hotel accommodations. Often it's sub-par food, being 'on' at meetings all day and dealing with flight delays. The traveler needs to understand that the partner at home has to deal with all the home chores, especially if they have kids, alone without support. Family routines and schedules may become more important when one person is a traveler. The extra steps are worth it for your relationship and your sanity.

For links and references to this chapter visit http://www.marceyrader.com/signup and login with your email address. Use the password provided via email for access to the online bonus page.

13. ACTION

You now have an arsenal of tools, ideas, hacks, tips, theories and nuggets to challenge your noggin. It's time to decide which ones you want to take action on, in what order and how you will hold yourself accountable. Some recommendations will work for you and others won't. Some you will try and others you will dismiss immediately. Get out your whiteboard or your Evernote and make a list of the changes you want to make. Put them in an order that makes sense and start working on one or two behaviors at a time. Once you have those mastered, move to the next one(s). If you're ambitious, try one behavior in each category.

What are your goals? Why do you want this goal? What will the result be?

What are your whines? Is this whine an excuse or reason?

What are your wins? What systems or people do you have in place to support you?

What's your plan?

Get an accountability partner or hire a coach. It can be me or someone else, but get the support you need. Books are great starting points but don't often make us change our behaviors. Several clients read my last book, but they didn't change their behaviors until they started working with me because they weren't sure how to make it personal for them. I would love to be part of your journey.

For links and references to this chapter visit http://www.marceyrader.com/signup and login with your email address. Use the password provided via email for access to the online bonus page.

About the Author

Marcey Rader is a Lifestyle Trainer with a B.S in Exercise Science and M.Ed. in Health Promotion. She holds multiple certifications including National Academy of Sports Medicine Personal Fitness Trainer, National Academy of Sports Medicine Fitness Nutrition Specialist, Institute for Integrative Nutrition Integrative Health Coach and formerly, the Productive Environment Institute Productive Environment Specialist. She partners with Extended Stay America Hotel as their Savve Travel Expert® to help their guests be healthy and productive. She is the creator of the Jetsetter Gym Kit, the 25 in 25® and 10 by 10® exercise challenges with Coach.Me and has three travel roadmaps with Sociidot. A professional speaker offering corporate health and productivity workshops, Marcey also provides customized health and productivity solutions to travelers and high achievers to declutter their mind, body and inbox, one habit at a time. Her primary goals in life are to *Work Well, Play More and feel like a superhero.* Find out more at www.marceyrader.com

Marcey lives with her musician-husband Kevin next to a beautiful state park in Raleigh, North Carolina and can often be found mountain biking, trail running or hooping blind-folded.

Made in the USA
Columbia, SC
14 March 2018